"This impressive volume edited by two gifted scholars demonstrates the seminal intellectual and theological leadership of Professor Edward Wimberly. Moschella and Butler illustrate the rich craft of Wimberly's evolved scholarship and spiritual formation. The breadth and depth of the writers confirm their solid capacity as scholar-practitioners who fully understand Wimberly as a pastoral theologian who is without question the 'Dean' of Black pastoral care theologians. Finally, this volume faithfully documents a perspective in the field of pastoral theology which merits attention, appreciation, and cultural affirmation."

—**VERGEL L. LATTIMORE**, *President and Professor of Pastoral Psychology and Counseling, Hood Theological Seminary*

"Butler and Moschella have captured the legacy of Edward Wimberly through their thorough and intriguing discussion and analysis of Wimberly's writings. Their exposition reveals the evolution of Wimberly's theological understanding of pastoral care. In addition, the significance of understanding the field through the cultural lens of the African American experience is clear. This is a timeless and relevant reader for pastoral theologians, pastors, and professional or volunteer spiritual caregivers."

—**BISHOP TERESA JEFFERSON-SNORTON**, *The Christian Methodist Episcopal Church*

"*The Edward Wimberly Reader* brings together significant essays from a giant in the field of pastoral theology. Edward Wimberly's scholarship displays rigorous reflection on the particularities of black churches, black communities, and black theological traditions to put forth understandings and practices for meaningful pastoral care. Whether one's interest involves emphasizing the embodied nature of the soul, discerning ways to faithfully embrace our woundedness, reauthoring our mythologies, exploring adolescent identity development, or outlining the deep connections between pastoral care and social justice, this book will remain an important contribution for scholars and pastors."

—**MONTAGUE R. WILLIAMS**, *Associate Professor of Church, Culture, and Society, Point Loma Nazarene University*

The Edward Wimberly Reader

A Black Pastoral Theology

Mary Clark Moschella

Lee H. Butler, Jr.

Editors

BAYLOR UNIVERSITY PRESS

Cover and book design by Kasey McBeath

Hardcover ISBN: ISBN 978-1-4813-1244-8
Library of Congress Control Number: 2020008729

Printed in the United States of America on acid-free paper with a minimum of thirty percent recycled content.

To Dr. Edward and Dr. Anne—Intellectual partners, Communicators of a tradition, Keepers of the faith.

Contents

Acknowledgments

First and foremost we thank the Reverend Doctor Edward Powell Wimberly and Doctor Anne Streaty Wimberly for their permission, support, and encouragement in the creation of this reader. It has been many years in the making, so we thank them for their patience as well. Numerous colleagues from the Society for Pastoral Theology conferred and contributed in various ways that led to the form of the project evolving over time. Our thanks to Elizabeth Johnson Walker, Rodney Hunter, Emmanuel Y. Lartey, Carolyn McCrary, the late Emma J. Justes, and many others who participated through a survey and through helpful conversations. Edward Wimberly's colleagues and students at the Interdenominational Theological Center (ITC) shared their time and reflections with us. We also thank his many friends, most especially Archie Smith, Jr., who contributed an insightful essay for an earlier version of the book. Although we could not include his contribution in this volume, we remain extremely grateful for his participation.

I, (Mary), thank Drs. Ed and Anne Wimberly for their trust, friendship, and care over the years as this project developed. The initial impetus for the book came when I taught a course on the history of pastoral care at Wesley Theological Seminary eighteen years ago and discovered the great paucity of recognition of African American authors in historical accounts of the field. I wrote to Dr. Ed at that time and asked him to send me a brief biography. My students wanted more, and thus a seed was planted. As a white scholar working in a racist society, it is a dicey thing to venture forth on this project, wanting to ensure that Edward Wimberly's scholarship is written into the historical record, while knowing that there is much I do not know, and many possible ways to err unwittingly. Therefore I am especially grateful to another distinguished African American scholar in the field, my co-editor, Lee Butler, Jr, for his willingness to join the project. The book has benefited enormously from his input and expertise. A side benefit is that we have gotten to know each other quite well. As always, I thank my friends, colleagues, writing groups, and family for their support in this project. To Beverly Mitchell, who has listened to and cajoled me along on this journey, merci beaucoup mon amie. Doug, Ethan, and Abbey, I love you.

I, (Lee) thank Drs. Edward and Anne Wimberly for modeling a love supreme as life and intellectual partners. Our interlocutors help make us who we are as scholars, and Edward Wimberly's contributions to the field of pastoral theology, care, and counseling would be very different if not for the loving support of Dr. Anne! They model true collegiality and demonstrate the care reflected in all that Dr. Ed has published. I thank him for being a steadfast presence as a senior scholar within the Society for Pastoral Theology (SPT). Years ago, at the close of an SPT annual meeting, Dr. Ed said, with my membership and active presence within the SPT, he felt he would leave our guild in good hands. I am grateful for the work of his hands and the ways his initial publications became formative articulations of the theories and practices of African American pastoral theology and care. I am grateful to my colleague and friend, Mary Clark Moschella. Our personal and professional relationship spans more than twenty years. It was my honor to be invited to join her as a co-editor, and my privilege to work with her on this unprecedented project. I am also thankful for all the African and African American voices from across the ages who have been embraced and represented by the voice of Dr. Edward P. Wimberly. And as noted by Mary, I too thank my friends, colleagues, students, and family for their support in this project.

We further offer our thanks to the amazing team at Baylor University Press. Our initial editor, Carey Newman, was the first to pick up on the importance of the project; he guided us through the evolutionary process that resulted in this reader. Thanks also to the three anonymous readers who offered their thoughtful and helpful feedback. David Aycock, Cade Jarrell, Jenny Hunt, and numerous others at Baylor have worked diligently with us. Special thanks go to two research assistants at Yale Divinity School, Jonathan Heinly and Helena Martin, for their outstanding work.

In honor of the Wimberlys, we will donate our royalties from this book to the ITC and the SPT.

Introduction

Edward Powell Wimberly, a tall, gregarious University of Arizona football player with his linebacker confidence, stepped on to the campus of Boston University School of Theology in 1965. Wimberly, however, had not come to play football. The son of a father in the ministry and a mother in education, he had left the gridiron to tackle the field of pastoral ministry.

Mentored by his father and inspired by a famous Boston University alumnus—the Reverend Doctor Martin Luther King, Jr.—young Edward Wimberly surveyed the scene. He may have paused as his eyes came upon Marsh Chapel, a striking Gothic structure at the center of campus, with its glorious lines and curves, and the afternoon sunlight glinting off its Indiana limestone. The venerable mystic, theologian, and civil rights activist, Howard Thurman, had been the recent dean in residence at Marsh Chapel. This historic United Methodist Church school of theology that had become a beacon for racial justice seemed full of wonder and possibility as Edward Wimberly pondered his future and calling. Though he had felt a call to the ministry since he was sixteen, now that he was there answering the call, where would God lead him? At this point in time, the young man could not have anticipated the vocational path that would open before him.

It would not be long before one crucial, maybe even providential, moment of inspiration marked his path. On the first Sunday morning he was in Boston, Wimberly chose to worship in Marsh Chapel. There he noticed a young woman he had never seen before. The next day as he was walking with a fellow student, George Anderson, he spotted her again as she was crossing Commonwealth Avenue. Trying to be coy to start a conversation, he asked "Didn't I see you see you at Marsh Chapel yesterday?" Her name was Anne Streaty. Wimberly recalls, "I found out she was a preacher's kid, and I was too." After Anne walked away, George Anderson remarked, "There goes your future wife."[1] The prediction proved accurate: Edward and Anne were engaged in December and married the following June. Their union was the beginning of a lifelong partnership in ministry and scholarship as well. They say they were "called in marriage and called in ministry together."[2]

While working on his Master of Sacred Theology, Wimberly became acquainted with a student from nearby Brandeis University, Archie Smith, Jr. With similar passions related to ministry, the two became fast friends and life-long colleagues. It was Smith who invited Wimberly to take clinical training at the Worcester Area Council of Churches Pastoral Counseling Center. Although Wimberly had already been introduced to the fundamentals of pastoral care by his father, it was within the Wooster program that Wimberly discovered a deep love for the practice of pastoral counseling. This experience, in concert with a pastoral position at the Winchendon United Methodist Church, helped form Wimberly into a warm and emotionally present pastoral care practitioner. Synthesizing the wonder of the practice of pastoral care and broad swaths of theological and psychological literature, Wimberly would make the field of pastoral theology his own.

The former football player, who had previously measured life in yards, would spend ten years at Boston University, earning not only his Bachelor of Sacred Theology (1968) and his Master of Sacred Theology in the Sociology of Religion (1971), but also a Ph.D. in the Division of Theological Studies, in the area of Pastoral Psychology and Counseling (1976). This was a remarkable transformation for one who had resisted learning to read until he was in eighth grade.

Boston University's Ph.D. program in Pastoral Care and Counseling, which emphasized personalism,[3] was a fit for Wimberly's approach and temperament. The city of Boston was a hotbed of racial tension with major protests against integration. With Black Studies programs beginning to enter the academy, and Black Theology pressing its way into theological education, the moment was ripe for black perspectives to emerge within

[1] Interview with Edward Wimberly, September 18, 2016.

[2] Yolanda Y. Smith, "Anne Streaty Wimberly," Talbot School of Theology, *Christian Educators of the 20th Century*, Biola University, https://www.biola.edu/talbot/ce20/database/anne-streaty-wimberly.

[3] Boston University Personalism was a philosophy based on explorations of personality. "The essential meaning of personality is selfhood, self-consciousness, self-control (self-determination), and the power to know . . . complete and perfect personality can be found only in the Infinite and Absolute Being." See Carolyn A. Warren, "Dynamic Interpersonalism and Personhood," *Journal of the Interdenominational Theological Center* 25, no. 3 (1998): 8–32.

other theological fields, including pastoral theology.[4] Although there had been other African American men who preceded him in the Ph.D. program, Wimberly's white professors now challenged him to write a dissertation on pastoral care in the black church.

Wimberly's initial scholarly reflections were informed by the nation's shift in consciousness during the Black Consciousness and Civil Rights Movements. While televised black bodies signified the flames of social unrest to be extinguished by firehoses, Wimberly sought to identify the system of care that had preserved the personhood of black lives in America. Integrating his early pastoral care experiences with his father, who took him to visit his congregants, and the personalism of the Boston school, Wimberly identified the black church as the locus of care for the black community.

After Wimberly earned his degree, one of his professors, Homer Jernigan, encouraged him to revise and publish his dissertation. *Pastoral Care in the Black Church* (1979) was the first book to argue that the black church's practice of pastoral care was something different, distinct: it had its own history, features, and traditions that could not be subsumed into white, Western practices. Elaborating on the four traditional functions of pastoral care—healing, sustaining, guiding, reconciling—as described by Clebsch and Jaekle,[5] Wimberly emphasized that sustaining and guiding had been the two most important dimensions of pastoral care in the black church, which he historically traced to the days of slavery. Rather than embracing the non-directive methods of psychodynamic care, Wimberly peered through the veil across time and saw that pastors in the black tradition must offer active and direct forms of sustenance and guidance to care for persons in contexts of racism, violence, and powerlessness.[6] His research and experience led him to conclude that the deep fissures to the soul resulting from living in the midst of unending traumatic assaults can only be mended by faith and the pastor's assurance of God's unending love. The book was a success, garnering interest in both the academy and the church. The United States Navy even bought one thousand copies for its chaplains.

[4] In 1966, the National Committee of Negro Churchmen issued a statement that was published in the *New York Times* supporting "Black Power" and in 1969 supported the "Black Manifesto" which called for reparations. See National Committee of Negro Churchmen, "Black Power," *New York Times*, July 31, 1966, E5. Also in 1969, James H. Cone published *Black Theology and Black Power* (New York: Seabury Press, 1969).

[5] William A. Clebsch and Charles R. Jaekle, *Pastoral Care in Historical Perspective*, revised edition (Northvale, N.J.: Jason Aronson, 1994).

[6] Edward P. Wimberly, *Pastoral Care in the Black Church* (Nashville: Abingdon, 1979), 18–38.

• • •

Living into his call from God, the Reverend Doctor Edward P. Wimberly has devoted himself to the field of pastoral theology and care for more than fifty years, making an impact that helped change the game. His twenty-one books and forty articles constitute a treasure trove of evolving insight, relationship counseling, and practical approaches to ministry. His work has both mirrored and informed developments in the wider field of practical theology. His critical reflections span the arenas of care, counseling, religious education, homiletics, and public theology. He speaks to individuals, marriages, families, and communities, always calling attention to the importance of cultural sensitivity in the midst of social malaise.

At the Interdenominational Theological Center (ITC), where he has taught during most of his career, and in meetings of the Society for Pastoral Theology (SPT), where he has participated regularly for more than 35 years, "Dr. Ed" is a well-known interlocutor. At SPT, one African American scholar refers to him as "God-Father," expressing affection and acknowledging his invaluable contributions to the development of African American pastoral care as a theological discipline. Edward Wimberly's persistent presence in guild meetings and professional gatherings, along with his prolific scholarship, helped pave the way during the initial reorganizing efforts to resist racial and gender oppression within the Society's theoretical reflections and praxiological interactions.[7] Wimberly's friendliness belies the struggle that he, Archie Smith, Jr., and others faced in breaking into the formerly all-white (and almost all-male) SPT. The challenge for them was not to find individual academic success but to give voice to the pastoral approaches of black care givers who wrestled with the oppressions of flesh and blood and systemic evil. Representing a tradition rarely regarded by the academy, their contributions changed the contours of the field: expanding and transforming its meaning, purpose, and practice in thorough-going ways. Their theoretical integrity participated in a movement of scholars bringing the cause of racial justice into the heart of the pastoral care field.

While a biography of Edward Wimberly is beyond the scope of this book, we do hope to show readers, through this collection, something of the person of Edward Wimberly and the lasting impression that he has made upon the field of pastoral theology and care. As one of the more prolific pastoral theologians, students of pastoral care will inevitably read one or two of his books. Yet his influence and importance to the field as a whole

---

[7] For an account of the Society for Pastoral Theology's early history narrating these challenges and power struggles over issues of race and gender, see Loren Townsend, *Introduction to Pastoral Counseling* (Nashville: Abingdon, 2009), especially chapter 2, "Genealogy Revisited: Euro-American Priority," 39–52.

has not yet been sufficiently narrated. We (the editors) offer this reader as a first step in the larger project of filling in the historical record, so that it will eventually include greater recognition of the contributions of Edward Wimberly and numerous other significant African American voices that have helped to reshape the field of pastoral theology and care.

This volume is a collection of some of Wimberly's most vital chapters and articles, highlighting the trajectory of his thought over time. We selected these pieces on the basis of their originality, their contribution to the larger field, their enduring value, and the way in which they convey Edward Wimberly's distinctive voice as an African American pastoral theologian. In these pieces, Wimberly stresses the importance of role models and mirroring (a concept he borrows from Kohut's self-psychology) and the necessity of a liberating praxis in the work of spiritual care. Through personal stories and anecdotes, he takes the risk of revealing himself openly, in order to demonstrate what it means to offer an authentic pastoral presence. In so doing he models the very care practices he describes, inviting his readers to do likewise.

Wimberly's corpus, like that of most pastoral theologians, emerges out of his social and political engagements. Whereas he continues to hold the gridiron close as a motivational metaphor, he never shies away but always faces the opponents that challenge living as social beings and tackles the issues that denigrate black life. He passionately attends to human suffering and peers through the veil of tears to describe the ineffable and name the unconscionable. Wimberly has confronted multiple social and generational crises within American life. With each socio-cultural shift, he has engaged the effects so as to remain a scholar for our times.

The articles in this volume have been organized around three major discernable themes found in Wimberly's writings. As a collection, they represent his reflective and insightful responses to the psycho-social shifts in the culture. They are: contextual care, narrative care, and prophetic care.

The first major theme, *contextual care*, heralds Wimberly's entrance to the field with his initial contribution being a new way for the guild to think about pastoral care as culturally and contextually determined. Pastoral theology, as an academic discipline, was grounded by the work of Seward Hiltner, who focused on the biblical image of "shepherding" and asserted that every minister should be a practical theologian.[8] As revolutionary as Hiltner's work was, it was not comprehensive enough in its reflective scope to include conceptions of care beyond those formulated by white scholars. Hiltner had not considered the degradation of racial oppression nor the

---

[8] Seward Hiltner, *Preface to Pastoral Theology* (Nashville: Abingdon, 1958).

survival resources required for African Americans to retain human dignity against the forces of racism. Wimberly's work gave voice to the conditions and practices overlooked by white mainstream pastoral care. Rather than researching and reflecting on pastoral care grounded in the exclusive thoughts of white pastoral theologians who universalized the white care tradition, Wimberly focused directly on the African American church as the context for describing pastoral care by black pastors.[9] Having come of age with an awareness of segregation in America, Wimberly had a social reference point for interpreting the segregation implicit in the context of slavery. Through this awareness, the importance of the context of care came into full view. Wimberly highlighted the work of black pastoral care practitioners, differentiating it from the work of white pastors, and gave the historical, social, and political contexts of care the full attention each deserved. This emphasis on context had wider implications that both reflected and contributed to a more general focus on communal and contextual models of care.

The second major theme, *narrative care*, marked a theoretical expansion in Wimberly's thought and work and offered a new methodological practice to the guild. He was among the first pastoral theologians to introduce narrative therapy concepts and methods to the field of pastoral care.[10] Narrative therapy is an approach that recognizes the fundamental role of stories and storytelling in human living. Family therapists Michael White and David Epston proposed narrative therapy in their key text, *Narrative Means to Therapeutic Ends*.[11] These authors took seriously the insights of critical theory, especially its recognition of the social construction of knowledge and the power of destructive cultural narratives to influence human lives. As family therapists were beginning to move "from systems to stories,"[12] Edward Wimberly laid out his adaptation of narrative therapy for the

[9] Archie Smith, Jr. was a significant conversation partner whose first text was published in 1982: *The Relational Self: Ethics and Therapy from a Black Church Perspective* (Nashville: Abingdon, 1982). See also Vergel Lattimore III, "The Positive Contribution of Black Cultural Values to Pastoral Counseling," *Journal of Pastoral Care* 38, no. 2 (1982): 105–17.

[10] Similarly emphasizing a challenge to harmful cultural narratives, Christie Cozad Neuger advocated for narrative pastoral care for women. See Christie Cozad Neuger, *Counseling Women: A Narrative, Pastoral Approach* (Minneapolis: Fortress, 2001).

[11] Michael White and David Epston, *Narrative Means to Therapeutic Ends* (New York: W. W. Norton, 1990).

[12] Jill Freedman and Gene Combs, *Narrative Therapy: The Social Construction of Preferred Realities* (New York: W. W. Norton, 1996), 1–18. See also Gene Combs and Jill Freedman, *Symbol, Story, and Ceremony: Using Metaphor in Individual and Family Therapy* (New York: W. W. Norton, 1990). Donald Capps describes a history of this shift, though he omits any reference to Wimberly's contributions, in *Giving Counsel: A Minister's Guidebook* (St. Louis: Chalice, 2001), 143–88.

purposes of pastoral care, drawing on the importance of the oral tradition and storytelling within the black church.

When asked how he came by his narrative therapy ideas, Wimberly said that he had met Michael White at a conference somewhere along the way, and they had gotten to talking.[13] Wimberly also explained that narrative ideas made sense to him because they fit so well with what he had learned from his father, a Methodist minister, about the power of telling stories.[14] And it is with a story of his father's that Wimberly begins his important text, *Recalling Our Own Stories: Spiritual Renewal for Religious Caregivers*.[15] Wimberly's topic is spiritual renewal for caregivers; the pastoral method he introduces derives from narrative therapy. He later highlights the power of narrative practices in caring for African American men in particular, as we shall see in this volume. Wimberly's impact in this area can be seen in the important work of one of his former students, Tapiwa Mucherera, who has advanced a "narrative, postcolonial approach."[16] Narrative care, with its emphasis on challenging destructive dominant stories, also leads logically to Wimberly's reflection upon liberating and prophetic dimensions of pastoral care.

Focusing on *prophetic care*, the third major theme in his work, Wimberly expounds upon the prophetic tradition of the black church which stresses individual, family, and community care. His work highlights the power of the people and the advocacy of God in a sinful world. Black church activism is commonly described as being theologically conservative and politically progressive. It is that "politically progressive" function that exemplifies the prophetic tradition of the black church. Many of the most charismatic black leaders in the struggle for freedom and justice have been ministers. Whereas Wimberly came to manhood in the context of the struggle for human and civil rights, he knows the importance of speaking truth to power. Black pastoral caregivers also resource the politically progressive tradition as central to care of persons. Relying on the biblical traditions of the exodus narrative and the proclamations of the prophets, many black

[13] Wimberly would later attend another conference where he participated in a workshop led by Michael White called, "Narrative Therapy." The conference was "The Evolution of Psychotherapy Conference" in Anaheim, Calif., May 25–29, 2000. Wimberly took copious notes at the workshop, notes that he has preserved.

[14] Edward Wimberly's father, Edgar Wimberly, was a member of the Delaware Conference of the Methodist Church, before segregation was abandoned and the United Methodist Church was formed.

[15] Edward P. Wimberly, *Recalling Our Own Stories: Spiritual Renewal for Religious Caregivers* (San Francisco: Jossey-Bass, 1997).

[16] Tapiwa N. Mucherera, *Meet Me at the Palaver: Narrative Pastoral Counseling in Postcolonial Contexts* (Eugene, Ore.: Wipf & Stock, 2009).

pastors have been prophetic preachers and care practitioners, leading their communities from states of suffering to be reconciled to God and neighbor through prophesying social justice and spiritual reconciliation.[17] Addressing the social injustices of a post-civil rights America, Wimberly advocates the importance of black pastoral care addressing the consequences of politics and policies that marginalize black people and create suffering as a new world order. A pastor at heart, Wimberly upholds the black prophetic tradition, emphasizing liberation and reconciliation through care for black life.

Edward Wimberly's evolution of thought and work began at BU School of Theology. From the very beginning of his time there, his intellectual journey was influenced by the blessing of companionship. Edward and Anne are life partners and scholarly collaborators. Socially, they have rarely been seen apart from one another. Intellectually, they have always supported one another through reflections and scholarly productivity. As with many prominent scholarly couples, very few theoretical ideas have been presented to the world without first being vetted by one another. Through this creative process of theoretical exchange and reframing conversations with Dr. Anne,[18] Edward Wimberly has presented new theology and care practices that were developed and enlivened by their collaboration. His entire scholarly career has been dedicated to the care of community he identified in his foundational text, *Pastoral Care in the Black Church*. As a scholar committed to black life, each time he was provoked by the new ideas of others, he worked day and night, supported by Dr. Anne, to reframe those provocations for the benefit of black people and black life.

We as editors offer this collection in order to distinguish and preserve Wimberly's voice, highlight his unique and original contributions, and show how he has been able to weave together insights from diverse fields and strands of thought into a vibrant pastoral theology. Although neither of the editors were students of Edward Wimberly, we have agreed that his stature and influence in the field of pastoral care are undeniable. As an African American pastoral theologian, Wimberly contextually focuses on the black church and black life and offers a social critique and cultural analysis that invites all caregivers to be attentive to the pain experienced by America's

---

[17] See, for example, Ella Pearson Mitchell, ed., *Those Preachin' Women: Sermons by Black Women Preachers*, vol. 1 (Valley Forge: Judson Press, 1985); and Kenyatta R. Gilbert, *Exodus Preaching: Crafting Sermons about Justice and Hope* (Nashville: Abingdon, 2018).

[18] The couple's joint works include, for example, *Liberation and Human Wholeness: The Conversion Experiences of Black People in Slavery and Freedom* (Nashville: Abingdon, 1986); and *The Winds of Promise: Building and Maintaining Strong Clergy Families* (Nashville: Discipleship Resources, 2007).

darker brothers and sisters.[19] We invite and challenge white scholars, in particular, to give attention to the issues that gave rise to Wimberly's thoughts, especially in light of the resurgence of white racism as it affects contemporary contexts of care in America. This collection, thoroughly grounded in a Wesleyan understanding of God, represents Wimberly's personal approach to pastoral theology and care and offers his prophetic vision of healing and hope to the community of faith.

[19] See Langston Hughes, "I, Too," in *The Collected Poems of Langston Hughes* (New York: Knopf and Vintage Books, 1994).

1

Pastoral Care in the Black Church (1979)

Edward Wimberly's first, groundbreaking book introduces a striking notion: that pastoral care in the black church has its own history, features, and traditions that differ from those described in the classic, white-authored pastoral care texts.* In the very first sentence of the first chapter, Wimberly challenges the clerical paradigm of care, noting that care in the black church is and has always been a communal ministry, involving members helping each other, and not a task restricted to the pastor of the local congregation. Further, Wimberly claims that pastoral care in the black church is broader in form: it involves "bringing to bear upon persons and families the total resources of the church" (13). Taking on the venerable work of William A. Clebsch and Charles R. Jaekle, who articulated four functions of pastoral care—healing, sustaining, guiding, and reconciling—Wimberly claims that care in the black church centers around two of these functions: sustaining and guiding. Sustaining is basic and holistic care, especially needed because of the ravages of racism through slavery, Reconstruction, and displacement during the Great Migration. Wimberly argues that these historical events and the current conditions of ongoing racism accentuate the need for sustaining care, which includes providing economic resources. He also describes a particular form of guiding, pastoral leadership, by which black pastors become symbols of their congregation's hope. Wimberly contrasts this description of black pastoral care with what he sees as a focus on healing in the dominant, white paradigm of the

* Edward P. Wimberly, *Pastoral Care in the Black Church* (Nashville: Abingdon, 1979); the first chapter, presented here, is "Pastoral Care in the Black Church," 17–38 and associated notes. © 2008. Abingdon Press. Used by permission. All rights reserved.

time that emphasized one-on-one pastoral counseling modeled on psycho-dynamic and Rogerian approaches. Wimberly's conception of the *contextual* nature of care is evident here.

The impact of the bold, straightforward claims that Wimberly unpacks throughout this book cannot be overestimated. Practical theologian Dale Andrews was quick to recognize Wimberly's insight into "corporate care" in the black church.* In contemporary pastoral theology and care, the "communal contextual paradigm" is considered fundamental.† The literature of the field now recognizes the critical importance of race, cultural identity, and social location to any notion of pastoral theology and care.

Further Reading

Wimberly, Edward P. "Pastoral Counseling and the Black Perspective." *Journal of Pastoral Care* 30 (December 1976): 264–72. doi:10.1177/002234097603000407.
Wimberly, Edward P. "Pastoral Care and Support Systems." *Journal of the Interdenominational Theological Center* 5, no. 1 (1977): 67–75.

• • •

---

* Dale P. Andrews, *Practical Theology for Black Churches: Bridging Black Theology and African American Folk Religion* (Louisville: Westminster John Knox, 2002), 24–30
† Nancy J. Ramsay, ed., *Pastoral Care and Counseling: Redefining the Paradigms* (Nashville: Abingdon, 2004).

Pastoral Care in the Black Church

Pastoral care is a communal concept. It exists whenever persons minister to one another in the name of God. In this light, pastoral care is not a new concept but has its theological roots in the Judeo-Christian tradition.

Pastoral care in the black church has a history. Many persons may have the impression that pastoral care does not exist in the black church because very little has been written about it. They may feel that pastoral care is a white-church phenomenon because of the many contributions made by white church people to its development in this country. But, to the contrary, any ministry of the church that has as its end the tender, solicitous care of persons in crisis is pastoral care. Pastoral care exists when the hungry are fed, when the naked are clothed, when the sick are healed, when the prisoners are visited. Therefore, it can be concluded that pastoral care has always existed in the black church because the needs of persons are ministered to by others all the time.

Following the premise that pastoral care exists wherever persons minister to the needs of others, our task is to examine the nature of pastoral care in the black church. For this purpose, pastoral care is defined as the bringing to bear upon persons and families in crisis the total caring resources of the church. Although such roles and functions as worship, church administration, preaching, and teaching are not generally considered pastoral care, they become resources for pastoral care when their dominant concern is for the care of individual persons and their families in crisis situations.

There are four functions that have characterized the way pastoral care has been practiced in the history of the Christian ministry. These four functions—healing, sustaining, guiding, and reconciling—have been examined and described by William A. Clebsch and Charles R. Jaekle.[1] *Healing* consists of binding up the wounds; repairing damage that has been done as the result of disease, infection, or invasion; and restoring a condition that has been lost. *Sustaining* refers to helping persons courageously and creatively endure and transcend difficult situations while preventing or lessening the impact of the situation; sustaining is offered when healing is not possible. *Guiding* seeks to help persons in trouble make confident choices between alternative courses of action that will help them solve the problems they are facing. *Reconciliation* seeks to reestablish broken relationships between a person and God on the one hand, and between a person and other persons on the other.

[1] William A. Clebsch and Charles R. Jaekle, *Pastoral Care in Historical Perspective* (Englewood, N.J.: Prentice-Hall, 1964), 8–10.

For our purposes, the emphasis and the descriptive definitions given by Clebsch and Jaekle have been slightly altered. For example, they emphasize the pastor's role in carrying out the four functions of pastoral care. Because this book defines pastoral care as the bringing to bear of the total ministry of the church upon persons and families in crisis, we shall herein explore the prominent role of the total caring resources of the black church, particularly in relation to sustaining. In this context, the sustaining function is a ministry of the whole congregation as well as of the pastor. Sustaining may therefore be defined as bringing to bear upon the person in crisis the total caring resources of the church in such a way that the person is enabled to transcend and endure circumstances that are not immediately alterable.

The second exception to the definitions provided by Clebsch and Jaekle concerns the guiding function of pastoral care. Guiding refers to helping a person make choices between alternative courses of action; but rather than focusing upon courses of action alone, we will also consider the person's choice of the appropriate skills for coping with a crisis. This change in focus reflects our understanding of crisis as obstacles persons face which they cannot overcome by their usual problem-solving skills. Therefore, guiding refers to helping persons in crisis to choose positive, healthy crisis-coping mechanisms.

Another consideration reflects the way sociocultural forces affecting the black church shaped the nature of sustaining and guiding in black pastoral care. Because of the cultural situation within the black community, the black pastor is a symbol reflecting the hopes and aspirations of black people for liberation from oppression in this life. Therefore, when the black pastor engages in the functions of sustaining and guiding, his or her symbolic significance is brought to bear upon the person and family in crisis. In this book, the symbolic role of the black pastor in sustaining and guiding will have a prominent position.

While four functions have characterized pastoral care historically, two functions have dominated pastoral care in the black church. Clebsch and Jaekle point out that all four functions of pastoral care are present in every period of history, but one function may dominate in a particular era because of historical conditions. This is not the general rule in the history of pastoral care in the black church. Guiding and sustaining have both been dominant functions at the same time in the history of pastoral care in the black church; there has been no dominance of one over the other. While sustaining and guiding dominated, reconciliation took a secondary position, and healing became very difficult because of the racial climate. Therefore, more attention will be given to the equal dominance of sustaining and guiding in black pastoral care.

The fact that social oppression existed did not mean that healing did not take place in the black church. Although the black person's personality was damaged by racism and oppression, wholeness did come for many through the experience of God's love toward them. When the caring resources were brought to bear upon persons suffering from low self-esteem and self-hatred, they experienced themselves as accepted and as "somebody" in the eyes of God and their black brothers and sisters. Healing did exist for some, but for others sustenance was all that could be accomplished. For many, the burden of oppression made the love of God which transformed the self a distant hope; for them God's love as mediated through the resources of the church prevented and lessened the impact of oppression.

Some explanation needs to be given concerning how sustaining and guiding became prominent in black pastoral care. The racial climate in America, from slavery to the present, has made sustaining and guiding more prominent than healing and reconciling. Racism and oppression have produced wounds in the black community that can be healed only to the extent that healing takes place in the structure of the total society. Therefore, the black church has had to find means to sustain and guide black persons in the midst of oppression. In this effort, much attention has been focused upon reducing the impact of racism upon the black personality, but it has been difficult to restore the wholeness of the person caused by the impact of oppression. People need guidance and hope in the present while making the most of their situation; at the same time, they look forward to a future time of ultimate healing.

Reconciliation among persons has had a place in black pastoral care just as healing has had a place. Its place has been to lessen the division among persons so that the caring resources within the caring community would not be disrupted. Public confession has been one of the chief means of reconciling broken relationships, and thus it has helped to maintain the integrity of the caring community. Thus, by preserving the integrity of the caring community whose resources were needed for the task of sustaining, reconciliation has served the end of sustaining.

Reconciliation with God has also served the sustaining function of black pastoral care, being subsumed under sustaining because of the nature of social reality. Reconciliation, or union, with God is the ultimate goal of the black Christian, but it must be viewed in the context of the oppression and powerlessness of black people. Because of oppression, union with God has meant uniting with the source of the power of the universe for the purposes of being supported and sustained in life.[2] Reconciliation has had an end beyond mystical union with God or life after death for the black

---

[2] Joseph Washington, *Black Sects and Cults* (Garden City, N.Y.: Doubleday, 1972). He introduces the concept of black religion's purpose of gaining power or uniting with sources of power in the world.

Christian. It has had implications for living, for being sustained in the presence of oppression.

Before concluding this section, there needs to be some indication of how black pastoral care differs from the modern pastoral-care movement in white mainline Protestant denominations. Owing to the historical circumstances of the black church, pastoral care has had a different focus than in mainline Protestant white churches. Healing has been the dominant function in these white denominations largely because of the absence of economic, political, and social oppression. The healing model of modern pastoral care goes back to the early 1920s, and it was predominantly influenced by the one-to-one Freudian psychoanalytic orientation to psychiatry.[3] To learn the methods and skills of the one-to-one healing model requires economic resources and extensive clinical and educational opportunities to which many black pastors did not have access until very recently. Therefore, healing could become a tradition in the mainline Protestant white churches because there were economic resources to provide clinical training for pastors, whereas the black church had to rely upon a tradition of sustaining and guiding fashioned in response to oppression.

The fact that the early roots of pastoral care in white Protestant denominations were largely nourished by the one-to-one model of medical psychiatry made such models difficult for the black pastor to appropriate in the local church. The black pastor needed an orientation that would help him or her utilize the resources within the black church in the care of souls. The creativity of many black pastors has been evidenced in their finding corporate and communal means to meet the needs of persons when theoretical models were inadequate.

In the remaining sections of this chapter, an examination of the historical roots of sustaining and guiding in the black church will be undertaken.

A Sustaining Ministry

Unlike the sustaining function in the healing tradition of mainstream Protestant pastoral care, sustaining in the black church tradition has not been the function of the pastor alone. The sustaining dimension of black pastoral care has been the function of the total church acting as the caring community. It was not just the pastor who looked after the spiritual and emotional needs of the church members; the whole caring community provided the

---

[3] See Edward E. Thornton, *Professional Education for Ministry* (Nashville: Abingdon, 1970), 31–33. See also William Hulme, *Pastoral Care Come of Age* (Nashville: Abingdon, 1970). These works show the influence of the one-to-one medical model orientation and the beginnings of a movement away from this orientation in pastoral care.

sustenance for persons and families in crisis situations. As a caring community, the black church has drawn upon many significant resources to enable persons to overcome and endure the numerous crises arising in the normal course of life exacerbated by oppression. For example, the caring community supported many of the personality needs of its members. It provided supportive structures for persons as they passed through the normal stages of the life cycle. It developed an important theological worldview that enabled the black person to find hope to endure the mundane problems of living in a hostile world. These caring resources will be examined in greater detail in the next sections.

Slavery

Slavery marked the beginning of the black person's journey in America. The slaves were forcibly removed from their native soil and sold away from their families in America. Forced to work without pay, they were stripped of any power to determine their own existence. They were viewed as property and regarded as subhuman. It was against this background that many of the important resources for sustaining were developed.

In the nineteenth century the black church came into existence as an independent institution. Prior to this time, it existed as an invisible institution meeting in clandestine fashion.[4] Many community resources emerged from the invisible and visible institution for the support of persons. These resources included the family, the extended family, peers, the social network, the church fellowship, and the rituals and ceremonies of the visible and invisible church. Sustaining as a function of pastoral care emerged as a corporate function of the community.

A theological worldview was one of the most important community resources for sustaining during slavery. A worldview is a system of symbols that integrates and synthesizes experiences in order to provide the meaning of existence.[5] In the context of pastoral care, a worldview undergirded the caring resources. In the case of the slave, a worldview emerged that not only gave meaning to the slave's existence but also provided the efficacious power that sustained the slave in a hostile environment.

The worldview of the slave projected God as the important resource of sustaining. For the slave, God was envisaged as being immanently involved in all of life, and he was the ultimate source of life. The worldview provided

    [4] E. Franklin Frazier, *The Negro Church in America* (New York: Schocken Books, 1964), 16. He examines the black church as an invisible institution during slavery.

    [5] E. Mansell Pattison, *Pastor and Parish: A Systems Approach* (Philadelphia: Fortress, 1977), 34. This work provides a helpful examination of the function of the community symbol.

explanations of how God had power over the universe, and held that faith in him provided the power to sustain the slave in the midst of chaos. The slaves believed God was in control of the matters of the world and in his own time would make things right in the world.

The Negro spirituals reflected much of the slaves' worldview. Through the singing of the Negro spiritual, the slave was actually participating in the sustaining power of God. As shared creations emerging out of a common condition, many of the Negro spirituals provided a view of the world that enabled the slaves to transcend the brutality of everyday existence. Some provided a faith in a sustaining power that transformed the slaves' despair over the cruelties of slavery into hope. The spirituals helped the slave find meaning and purpose for existence. Through the worldview expressed in the spiritual, the slave was provided with a deep capacity for endurance in spite of suffering. It was the faith expressed in many of the spirituals that sustained the slave through life.

The uniqueness of Negro spirituals lies in their reflection of the faith that undergirded the caring life of the black church. Their worldview provided not only sustaining power for individual persons, but also the glue that held the caring community together. Many of the spirituals reflected a faith that God was intimately involved in the life of specific communities and that he had not exhausted all his resources for conquering evil. Some of the spirituals reflected an incarnational faith that God became the companion of persons within the community for the purposes of caring for a suffering humanity. This belief sustained the care that persons gave one another.

In addition to this worldview, another community resource for sustaining during slavery was the ritual of baptism. Baptism, in most mainline white churches, would fall into the category of reconciliation; but, as we indicated earlier, in the black church, reconciliation was subsumed under sustaining for historical reasons.

One function of sustaining in the black church during slavery was to provide symbolic means for the slave to unite with the source of power and care in the universe. It was through the symbolic means of baptism that the slave sought to be put in touch with God. It was through *immersing* that the slave found symbolic unity with God and obtained the power for survival. It was through the power of God working through the caring community that persons being baptized found the power to live a new life in a strange world.

Not only was the ritual of baptism an important means of sustaining, but the black church as an extended family for the slave was also a tremendous resource. The black church provided surrogates to replace the slave's relatives who had been sold away. Within the church, children who had been sold away from their parents could find substitute parents and parental images. Moreover, the black church attempted to provide moral support for the restoration of the black male to black families. The black church tried to emphasize the Old Testament cultural ideal of the responsibility of the father in the Jewish family.[6] In addition, the church served as an agency of social control whose aim was to strengthen and stabilize the black family by emphasizing patterns that were healthy to family and community life.[7] The total ministry of the black church was thus concentrated on the attempt to heal the wounds in black families during slavery.

The black church also provided community resources to support persons during life crises. One crisis in the black community during slavery was death. Because the slaves were viewed as property that could be expendable, they lived in the constant shadow of death. Consequently, they sought to create social structures within the life of the community and the church to help them deal with death when it came.

During the eighteenth century, mutual-aid societies and burial societies emerge in the black church to provide economic and moral support systems for persons during bereavement. According to Frazier, the earliest mutual-aid society was the Free African Society organized in Philadelphia in 1787 by Absalom Jones and Richard Allen.[8] This society's purpose was to support its members in sickness and to benefit the surviving spouse and the children of the deceased. Financial aid as well as caring concern was offered. Another beneficial society was the Brown Fellowship Society in Charleston, South Carolina, which was designed to relieve widows and orphans during distress, sickness, and death.[9] These mutual-aid societies developed significantly during the emancipation of the slaves and continued to expand for many decades in black churches. Through these societies, the community emphasis in pastoral care in the black church can be visualized.

Another important resource of the black church for sustaining was the therapeutic nature of black worship. Because of the holistic view of persons in black religion, people's feelings were not ignored or considered unimportant. In fact, the black church helped the slaves to realize that their feelings were essential to their very being, for it was through the slaves' feelings that they recognized what they valued most and what they aspired to in life. The slaves desired more than anything else their freedom and the

[6] Frazier, *Negro Church*, 33.
[7] Frazier, *Negro Church*, 34.
[8] Frazier, *Negro Church*, 35.
[9] Frazier, *Negro Church*.

right to determine the directions for their own lives. However, freedom and self-direction were denied, and, as a result, the slaves had to find an outlet for their frustrated feelings. The black church provided an avenue for the expression of their shattered dreams. Black worship served as a catharsis by which the slaves could release pent-up emotions. It served as an important avenue of expression for the whole personality.

The therapeutic value of black worship as a resource of pastoral care is pointed out by Melville Herskovits. "That repression is a cause of neurosis is an elementary tenet of psychoanalysis; the fact, explained in different terms, has been recognized by Negroes."[10] In worship, persons' feelings of frustration with the conditions of life were accepted as real. Such feelings were not ignored by others who shared the same situation in life; and through the acceptance of their feelings, individuals found they were loved and cared for by others. In the context of worship, persons' feelings of frustration were shared and accepted, and they administered pastoral care to one another.

In summary the community resources for sustaining the slave included symbols, rituals, and social groups. These resources helped sustain the slave in the face of injustice, but they could not heal the wounds from the injustice that was inflicted. It must be pointed out, however, that forces for liberation were operating in slavery through violent rebellions and the underground railroad. For the slave, healing meant liberation from oppression; therefore, it was impossible to repair the damage done by slavery without manumission.

Sustaining between 1910 and 1950

The basic resources for sustaining during slavery existed also in the period from 1910 to 1950. The caring resources of the community continued to support persons during crisis situations. The same worldview, which portrayed God as immanently involved in the life of the community, continued. However, many of the social conditions that existed during slavery changed in this period, and this meant that the community resources had to be applied to different circumstances.

Although slavery was abolished by the Emancipation Proclamation, racism continued into the twentieth century. White people's attitude toward black people continued to reflect the assumption of inferiority. More violence replaced the slave system as one of the mechanisms to reenslave the black person. Jim Crow laws were enacted to support segregation. By 1921,

---

[10] Melville J. Herskovits, *The New World Negro* (Bloomington: University of Indiana Press, 1966), 141.

all the political, social, and economic gains made by black people during the Reconstruction period became null and void.

Against this backdrop of racism, violence, and disfranchisement, many Southern black people turned Northward to attempt to secure freedom. In 1900, the rural black population in the United States was 77 percent of the total black population. By 1910, the rural part of the black population had dropped to 72 percent, and by 1920 to 66 percent. It is obvious that the rural population was changing.

Migration of the rural Southern black people to Northern urban areas took place during this period. Not only was freedom an attraction for rural Southern black people, but job opportunities also lured them to the city. Many jobs were created after the end of World War I and the influx of European immigrants halted. This migration of rural black people was also accelerated by the collapse of the cotton crop due to the boll weevil and the unusual floods in 1915. The end result was the Great Migration, which continued through the Depression and World War II unabated.

Naturally, the black church expanded into Northern cities as a result of the Great Migration. Many new black churches emerged during this period to meet the emotional needs of persons.

The migration to the urban North and the continuation of racism exacerbated the problems of black people. The black person's self-esteem was threatened because of negative feedback from the wider society. There was a crisis of powerlessness caused by exclusion from full participation in the wider society, and there were the problems associated with adjusting to the depersonalized city. The sustaining ministry emerged during this period to help the black person adjust to these new circumstances.

The black church became a community resource for sustaining the black person's self-esteem in the midst of powerlessness. In fact, the black church became an alternative structure which substituted for economic and political participation in the wider society. Many parishioners found sustenance for their self-esteem by being part of a successful institution that was able to support itself and provide economic support through small business ventures and credit unions. Moreover, people could exercise political awareness through participation in the decision-making processes of the local church. As an alternative structure, the black church did not heal the problems associated with exclusion from full participation in the wider society; however, it did prevent further damage to black self-esteem.

Perhaps the greatest sustaining ministry of the black church during this period was the care given to the uprooted Southern migrants that helped them adjust to the depersonalized urban environment. This care was manifested through the community support systems which the black church provided. Large, established churches in the urban North provided many types of supportive activities during this period.[11] These activities included scouting, recreation, youth programs, and camping. Some of these churches had community workers, day nurseries, community houses, and clinics. All these churches offered the migrants such traditional services as Sunday school, choir activities, and prayer meetings. Moreover, remnants of the old benevolent burial societies, which were developed during slavery, continued.

These resources provided a stabilizing influence for the uprooted Southern migrants by helping to support a sense of family unity among the migrants. Many left their families behind and sent for them later, after they found jobs. These people suffered feelings of being uprooted and isolated. The church's resources helped these black persons overcome feelings of isolation by helping them relate to others.

Moreover, the black church functioned as a port of entry for the migrants, helping them adjust to urban life. Many of the migrants had never been to the city; they were straight from the rural areas and farm economy. They needed help in finding housing and jobs. Since the black church was the gathering place for the whole black community, it served many of the needs of persons by helping them find housing and jobs.

The black church also provided opportunities for persons to find emotional support for coping with urban ills. One such opportunity was the prayer meeting. The average attendance at prayer meetings during this period was thirty-nine.[12] These meetings, characterized by a warm interpersonal environment, were conducted in an atmosphere of freedom of expression. Extemporaneous prayers, songs, and personal testimonies contributed to the air of spontaneity and support. Biblical instruction was an undergirding influence in these sessions. In these surroundings, individuals found themselves cared for and accepted. This acceptance provided an important experience in the lives of those adjusting to an impersonal urban environment.

The storefront church performed a significant ministry of sustaining during this period. Many migrants suffered from cultural shock as a result of migration. The urban environment was much different from the rural environment: people lived on top of one another; there were no farms, only paved streets. It was impossible for the migrant to know everybody as he did in the rural areas. The drastic change in culture presented the migrant with an extremely difficult psychological adjustment. Many persons turned

---

[11] Benjamin E. Mays and Joseph W. Nicholson. *The Negro's Church* (New York: Institute of Social and Religious Research, 1933; reprinted, New York: Arno Press, 1969), 14.

[12] Mays and Nicholson, *Negro's Church*, 110.

to the traditional established denominational church for a sense of community. However, once the migrants were settled, they became dissatisfied with these traditional denominations, because they were too different from the churches they had left in the rural South. Many migrants began to develop their own churches as a result, patterned after those which were most familiar to them, the rural churches. These churches were very small and usually met in small storefronts. Thus, the storefront phenomenon emerged in the city.

The basic function of the ministry of sustaining in these storefront churches was to help the migrant feel at home in the city. The migrant had difficulty adjusting to the impersonal urban environment. Therefore, the storefront church sought to gear its sustaining ministry to attempting to help the migrant feel comfortable in a strange new world.

These small storefront churches helped prevent a feeling of isolation through the social nature of the worship experience and through the opportunity for fellowship and personal recognition.[13] Within the storefront church, the migrants could sing the same songs they sang in the rural areas. They could be expressive in worship. They could gather with friends. The migrants found the storefront church very supportive in making their adjustment to urban living.

Sustaining since 1960

Beginning in the mid 1950s, events in the United States laid the groundwork for the full participation of black people in American society. The civil rights movement, the black power movement, the involvement of Congress, the executive branch, and the Supreme Court introduced a new era of race relations in America.

The doors of full participation have been opened to many black people, although some of the old racist attitudes still prevail. Because of the entry of black people into the mainstream, some of the functions performed by the black church have been relinquished to secular agencies. The centralized role of the black church in the black community has been weakening; and the old supportive resources for sustaining black people, though still in existence, are disappearing. The task of ministry in the future is to revitalize many of the supportive structures of the black church and give them new meaning in the light of a changed condition. Many economic, social, and emotional problems still exist for black people, even though oppressive structures have been modified and secular agencies exist to respond to

[13] Vattell E. Daniel, "Ritual and Stratification in Chicago Negro Churches," *American Sociological Review* (June 1942): 360–61.

these needs. Therefore, a ministry that will sustain people in their pursuit of a meaningful life within American society is still relevant.

The Symbolic Role of the Pastor

Sustaining and the Black Pastor

The discussion so far has emphasized the role of corporate caring resources in sustaining persons. There needs to be some explanation of the role the black pastor has performed in sustaining persons. This role has largely been that of a symbol—that is, he or she has been an articulator of the theological worldview and a presider over the rituals and ceremonies that provided sustenance. The major function of the black pastor has been to be the leader of the corporate community in utilizing its resources; and when these resources were brought to bear upon the lives of persons in crisis, the symbolic role of the pastor became a function of pastoral care.

As a leader of the community, the black pastor has been the custodian of the community worldview. From the pulpit he or she expounded the faith of the community that enabled persons to endure the hardships of life and proclaimed a faith in a God who was incarnate in life and whose purpose was tied to the lives of black people. The pastor made sure that the faith of the community was constantly before it so that the people found meaning for life. In presiding over baptism and communion, the pastor made the worldview and its power to sustain available to the parishioner. The role of the pastor as leader was crucial, because without such leadership, the corporate resources for sustaining persons in crisis lost some of their meaning. More will be said about the symbolic role of the black pastor in the next section.

Guiding and the Black Pastor

The black community has given a significant place to the black minister historically, and the leadership role of the pastor has been significant in shaping the sustaining and guiding functions and making them the major emphasis in pastoral care in the black church.

Every living system possesses an identity. This identity is expressed in goals and values that are embodied in symbols. These symbols are standards of reference to which the people look to find meaning, purpose, and guidance. In this context the pastor, by virtue of his or her office, is the major symbol of the church, according to Mansell Pattison.[14] His or her function as a symbol provides a continuing affirmation of the community's identity, its goals, its values, and its purposes. Pattison comments on the

---

[14] Pattison, *Pastor and Parish*, 63.

importance of the symbolic significance of the minister: "The minister's very presence carries with it an implicit message. The pastor is a systemic reminder of what the system is."

The black pastor is and has been the symbol of the black church. The presence of a minister in the black community evokes many responses, both positive and negative. In either case the emotional response is strong, and no other person has been given a more centralized role in the black community.[15] The black pastor reminds the people of who they are—children of God living in a hostile environment. More than this, he or she symbolizes for some people God's engagement in the life of humankind, while for others he or she symbolizes God's absence or hiddenness from humankind. For many black people, however, the minister is a representative of God and therefore should be accorded respect.

Because of the symbolic nature of the role of the black minister, he or she has been accorded leadership authority of great magnitude. Many people in the black community have assigned to the black pastor wisdom and competence in all matters of living. He or she is expected to provide a worldview so that the parishioner can integrate his or her own experience. Because of this assignment, many of the laity have expected the minister to be omniscient, omnipotent, and omnipresent, and to provide solutions to many earthly problems as well as to be a custodian of the values connecting them to God. Although no human could live up to these expectations, they have been operative among the laity, and the pastor has tried to live up to them as much as possible.

Because of this leadership expectation by black people, the guiding function of pastoral care became dominant. The black pastor, namely the male, became the spiritual father and leader of the black people, and was expected to guide the congregation. He was expected to display no weakness at all, and he was expected to be in full charge and control of the church. In personal matters of pastoral concern, the pastor was expected to take charge and provide answers and solutions. Many people looked to the minister as a father in pastoral concerns, and this included elderly people. The prominence of the black pastor's authority came as a result of the fact that the church was the center of the community and that this church was full of persons whose earthly power had been frustrated.[16]

Recently, the central role of the pastor in leadership has changed in the black church. Since the 1950s, progress in race relations has opened new

---

[15] This is the conclusion made by Charles V. Hamilton, *The Black Preacher in America* (New York: Morrow, 1972), 14–15.

[16] Floyd Massey, Jr. and Samuel B. McKinney, *Church Administration in the Black Perspective* (Valley Forge, Pa.: Judson Press, 1976), 34–35.

opportunities for black leadership in the wider society. Slowly, black people have begun to look away from the church for leadership, because more and more black people are being educated and trained. Opportunities for black lay people outside the church have been lessening the influence of the black preacher. As a result of this new development, many pastors are in the midst of an identity crisis and need help in developing new skills of guiding. In the future, the black laity will need guidance, but the guidance will have to take more cognizance of the parishioner's internal abilities. The pastor's guidance will be less authoritarian and more enabling of persons' own abilities and potential for making their own decisions.

Summary

The sustaining and guiding functions of pastoral care have had equal prominence in black pastoral care. Unlike the alternating dominant-function hypothesis described by Clebsch and Jaekle, there have been two functions, not one, operating simultaneously in black pastoral care. This has been true because of socio-cultural circumstances. It was very difficult for the healing function to emerge because oppression made wounds almost irreparable, and reconciling became a function performed under sustaining.

Historically, sustaining has been the function of the total church in black pastoral care. In this context the pastor and the congregation have worked together to sustain persons in crisis. Not only have the congregation and the pastor represented significant resources for pastoral care, but other cultural religious resources have been drawn upon for the care of persons. Among these resources have been the religious worldview, ritual practices, and the symbolic significance of the black pastor.

2

African American Men:
Identity, Marriage, and Family (1997)

Edward Wimberly continues to develop his distinctive black pastoral theology in these readings from *Counseling African American Marriages and Families** and *The Care of Men.*† In the first, Wimberly puts forth a challenge to norms of male leadership over women in African American marriages, utilizing biblical, feminist, and womanist scholarship in the field of pastoral theology to challenge sexist assumptions and encourage more egalitarian marital relationships.

In his chapter in *The Care of Men*, edited by Christie Neuger and James Poling, Wimberly identifies significant critiques of the mythopoetic men's movement associated with Robert Bly: class and race biases, sexism, and a tendency to appropriate indigenous practices such as drumming and sweat lodges. Wimberly goes on to articulate the need for an African American men's movement that resists stereotypical notions of masculinity and instead nurtures the "egalitarian, androgynous, and spiritual impulses that characterized African American maturity in the past" (57). He identifies preferred models of male personhood culled from the Scriptures and informed by

---

* Edward P. Wimberly, "Beyond African American Male Hierarchical Leadership," in *Counseling African American Marriages and Families* (Louisville: Westminster John Knox, 1997), 1–10; Wimberly, "Male and Female, God Created Them to Be Whole," in *Counseling African American Marriages and Families*, 11–24.

† Edward P. Wimberly, "The Men's Movement and Pastoral Care of African American Men," in *The Care of Men*, ed. Christie Cozad Neuger and James Newton Poling (Nashville: Abingdon, 1997), 104–21.

womanist critiques of compulsive masculinity. Wimberly's chapter, like the rest of the essays in Neuger and Poling's volume, begins to explore a *narrative* model of pastoral care for men that revolves around the stories of particular communities and their distinct spiritual and religious sensibilities.

In each of these contributions, we see more clearly Edward Wimberly's ability to address both the church and the academy in his writing. Wimberly's primary sense of call is to serve the black church, and it is out of his concern for the everyday struggles of African American men and their family relationships that his work develops.

Further Reading

Wimberly, Edward P. "Pastoral Counseling with African American Men." *Urban League Review* 16, no. 2 (1993): 77–84.

Wimberly, Edward P. "African American Spirituality and Sexuality: Perspectives on Identity, Intimacy and Power." *Journal of Pastoral Theology* 4 (Summer 1994): 19–31. doi:10.1080/10649867.1994.11745311.

Wimberly, Edward P. "Compulsory Masculinity and Violence." *Caregiver Journal* 13, no. 1 (1997): 18–19. This is a response to Vincent Reyes, "The Widening Circles of Violence." *Caregiver Journal* 13, no. 1 (1997): 14–17.

● ● ●

Beyond African American Male Hierarchical Leadership *

This book is intended to help practitioners of marriage and family pastoral counseling to be aware of the religious worldview and metaphors that many African American spouses and family members bring to pastoral counseling. Such an awareness will influence the assessment and intervention strategies that might be used when working with these marriages and families. Nancy Boyd-Franklin, Henry Mitchell, and Nicholas Lewter have talked about these religious values and worldviews that often accompany African Americans when they come for individual, marital, and family counseling.[1] This work will explore such religious and spiritual values and their function in the therapeutic relationship.

One major theological phenomenon is emerging that some African Americans bring to marriage and family counseling. It has to do with biblical images of the ideal marriage and family. Following many evangelical and conservative Christian movements, some African Americans come to pastoral counseling emphasizing the traditional male leadership within the home, and this emphasis does not seem to help the family achieve its intended goals. In such marriages and families, spouses are engaged in a power struggle in which the husband seeks to dominate and the wife seeks to be out from under the husband's domination. While it appears to me that there are deeper marital and family dynamics at work in these marriages and families than the religious values that are articulated, the fact is that some marriages and families organize their conflict around religious values.

Given the history of racism and discrimination and some experts talking about the emasculation of African American men, it does seem that male leadership in the home is very important. However, this male leadership is often expressed through utilizing stereotypical images of masculinity and femininity that permeate all of society.[2] Drawing on these stereotypical images, many African American men have sought the sanction of religion to support a particular type of domineering leadership style in the home that is oppressive rather than liberating to the growth potential of their

---

[1]   Nancy Boyd-Franklin, *Black Families in Therapy: A Multisystems Approach* (New York: Guilford Press, 1989); Henry Mitchell and Nicholas Lewter, *Soul Theology* (San Francisco: Harper & Row, 1986).

[2]   Edward P. Wimberly, "Pastoral Counseling with African American Men," *Urban League Review* 16, no. 2 (1993): 77–84.

*   This selection was previously published in Edward P. Wimberly, *Counseling African American Marriages and Families* (Louisville: Westminster John Knox, 1997), 1–10.

spouses and children. Rigid role definitions are enacted and scripture is drawn on for authority. Such dynamics present real problems for marriage and family therapists.

Often wives also want to be accommodating to the religious values that they feel are important. However, they are in conflict because they feel that what they are expected to do does not lead to their growth and development. Consequently, many are in a spiritual quandary.

Theologically, this use of scripture to support stereotypical and hierarchical roles of males and females within African American marriages and families raises the question about how scripture is being used. Three alternative approaches are possible.[3] The first approach is the *propositional model*. This model emphasizes cognitive uses of scripture that formulate truth into objective realities and call for rational and behavioral allegiance by its adherents. The second approach is the *experiential-expressive model*. This model puts emphasis on the inner feelings, attitudes, and experiences of people. It draws on the experiences of people and makes scripture secondary when understanding family relationships. The third approach is the *cultural linguistic or narrative model*. This model emphasizes the narrative orientation to life and demonstrates how narrative organizes life and informs experience.[4] Rather than seeking sanctions for marital and family relationships in theological propositions or in the experience of marital partners or family members, this approach looks to scripture as narrative to inform marital and family relationships.

The relationship among these three forms of organizing marital and family experience is not necessarily exclusive. They represent divergent aspects of organizing experience and can inform how people in marriage and families utilize religious values. The concern here is that propositional statements are made about male and female relationships and relationships between family members that exclude the experiences of other family members and produce dysfunctional families. Moreover, focusing on individual experiences of family members could lead to making one family member's experience normative for all family members. This too could end up in marital and family dysfunction. However, the narrative approach to utilizing scripture holds out the potential for developing marital and family interactive patterns that allow for each family member to grow and develop.

---

[3] These three approaches are modifications of the approaches to doctrine found in the work of George A. Lindbeck, *The Nature of Doctrine: Religion and Theology in a Postliberal Age* (Philadelphia: Westminster John Knox, 1984), 16–29. The modifications relate to how individual marriages and families formulate their approach to using scripture.

[4] Lindbeck, *Nature of Doctrine*, 32–33.

Scripture is much more dynamic in quality than either propositional or experiential-expressive approaches allow. The narrative model captures better the dynamic way scripture can work in the lives of people. The narrative approach to scripture challenges both the nongrowth-producing propositions that people make and the self-centered use of experience.[5] Therefore, a narrative approach that understands the function of scripture in interaction with human beings offers an important way to approach marriages and families. It is especially useful with families that have a tendency to make rigid propositions about male and female role relationships. Consequently, narrative theology and narrative approaches to scripture will be utilized to give direction for assessing and intervening with African American marriages and families that have the tendency to develop inflexible role boundaries rooted in propositional understandings.

Narrative approaches to marital and family life are more consistent with how African American families have brought meaning to their lives in the past. Scripture has been very important in the African American church and in African American families, and the method of bringing meaning to the lives of people has been relating their lives to the dominant stories of the Bible. For example, it is not unusual to hear the storytellers of family history tell the family history in relationship to the Christian story especially the exodus story. Consequently, narrative approaches, where people bring meaning to their lives by relating them to biblical stories and plots, have been very important in African American family traditions.

This does not mean, however, that propositional approaches are not necessary. Rather, it emphasizes a more holistic approach that involves both sides of the brain. Propositional or rational uses of scripture alone are not sufficient to inform the marital and family life of many African Americans. Consequently, the narrative perspective permits African American marriages and families to be more flexible with regard to roles and family patterns as they respond to the problems that they confront.

The next section will lay the foundation for utilizing narrative in pastoral counseling with African American marriages and families.

Narrative Theology

Narrative is the telling and retelling of a community's story, the meaning of which unfolds through the interaction of characters over time.[6] A narrative

---

[5] Edward P. Wimberly, *Using Scripture in Pastoral Counseling* (Nashville: Abingdon, 1994).

[6] Michael Goldberg, *Theology and Narrative: A Critical Introduction* (Nashville: Abingdon, 1981), 35.

theology focuses on the elucidation, examination, and transformation of the religious convictions that make up the faith of a given community.[7] In the process of reflection on the faith and beliefs of a given community, the narrative theologian attends to the linguistic structures that represent the source and ground of the community's convictions.[8] The narrative theologian not only attends to the propositional level of the belief systems of a faith community, but also keeps the underlying narrative and the events and activities surrounding it in focus.[9] Consequently, narrative theology is an abstraction from the concrete life and interaction of a community of faith.

From the point of view of the Christian faith, *narrative theology* is reflection on the Christian faith story as told and retold in scripture and in the traditions that proclaim Jesus Christ as Savior and Lord. For many Christians this story is about God establishing God's rule in history, and scriptures are viewed as a narrative recording of the events that unfold in God's establishing salvation history.[10] In this historical view of faith, scriptures become the living memory of the faith community to which they return over and over again in the retelling of its story.

For the purposes of this book, the rule of God is the primary metaphor used to understand the unfolding of God's purposes in history. This metaphor is a level of abstraction from the concrete history of the Christian faith community as it is expressed in the Hebrew scriptures and in the New Testament. Therefore, the present canon in scripture is normative, and the traditions utilizing this narrative memory are also sources for interpretation of the church's faith and practice. The term "normative" here refers to the present canon as the major source for understanding God's history of salvation beginning with creation and moving to the eschaton.

The narrative theology articulated here takes very seriously the embodiment of the rule of God in Jesus Christ. The Gospels proclaim Jesus as the incarnation of God who inaugurated the rule of God concretely in history. This was the preaching of the Gospels and the entire early church. This incarnation of God in history did not end with the death of Jesus. It continues today within the church through the power of the Holy Spirit.

[7] Goldberg, *Theology and Narrative*, 34.
[8] Goldberg, *Theology and Narrative*, 35.
[9] Goldberg, *Theology and Narrative*, 35.
[10] The view that makes the rule of God or kingdom of God central in the narrative history of the Christian church comes from the work of Stanley Hauerwas. See Stanley Hauerwas, *A Community of Character: Toward a Constructive Christian Social Ethic* (Notre Dame: University of Notre Dame Press, 1981), 37. I am also indebted to H. Richard Niebuhr, *The Meaning of Revelation* (New York: Macmillan Co., 1941), 32–66 for his understanding of revelation in history.

Theologically, the narrative of God's unfolding purposes and God's establishing God's rule in history continues through the church.

In order for this narrative memory and history to be relevant for marriage and family life, it is necessary to further reflect on the nature of God's
rule and reign. Further abstractions are needed on the narrative history
of the faith community in order to make a connection between the flow of
what H. Richard Niebuhr calls the external history of a community of faith
and the internal history of people who live in particular communities.[11]
External history has to do with the ongoing thrust of God's unfolding history,
and *internal history* has to do with how this history impacts the lives of people
in community.

Narrative Theology and Marriage and Family Counseling

The implication of narrative theology for marriage and family life must be
explored in relationship to another metaphor. The metaphor eschatological
community is closely related to the rule of God. The *eschatological community*
is the faith community that exists between the time Jesus inaugurated the
rule of God and the time it is finally established at the end of time. This
community is made up of the persons who have consciously decided to
participate in God's unfolding story of salvation and who have given their
lives over to the rule and reign of God. In Niebuhr's terminology, these people have taken the leap of faith; they have moved from observers of God's
story to participants in it.[12] In other words, the external history of God has
become their inner history.

In the eschatological community, how people live in relationship to
one another is essential as God's purposes continue to unfold in its midst.
The scriptures emphasize that the quality of relationships among people is
extremely significant for the fulfillment of God's purposes. Therefore, communal ethics and the kind of communal atmosphere created are important
within the eschatological community.

Abstracting further from the narrative history as recorded in scripture,
the ethical norm of love seems to be central, especially to the early church
as an eschatological community. This is found particularly in Paul's thinking as he reflects on the significance of the theology of the cross and Jesus'
life, death, and resurrection. This same love motif is found in the Gospels
and Johannine biblical literature. Jesus' relationships with others were to
be imitated and the quality of relationships of support and care was to
be primary in the eschatological community. Welcoming strangers to the

---

[11] Niebuhr, *Revelation*, 59–66.
[12] Niebuhr, *Revelation*, 61.

eschatological community regardless of race or gender was very important in the early church, particularly in the house churches in Rome.[13] Brotherly and sisterly love extended beyond cultural and racial lines. Participation in God's salvation history was viewed as a family affair, and all were invited to be members of this eschatological family without regard to gender, race, or cultural background.

Through the power of the Holy Spirit, the early church saw itself empowered to live a faithful life of love as it patiently awaited the completion of God's rule. This same love ethic and quality of caring in relationship are informative for the eschatological community today. It is possible to draw an analogy between the eschatological community and individual marriages and families that make up the eschatological community, that is, marriages and families also are to live under the love ethic. Marital partners and family members are to live in such a way in their relationships that care and support of others are central. Quality living is essential to the fulfillment of God's purposes even today.

An additional abstraction is necessary to be specific about the love ethic. This specificity has to do with developing a norm from the narrative history of the eschatological community. The norm I have abstracted from the love ethic for guiding marital and family relationships is: *Family members and marital partners are to live in their relationships in such a way that all family members are free to grow into their full possibilities as full participants in God's unfolding drama of salvation and as members of the eschatological community.* This refined norm will serve as the basis of the pastoral theology needed to assess and intervene in African American marriages and families.

From the above principle, it can be visualized that narrative theology also has its propositional elements. Propositional dimensions of thought cannot be eliminated. From my vantage point, propositional statements need to be minimal, and they also need to be stated at the nonnegotiable normative level of abstraction to give guidance to human interaction. Therefore, normative statements need to be made to provide goals toward which African American marriages and families need to move. However, specific roles can only be defined by marital partners and family members as they interact in concrete life situations as they move toward the goals.

Theological Method

In the above information, the beginnings of a theological method are outlined. *Pastoral theological method*, for the purposes here, refers to the level of

[13] Anne Streaty Wimberly and Edward Powell Wimberly, *The Language of Hospitality: Intercultural Relations in the Household of God* (Nashville: Cokesbury, 1991), 42–47.

abstract reflection needed to assist pastoral counselors working with African American marriages and families. This method involves attending to themes, values, and traditions that have nurture African American families historically: communalism, extended family emphases, egalitarian roles, and a religious orientation. The method also involves establishing abstract norms from the narrative faith history of scripture and the historical values of African American family experience that will serve as the basis for critical analysis of marital and family relationships of African Americans. The norm also needs to be adequate enough to critically analyze the social and cultural forces influencing the lives of African Americans. Finally, this norm needs to serve as a basis on which to draw from the behavioral sciences methods and theories that might help in assessing and intervening in African American marriages and families.

The norm I have chosen has been stated as family members living in ways that liberate the growth potential of each family member. This means that no family member or marital partner lives at the expense of other family members. This norm will be spelled out further focusing on the specifics of what this means in concrete situations. Moreover, it will be the basis on which to interpret scripture and draw from the behavioral sciences.

The specific method of interpreting scripture is called Scripture Interpreting Scripture.[14] This method refers to reading specific parts of the Bible in light of other more definitive aspects of the Bible. Here the emphasis is on the ethic of love abstracted from the experienced narrative of the eschatological community of faith. This norm has been spelled out for its meaning within marital and family relationships. Consequently, this ethical norm of love will help to interpret particular passages of scripture dealing with family and marriage relationships. This method of interpretation seeks to interpret particular passages m their original context and meaning while also using the abstracted norm of love emerging out of the narrative thrust of God's salvation history.

In summary, the overarching theological and ethical norm that informs pastoral counseling with African American marriages and families is the love ethic. This ethic has been refined to involve each family member living in ways that liberate the growth and development of each family member as full participants in God's unfolding drama of salvation. In other words, the emphasis will be on marriages and families as environments for encouraging the holistic growth of marital partners and family members. This norm will be used to interpret scripture and to draw from the behavioral sciences; to evaluate the history of marital and family relationships within

[14] This method is used by William B. Oglesby in *Biblical Themes in Pastoral Care* (Nashville: Abingdon, 1980), 33.

the African American community; and to deal with sexism within the African American community. On the basis of this norm and the results of using it, implications for assessing and intervening in African American marriages and families will be drawn.

The significance of the norm of love, expressed through liberating holistic growth dimensions for marriages and families, relates to how marriages and families utilize scripture. The criteria is whether or not scripture is used in ways that promote the holistic liberated growth of each family member. If the propositional use of scripture seems to benefit some family members and not others, then such uses need to be revised.

The second significance of this norm is that it gives guidance to pastoral counselors who work with people who utilize scripture. The pastoral counselor can help counselees to explore whether or not their uses of scripture promote or hinder the liberated holistic growth of each marital partner and family member.

The major concern of this book is to help promote the development of healthy personal, marital, and family stories or mythologies that facilitate the growth and development of each family member. Further, such liberated growth is not envisaged as an end in itself. Rather, the ultimate end of growth facilitation is participation in the unfolding drama of God's salvation. The purpose of the eschatological community is to make people ready to assume their roles and vocations in God's salvation endeavor. Consequently, marital and family relationships serve a greater end.

Pastoral Counseling with African American Marriages and Families

This book is addressed to pastoral counselors and religious counselors who are interested in marriage and family counseling with African Americans. Therefore the uniqueness of African American marriages and families must be identified. Moreover, the distinctiveness of the approach for working with African American marriages and families needs to be identified as well.

The distinctiveness with regard to African American marital and family life can be identified in terms of themes, values, and emphases. For example, the themes, values, and emphases are communal and extended-family-oriented as opposed to individualistic thrusts that are characteristic of wider cultural emphases. This does not make African American marriages and families unique from other marriages and families that are ethnic. However, communal and extended-family values are unique when compared to wider cultural emphases on individualism.

In addition, the communal and extended-family orientations are legitimate for African survival in the Western world. This means that it is very difficult for African American families and marriages to survive without connectedness to extended-family traditions.

A second value is the historical presence of two marital and family life traditions of African Americans. The first tradition is the emphasis on the patriarchal male leadership in marriage and family life that goes back to slavery as a means to reclaim the African American family. The second tradition is a mutuality and androgynous tradition that envisages husbands and wives working together in order to survive oppression and racism. Here again the two traditions are not necessarily distinctive from other traditions in wider culture. Yet the cultural context that gave rise to these traditions is unique, that is, oppression and racism helped to foster responses that eventuated in unique emphases for African American marriages and families.

Patriarchalism is also an African survival form. Its nature is different from Western patriarchalism according to some scholars, for example, I find the work of Charles Finch helpful in this regard.[15] Summarizing his views in an article, I state:

> He illustrates that patriarchy was an inevitable outgrowth of the development of human consciousness related to a number of economic and social factors. He indicates that matriarchy lost ground because it was one-sided, all consuming, and unhealthy in the same way that patriarchy has become today. According to Finch, Africa, particularly Egypt, avoided the split between matriarchy and patriarchy that dominated the rest of the world. He notes that there was a creative reconciliation between matriarchy and patriarchy in lower cultures of the Nile where patriarchy did not overcompensate for the abuses of matriarchy.[16]

Finch points out that matriarchy preceded patriarchy prior to written history and was as abusive as patriarchy is today.[17] His point is that African patriarchy was more androgynous and egalitarian than Western forms of patriarchy.

While African Americans inherited a more mutual form of patriarchalism, we are being influenced to adopt a more deadly form of patriarchalism that is destructive of African American females. That is, African American men are abandoning androgyny and mutuality of African patriarchalism for a model that is destructive to the growth of African American women.

---

[15] Charles S. Finch III, *Echoes of the Old Darkland: Themes from the African Eden* (Atlanta: Khenti, 1991).

[16] Wimberly, "Pastoral Counseling with African American Men," 79.

[17] Finch, *Old Darkland*, xiii.

Consequently, part of the need is to be more in touch with the mutuality traditions that are part of our African and African American past.

One way to do this is to help African Americans to be *bicultural*. This means that they need to live in two cultures at the same time. They must appropriate the mutuality and androgynous traditions of the African and African American past while living in a culture that has a different focus.

The major themes from the African American past that this book appropriates are (1) the communal nature of African American marital and family life and (2) the mutuality and androgynous models of our heritage of male and female relationships.

In addition to these two themes there are healing traditions of care that make up the heritage of African Americans. The healing tradition consists of a communal support systems approach to marital and family life. This means finding the sources of care for marriages and families from within the extended family.

It is my belief that the healing power of the African American extended family can be enhanced by the modern family systems approaches to marriage and family life. Consequently, cross-generational emphases will be the constant thrust of this book, and family systems theories that feature cross-generational connections will be emphasized.

A valid criticism can be launched that what this book is doing is not much different from what some textbooks do in marriage and family therapy. While this criticism has some validity, it must be recognized that a cross-generational emphasis is nothing new to African Americans. This has been a consistent theme for us emerging out of our African roots. It is not a new therapeutic trend. Consequently, I draw on contemporary cross-generational theories to assist in helping African American marriages and families continue a distinctive historical thrust.

In my mind, making cross-generational connections is living biculturally, that is to say, connecting cross-generationally puts African Americans in touch with a heritage of mutuality and androgyny that is unique and different from wider culture. Moreover, connectedness to the extended family brings with it resources from the past that are necessary for marital and family survival in contemporary life. Being in touch cross-generationally enables African Americans to live in a culture far different from itself.

I see many African Americans who do not realize the value of extended-family connections. They seem to feel that cutoffs from the extended-family are what is needed to survive in the corporate segments of our economy. However, the opposite is proving to be true. Many African Americans are discovering that connectedness with the cross-generational extended family is not a luxury but an absolute necessity. Therefore, the role of pastoral counseling with African American marriages and families focuses on helping them to recover extended-family connections. Using modern cross-generational methods of therapy are not novel, but they are essential in recovery of a vital African American marriage and family life. What makes this book distinctive is that it seeks to recover a unique and distinctive historical thrust rooted in African and African American communalism and the extended family.

The recovery of the egalitarian and androgynous past is consistent with the narrative theological thrust of this book. These models are very compatible with the growth norm and the ethic of love. This book, however, does not emphasize African patriarchalism. Rather, it lifts up the egalitarian and androgynous traditions of the past that have facilitated growth and love. Therefore, the emphasis is on equality and growth for both marital partners and for each family member.

In summary, the values that inform African American marriages and families are biblical views regarding male and female relationships, affinity for narrative more than propositional approaches to theology, communalism, extended-family orientation, healing tradition of support systems, cross-generational connectedness, and a religious orientation. None of these values represents anything unique to African American marriages and families. However, taken together as a coherent worldview undergirding African American marriages and families, these relationships are unique and distinguishable from orientations in wider culture.

Additional values that are related to the religious orientation will be covered in the next chapter in greater detail.

• • •

Male and Female, God Created Them to Be Whole *

An African American mother came to counseling initially because she felt she was an inadequate mother. She had just discovered that her seventeen-year-old daughter had been molested when she was eight years old. Her daughter was having difficulty in school and at home. The daughter told her mother that part of the problem was that the mother was inadequate, because the mother had not protected the daughter from the molestation. The mother was devastated, and she felt that the daughter had told the truth. The mother also recalled that she too had not been protected from molestation by a close family member when she was a child. The mother also discovered that the molestation pattern occurred with her own mother. Therefore, she discovered that the pattern of molestation was a multigenerational pattern. For three generations, and perhaps more generations, the female family members were molested by male family members.

The mother came to counseling to help get her relationship with her daughter on a better footing. She also wanted to work on personal issues that could help her come to grips with family of origin issues related to victimization at the hands of male family members. In the process of counseling she confronted a major form of helplessness that was passed on from generation to generation by her mother. This helplessness said that you must remain quiet in the face of sexual molestation, and it was impossible to do anything about it. Early in counseling she learned to confront her mother about her own feelings about molestation. She was also able to allow her daughter to work through her daughter's feelings about her ineptness as a parent. After a year, she was able to confront her daughter's perpetrator and her family that allowed this to happen. She had made up her mind that the cycle of family silence had to stop, because there were other young girls at risk in the extended family.

One of the reasons why this counselee was able to break the silence after several generations relates to her desire to be better connected to her family of origin. Because of the molestation, she felt alienated from her mother and her relatives. She withdrew from them as a protective measure; however, she felt like she was dying inside. Being cut off from her family of origin felt like "soul murder." She did not feel like a whole person as a result. Consequently, she desired to reconnect with her family, and she felt she had to confront the silence about sexual molestation as part of her reconnecting to her family of origin.

*   This selection was previously published in Edward P. Wimberly, *Counseling African American Marriages and Families* (Louisville: Westminster John Knox, 1997), 11–24.

The sexual molestation also resulted in her alienation from the church. She had a very deep faith in God. However, because of the history of sexual molestation, she was vulnerable to sexual exploitation. Often, this sexual exploitation came at the hands of church leaders. She withdrew from the church to protect herself from this form of sexual exploitation and to gain more control of her life. The point is that she desired to reconnect with the church because she felt cut off from another source of her identity. She was a very spiritual person and felt the need for spiritual nurturing through the church.

Throughout my counseling with this mother and her daughter several religious themes were prominent. Among these themes was the need for connectedness to a family tradition and a religious tradition. Pivotal in the themes was the need for wholeness. The need to overcome past abuse, the need to be in charge of one's own physical body and to protect it from abuse from others, the need to have spiritual integrity, and the need for family connectedness are themes of wholeness.

The theme of wholeness and its subthemes are present in the lives of many African Americans with whom I do pastoral counseling. The dominance of these themes relates largely to the presence of a theological worldview that nurtures African Americans' understanding of themselves as whole persons. This theological worldview also helps to distinguish what African Americans bring to pastoral counseling from what non-African Americans bring. My presupposition is that the theological themes and spiritual issues that African Americans bring to pastoral counseling are unique, because the themes and issues are shaped by a unique theological worldview. Therefore, this chapter will explore the themes of this theological worldview and their implications for pastoral counseling with African American marriages and families.

The uniqueness of African American marriages and families is in the theological worldview that undergirds their marriage and family life. The worldview has many religious themes that emerge from the African American religious experience and help to shape how many people behave within African American marriages and families. The themes that dominate this worldview include:

1. the embodied soul
2. the uniqueness of persons
3. the family of God

These three themes undergird the values that were identified in chapter 1, namely, communalism, extended-family orientation, cross-generational connectedness, religious orientation, and living biculturally. This chapter will explore these themes in detail. The goals of this exploration are to:

1. identify the theological content of these themes

2. identify the biblical and theological traditions undergirding these themes

3. examine the theological and biblical scholarship related to these themes that support a narrative orientation rather than a propositional orientation

4. draw implications of the examination of these themes for pastoral counseling with African American marriages and families

5. make constructive theological statements about the nature of persons rooted in extrapolations from the vision of the eschatological community and to balance self-love and other-love.

An Embodied Soul

In 1982 my wife and I took a sabbatical leave from the School of Theology at Claremont in Claremont, California, where we worked with Howard Clinebell and John Cobb. I remember using the term "soul" on one occasion with John Cobb. His response to me was that African American theologians were fortunate to be able to use the word "soul." He pointed out that Western theology abandoned the word, primarily because of the Greek influence. The concept of the self took the place of the soul.

The concept of the soul remains significant for many African American theologians. The word "soul" appears prominently in the titles of significant books by such people as James Cone, Henry Mitchell, and Nicholas Cooper Lewter.[1] Some African American psychologists also use the concept in their book titles. The most notable is *Roots of Soul* by Alfred Pasteur and Ivory Toldson.[2] Linda Hollies includes the word "souls" in her edited work by womanist writers, *Womanist Care: How to Tend the Souls of Women*.[3] Anne Wimberly uses the concept of soul in her work *Soul Stories: African American Christian Education*.[4]

---

[1] James H. Cone, *My Soul Looks Back* (Maryknoll, N.Y.: Orbis Books, 1986); Henry Mitchell and Nicholas Lewter, *Soul Theology* (San Francisco: Harper & Row, 1986).

[2] Alfred B. Pasteur and Ivory L. Toldson, *Roots of Soul: The Psychology of Black Expressiveness* (Garden City, N.Y.: Anchor Books, 1982).

[3] Linda H. Hollies, ed., *Womanist Care: How to Tend the Souls of Women* (Joliet, Ill.: Woman to Woman Ministries, 1991).

[4] Anne Streaty Wimberly, *Soul Stories: African American Christian Education* (Nashville: Abingdon, 1995).

Of great significance is the fact that the concept of soul within African American theology largely avoids the ancient Gnostic dualistic split between soul and body or flesh and spirit. Mitchell and Lewter point this out. They believe that the soul is embodied, because it is both physical and related to its social context.[5]

For Mitchell and Lewter *soul theology* forms a belief system that sustains and supports African Americans' journey in the United States.[6] This belief system is made up of core beliefs that enable African Americans to function at full capacity physically, intellectually, emotionally, and spiritually.[7] Mitchell and Lewter point out that these core beliefs enable African Americans "to affirm their own gender, ethnicity, and peculiar personhood and still be other-centered and self giving."[8] This belief system fosters a positive sense of relationship both to God and God's creation and to the family, extended family, and community. The various affirmations have their roots in the Bible that reflect African and biblical wisdom.[9] Oral tradition forms soul theology and passes it on from generation to generation. Mitchell and Lewter call soul theology "doctrine-in-narrative form."[10] About the narrative basis of soul theology Mitchell and Lewter say:

> Soul theology speaks also to the idea of the canon, the corpus of narratives deemed worthy of memory and transmission to succeeding generations. There is little question that the most popular tales in African tradition were told for their usefulness and effectiveness. Likewise, Moses, the emancipator, and Jesus, the suffering Son of God and link to heaven, were themes chosen by African-Americans in the crucible of need.[11]

The embodied nature of the soul is envisaged through defining what I mean by this concept. By *soul* I mean a purposive entity that pushes and pulls the person toward self-transcendence and unity with God, the ultimate source of the soul's activity. This understanding of the soul derives from and is consistent with the black Christian understanding of the soul.[12]

This definition reflects the African past of African Americans where the physical and spiritual worlds were mutually related and influential and

---

[5] Mitchell and Lewter, *Soul Theology*, ix–x.
[6] Mitchell and Lewter, *Soul Theology*, 5.
[7] Mitchell and Lewter, *Soul Theology*, 5.
[8] Mitchell and Lewter, *Soul Theology*, 5.
[9] Mitchell and Lewter, *Soul Theology*, 6.
[10] Mitchell and Lewter, *Soul Theology*, 8.
[11] Mitchell and Lewter, *Soul Theology*, 8–9.
[12] Edward P. Wimberly, *Pastoral Counseling and Spiritual Values: A Black Point of View* (Nashville: Abingdon, 1982), 42–43.

were not mutually exclusive as in Platonic dualism or ancient Gnosticism.[13] With no fixed boundaries, the physical and spiritual worlds interpenetrated each other and were in constant feedback. The soul permitted this mutual feedback and was in constant relationship to God. The soul was not confined to the physical world or to the body, but it traveled within both.

The definition of soul that I am lifting up moves toward an understanding of soul closely akin to the biblical understanding of soul relating to the whole person. Biblically, the concept of soul relates to the entire person as a spiritual and physical unity. The soul is not abstracted from the body but related to the entire person.[14]

It has been pointed out that soul has almost been universally rejected except for Carl Jung.[15] This has not been the case, however, for African Americans. Neither the word "self" nor "ego" dominates the African American's definition of personhood. Rather, the word "soul" seems more inclusive of what psychologists today call the self. For African American Christians soul is essential to understanding the worth and dignity of human beings.

Alice Walker believes that the emphasis on soul is essential for creating an environment for home life of African Americans. She comments on the significance of soul and its definition as she reflects on the enmity between African American males and females:

> In a society in which everything seems expendable, what is to be cherished, protected at all costs, defended with one's life? I am inclined to believe, sadly, that there was a greater appreciation of the value of one's soul among black people in the past than there is in the present; we have become more like our oppressors than many of us can bear to admit. The expression "to have soul," so frequently used by our ancestors to describe a person of stature, used to mean something. To have money, to have power, to have fame, even to have "freedom," is not at all the same. An inevitable daughter of the people who raised and guided me, in whom I perceived the best as well as the worst, I believe wholeheartedly in the

---

[13] For a discussion of the Platonic and Gnostic view of human beings, see A. W. Richard Sipe, "Sexual Aspects of the Human Condition," in *Changing Views of the Human Condition*, ed. Paul W. Pruyser (Macon, Ga.: Mercer University Press, 1987), 81–100.

[14] Rodney J. Hunter, ed., *Dictionary of Pastoral Care and Counseling* (Nashville: Abingdon, 1990), 1201–2. For a discussion of how some of the biblical material in the New Testament was a reaction to a mind and body dualism, see Khiok-Khng Yeo, "Rhetorical Interaction 1 Corinthians 8 and 10: Potential Implications for a Chinese, Cross-Cultural Hermeneutic" (Ph.D. diss., Northwestern University, 1993), 198–215.

[15] Hunter, *Dictionary*, 1202.

necessity of keeping inviolate the one interior space that is given to all. I believe in the soul.[16]

For Walker soul is that part of the person's life that could not be enslaved unless one permits its enslavement. She believes that one has to make a choice to allow one's soul to be contaminated by what surrounds it. Each person has the responsibility to keep his or her soul in proper shape, because it is the center of our character and ability to live with dignity.

From the above statement a general summary can be made about the nature of the soul for many African American Christians. First, the soul is the center of the person's life.[17] It is that part of the person that encounters God and through which God enlivens the entire person. Second, the soul and the body are intricately connected, and the resources of the spiritual world interpenetrate with the material world.[18] In this view the spiritual world and the material world are not enemies; rather they interpenetrate and are mutually influential. This follows the African religious heritage that envisages the world as a union of spiritual and material. Third, the body and the soul are interrelated.[19] Fourth, the soul not only has a rela-tionship with the body, it also has a relationship with communities. The soul is what enables the person to become a full participant in the life of the community even when that community is continually oppressed. God's empowerment of the soul and spirit in community provides the person the ability to transcend and live in spite of oppression. Fifth, the person is a whole being, and this includes a soul, a body, and relationships with others. In other words, undergirding the personality is a soul that is relational in nature. Finally, the soul is the center that gives meaning to life and helps to shape the core beliefs that sustain lives.

The key constructive statement growing out of this discussion of the soul is that the soul is embodied. It is not isolated from its relational and social context. The view of the embodied soul presented here does not lend itself to individualism that seeks to take human beings out of their relational and social contexts.

The view of the *embodied soul* as relational and participatory in historical events is harmoniously consistent with the liberated growth of persons and

---

[16] Alice Walker, *The Third Life of Grange Copeland* (New York: Pocket Books, 1988), 345.

[17] For a discussion of the soul as center of the person's life, see Edward P. Wimberly and Anne Streaty Wimberly, *Liberation and Human Wholeness: The Conversion Experiences of Black People in Slavery and Freedom* (Nashville: Abingdon, 1986), 99–100.

[18] Wimberly and Wimberly, *Liberation and Human Wholeness*, 99–100.

[19] Riggins R. Earl, Jr. explores in depth how the slaves developed an embodied soul. See his *Dark Symbols, Obscure Signs: God, Self and Community in the Slave Mind* (Maryknoll, N.Y.: Orbis Books, 1993), 4–7.

the ethic of love growing out of the eschatological community. The concern for the growth of each family member and the concern for one's own growth is related to the embodied soul. The whole person is an embodied soul. The person grows and develops within relationships with others and within particular social contexts. These relationships also include relationships with others across generations. It is impossible for the embodied soul to live in isolation, even though its fundamental orientation begins with the relationship with God. Placing the embodied soul in its relational and social context is essential to its very nature. In short, soul is embodied in physical and social contexts; being relational the soul seeks growth in relationship to God, self, and others.

With regard to the implication for pastoral counseling with African Americans, it needs to be emphasized that connections are important. These connections include family, extended family, and church. Therapists need to keep these connections continuously in mind and use them as therapeutic resources when possible.

The Uniqueness of Persons

Mitchell and Lewter point out that the soul appears before God and receives its unique character.[20] Of great significance is the belief that one is not defined externally nor does one receive his or her uniqueness externally. Uniqueness is a gift of God bestowed by God through God's relationship to persons. In the process of being known by God one receives one's uniqueness.

African Americans believe that the source of one's uniqueness is that they are made in the image of God. They take very seriously the biblical support for this notion that is found in Genesis. The doctrine of the uniqueness of persons generally begins with Genesis 1:26-28. We were created in God's own image and likeness. What does this mean?

First, Adam refers to all humanity. All human beings are God's creation and created in God's own image, both males and females. Second, image and likeness are not separated according to maleness and femaleness in this first creation story. Both males and females share godlikeness. *Godlikeness* also refers to resemblance, representation, similar form—a replica. Likeness and image therefore have to do with the godlikeness that exists in all human beings that are part of creation.[21]

---

[20] Mitchell and Lewter, *Soul Theology*, 113.

[21] Phyllis Bird, "Male and Female He Created Them," *Harvard Theological Review* 74 (April 1981): 129–59.

This understanding of likeness and image, I believe, is the source of Alice Walker's notion of soul. It is that dimension of each person that is given by God as part of the created order. This concept also identifies our capacity to transcend the purely animal level or instinctual level. It makes possible our living as God's representatives on earth with the task of assisting God in ruling.

Godlikeness is, indeed, the source of the African American's concept of soul. However, the second creation story in Genesis 2 raises a significant question for African American marriages and families. The issue raised is whether women are derivative of males, and therefore, subject to male leadership. A propositional view of marriage often has drawn on the second creation story interpreted to say that men are viewed as leaders over women. Consequently, this creation story could present some difficulties for African American women and men who want an egalitarian marriage and family. A fresh examination of this passage is important. The work of Phyllis Trible will be explored to bring a different perspective on this issue.

In her book *God and the Rhetoric of Sexuality*, Trible points to some of the common and popular notions about woman being formed from man and being man's helpmate. She makes the following list of popular ideas:

> A male God creates first man (2:7) and last woman (2:22); first means superior and last means inferior or subordinate.
>
> Woman is created for the sake of man: a helpmate to cure his loneliness (2:21-22).
>
> Contrary to nature, woman comes out of man; she is denied even her natural function of birthing and that function is given to man (2:21-22).
>
> Woman is the rib of man, dependent upon him for life. Taken out of man, woman has a derivative, not an autonomous, existence.
>
> Man names woman and thus has power over her.[22]

Trible points out that these traditional notions supporting male superiority and female inferiority are not accurate and are not present in the story itself. She says that these ideas do not respect the true meaning of the text when one looks at the grammar, themes, and images from the point of view of the overall purpose of the story.

Trible points out, and I agree, that the story is divided into three scenes. The first scene is God's creation of the earth and human beings; the second scene is the disobedience of human beings; and the third scene is the

[22] Phyllis Trible, *God and the Rhetoric of Sexuality* (Philadelphia: Fortress, 1978), 73.

disintegration of God's handiwork. The story conveys the destruction of a harmonious whole created by God. Thus, the story is not about the subjugation of females to males but the nature of human tragedy. The plot is about how God's original intention for human beings and for the world was disrupted. The original intent was for men and women to live in harmony with each other, with the earth and all earth creatures as well as with God. The Fall, however, introduced the tragic element of sin into human existence.

The third concern of this second story is the damage that came to human beings as a result of the Fall, that is, God laid a curse on human beings and the order of creation because of human disobedience. Remember that God had created human beings to live in harmony with each other. Both males and females were created equal in the image and likeness of God. Gender was part of the created order, but in neither story was there any presupposition of superiority or inferiority. The fact that Adam was nonsexual in both stories is crucial. Moreover, Eve's being created from Adam's rib does not mean that Adam was male. It only points to the fact that Adam was an earth creature and that to become reproductive Adam, or human nature, had to be divided into sexes.

In the Fall the inequality between men and women was created. The hostility and enmity between male and female came into existence. The animosity is the result of the curse, and is not the way it was intended to be. Trible comments on the nature of the relationship between males and females after the Fall.

> Alas, however, union is no more; one flesh is split. The man will not reciprocate the woman's desire; instead, he will rule over her. Thus she lives in unresolved tension. Where once there was mutuality, now there is a hierarchy of division. The man dominates the woman to pervert sexuality. Hence, the woman is corrupted in becoming a slave and the man is corrupted in becoming a master. His supremacy is neither a divine right nor a male prerogative. Her subordination is neither a divine decree nor the female destiny. Both their positions result from shared disobedience. God describes this consequence but does not prescribe it as punishment.[23]

The story ends with Adam and Eve being thrust from the Garden of Eden. Their mutuality is gone. The ground for a life of animosity was established permanently.

Biblically, the key for African American marriages and families is that stereotypical and hierarchical images of males and females are not part of the structure of essential reality. Rather, they are the result of human

---

[23] Trible, *Rhetoric of Sexuality*, 128.

limitations and frailty. Therefore, the emphasis theologically needs to be on what is possible for males and females in terms of mutuality and sharing. Settling for the stereotypical and hierarchical images of males and females is to limit human possibilities.

Trible's work also helps to envisage the stories in Genesis as narratives rather than as propositions for the relationships. This means that marriage and family life unfolds like narratives, and it is hard to script marital and family life according to rational propositions. Marriage and family life is dynamic, and biblical narrative helps to inform the interactions taking place in marriage and family life.

With regard to marital and family therapy with African Americans, the significance of Trible's interpretation is that therapists need to help counselees envisage possibilities beyond hierarchy. Moreover, the pastoral counselor needs to help African American couples and families to see that there are different traditions of interpretations of Genesis 1–3.

This discussion of Genesis 1–3 needs to be summarized and related to the norm of liberated holistic growth and the ethic of love. The basic question governing this summary is, How does the discussion of these biblical passages help us to expand our understanding of the norm of growth and the ethic of love?

First, both males and females are created in the image of God. Women are not derivatives of men. Thus, males and females share a common humanity and, therefore, they share similar growth needs.

Second, there is no basis at all for making male experience normative for everyone. Rather, males and females have experiences that are gender specific as well as experiences that are common. Particular gender differences, though hard to define, ought not be placed in any hierarchical order or valued more than the other. Experiences of both females and males should be valued and form a complementary interaction to enrich the life of those in the eschatological community.

Finally, gender-linked roles are *not* ontologically established. Rather, they are established socially and should function to make the life of the community better for all who participate. Women attending to the needs of others without thought of developing their own selves, for example, is not consistent with the norm of liberated holistic growth. Moreover, men attending to their own needs without thought of the needs of others is inconsistent with the ethic of love and the norm of liberated holistic growth. Roles exist to serve the needs of individuals and the needs of the community. People are not created to serve the roles.

New Testament Views on Hierarchy

It is not enough to focus on perspectives on Genesis as a way to inform working with African American marriages and families. New Testament perspectives on male and female relationships need to be examined as well.

Robert Jewett, a scholar on Pauline writings, in a chapter entitled "The Sexual Liberation of Paul and His Churches," says that Paul believes that sexual differences were overcome in Christ.[24] Jewett goes on to describe a progression in Paul's thinking from a patriarchal or male-dominating model toward a more egalitarian model of male and female relationships. This can be seen in 1 Corinthians 7:7 where Paul outlines an egalitarian model of male and female relationships. Jewett points out that the Corinthian churches took equality of males and females being copartners in ministry seriously. He identifies androgynous impulses such as women taking on male hairstyles as a sign of their equality. Corinthians viewed males and females as equal and both subject to God.

Jewett points out that Paul's views were altered by later writers from the Pauline school in terms of moderate subjection and later repression of women as reflected in the pastoral epistles. Elisabeth Schüssler Fiorenza supports this by pointing out that Paul leaves the door open for his successors to reinstate the patriarchal relationships.[25] Commenting on Galatians 3:28, she indicates that Paul unequivocally affirmed the equality and charismatic gifts of males and females. She points out that he affirmed women in their leadership roles in the church, their call to a marriage-free life, as well as equal rights for males and females within sexual relationships in marriage. However, Paul left the door open to later reintroduction of patriarchalism, in Fiorenza's mind, when he valued the nonmarried state higher than the married state with regard to missionary work. She feels this restricts the active participation of Christian wives within the Christian community. She concludes that Paul's impact on women is double-edged, emphasizing Christian equality and freedom of women, but subordinating women's behavior in marriage and participation in the church.

The Gospels are clear that the historical Jesus also challenged the male and female stereotypes by the way he related to women. Jesus came announcing that a new order of reality was emerging. This order was different from the reality that existed. The consequences of the Fall had been overcome, and the original creation of males and females in God's own image was restored.

[24] Robert Jewett, *Paul the Apostle to America: Cultural Trends and Pauline Scholarship* (Louisville: Westminster John Knox, 1994), 45–58.

[25] Elisabeth Schüssler Fiorenza, *In Memory of Her: A Feminist Theological Reconstruction of Christian Origins* (New York: Crossroad, 1992), 235–36.

The use of Trible, Jewett, and Fiorenza does not exhaust the scholarship on the various biblical texts that have been discussed. However, the concern here is to attend to those scholars whose hermeneutical interpretations of selected biblical texts are closely associated with narrative models of interpretation, the norm of liberated holistic growth, and the ethic of love. These scholars find traditions within the canon of scripture that transcend the patriarchal model. Within scripture exist egalitarian and mutuality traditions where men and women participate equally in partnership within the household of God.

The point of this discussion for pastoral counseling with African American marriages and families is that scripture moves beyond stereotypical roles of males and females in selected traditions. Consequently, it is possible to help couples and families to move toward a functional understanding of roles in terms of their utility functions for the sake of the marriage or family rather than for the sake of the role itself.

The traditions of scripture emphasized here are consistent with the norm of liberation and the love ethic. The interpretations reviewed here help to free the growth possibilities of each marital partner and family members.

The Family of God and Humanity

Mitchell and Lewter point out that another core soul belief is the affirmation that African Americans are part of the family of God.[26] The sources for this affirmation have biblical bases. The biblical bases for understanding persons as members of the household of God are numerous.[27]

The foundation for the doctrine of the family of God is rooted in the theological metaphor of household. Ephesians 2:19-22 is one scripture that lifts up the household imagery:

> So then you are no longer strangers and sojourners, but you are fellow citizens with the saints and members of the household of God, built upon the foundation of the apostles and prophets, Christ Jesus himself being the cornerstone, in whom the whole structure is joined together and grows into a holy temple in the Lord; in whom you also are built into it for a dwelling place of God in the Spirit.

[26] Mitchell and Lewter, *Soul Theology,* 127.

[27] Most of the references used here are found in two sources that my wife and I have written: Anne Streaty Wimberly and Edward Powell Wimberly, *One Household and One Hope: Building Ethnic Minority Clergy Family Support Networks* (Nashville: General Board of Higher Education and Ministry, United Methodist Church, 1988); and Anne Streaty Wimberly and Edward Powell Wimberly, *The Language of Hospitality: Intercultural Relations in the Household of God* (Nashville: Cokesbury, 1991).

The metaphor of *household* was used by the writer of Ephesians to describe the inclusion of certain people within the family of God who did not previously belong to this family by tradition. In Jesus Christ the partition that separated persons was broken down (Eph 2:14) and he declared that strangers are part of the family. Since the time of the writing of Ephesians, many Christians across the centuries have drawn on this image of the household of God to support their own inclusion and participation in the family of God. This is true also for African American Christians.

Deotis Roberts, in *Liberation and Reconciliation: A Black Theology*, addresses this very issue of how the black church drew on Ephesians 3:14-15 and Galatians 6:10 for their inclusion in God's family.

> It is the image of the family which best describes our peoplehood, that offers, I believe, the most constructive possibilities for a theological understanding of the church in general and the black church in particular. Paul, speaking to the church at Ephesus, says: "For this reason I bow my knees before the Father, from whom every family in heaven and on earth is named" (Eph 3:14-15). Elsewhere he says: "So then, as we have opportunity, let us do good to all men, and especially to those who are of the household of faith" (Gal 6:10). These words of Paul seem to be written especially for a homeless, hopeless, powerful people.[28]

African American Christians have understood themselves to be included in God's household. Such a sense of belonging has empowered African American Christians' belief that they have worth because God invited them to be participants in the ultimate family, the household of God.

In God's household there is room for all.[29] Members of the household feel not only a kinship toward one another but also a responsibility toward one another. Such a household is patterned after the caregiver Jesus, who is the head of the household of God. One does not receive membership in the household based on one's own effort, but only through the initiative of God. Membership is a gift that cannot be earned; it is bestowed.

Being members of the household of God also brought with it the gift of seeing others within the household as brothers and sisters under the parentage of God (Matt 12:50; 25:40; Mark 3:31-35; 1 Cor 1:10-17; 2 Cor 13:11-12; 1 Tim 5:1-2).[30] Roberts points to the fact that membership in the household of God transcends the limits of blood relationship.[31] Membership in the

---

[28] J. Deotis Roberts, *Liberation and Reconciliation: A Black Theology* (Philadelphia: Westminster John Knox, 1971), 66.

[29] This paragraph reflects conclusions that are found in Wimberly and Wimberly, *One Household*, 9.

[30] Wimberly and Wimberly, *Language*, 74.

[31] Roberts, *Liberation*, 68.

household of God, the bestowing of self-acceptance, and the brotherhood and sisterhood of all under the parentage of God are gifts of God that are to lead toward ministry. These gifts are free, but the intent of bestowing them is for those who receive the invitation to enter into God's salvation drama. Roberts, with this understanding, emphasizes that the household of God is a messianic and christological community.[32] Those who accept the invitation become disciples who are to reproduce the activity of God. Those who are invited are to produce fruit and good works. As family members, they become joint workers (1 Cor 3:9; 2 Cor 6:1-10). They are fellow servants seeking to do the work leading to God's reign.

African Americans envisioning themselves as members of the household of God has foundation within the New Testament, particularly in Pauline theology. In his article entitled "Tenement Churches and Pauline Love Feasts," Robert Jewett makes the following conclusions:

1. there were inner-city, lower-class tenement churches in addition to more middle-class house churches in the early church

2. these churches were not governed by an hierarchical model of leadership, but by a form of egalitarian leadership

3. the attenders at the tenement houses were slaves, ex-slaves, and laborers in a variety of trades

4. the structure of the tenements was that of high-rise slum dwellings; and

5. many had immigrant status.[33]

Commenting on these tenement churches and their communal life, Jewett says:

> They fused sacramental life with regular sharing of material resources in the context of celebrative meals; they joined ecstatic joy at the presence of a new age by forming new families of brothers and sisters to cope with the poverty and alienation in the slums of the inner cities; they united care for the poor with worshipful celebration of Christ as the Lord of the Banquet.[34]

The point is that the egalitarian and sharing traditions of the scripture attracted African American Christians. Just as the early church attracted the poor and oppressed, the scriptures also drew African Americans and helped to meet the religious and spiritual needs of African Americans.

---

[32] Roberts, *Liberation*, 67.

[33] Robert Jewett, "Tenement Churches and Pauline Love Feasts," *Quarterly Review: A Journal of Theological Resources for Ministry* 14, no. 1 (1994), 46–50.

[34] Jewett, "Tenement Churches," 55.

Consequently, African Americans saw themselves as part of God's eschatological community where participation was not based on hierarchy, race, or class.

The significance of the doctrine of the household of God for African Americans is manifold. First, membership in God's household confirms that African Americans have worth and value as human beings and as children of God. Second, it supports the idea of extended-family relatedness beyond bloodlines. Third, membership in the household helps to affirm that individuals are not alone and isolated. Fourth, membership also means that individual souls are connected to other souls; these connected souls need to be participants in God's salvation drama. In short, membership within the household of God affirms the worth of each individual soul and helps each individual soul to see himself or herself in relationship with others who participate in a common mission.

The implication of belonging to the household of God for pastoral counseling with African American marriages and families is that pastoral counselors need to call marital partners' and family members' attention to their connectedness to God's household. My wife and I lead many marital enrichment groups with African Americans. We have found that couples with functional or dysfunctional marriages often find their connections with other couples to be very comforting for them. They realize that they are not alone in their struggle and they can find resources from others for their marital journey.

One of the limitations of marital and family counseling is that it does not often involve other couples having similar problems. Finding models where there can be multiple couples and families in pastoral counseling is very important.

Toward a Doctrine of Human Beings

This chapter has explored several key themes undergirding the life of African American marriage and family life. The conclusions of this exploration for a constructive statement about the nature of persons are important. On the basis of this constructive anthropology implications for pastoral counseling with African American marriages and families can be drawn.

1. The soul in the African American Christian experience is a way to talk about the whole person related significantly to God, to the self, to others, and to the community. Therefore, the soul is relational and contextual. The concept of the embodied soul embraces this contextual and relational understanding.

2. The embodied soul participates in a variety of relationships and shares godlikeness. This godlikeness is bestowed on females and males alike without distinction. Because of this equality of bestowal, male experience is not normative for females. There are experiences that females and males share in common, but there are also experiences that are unique to females and to males.

3. The soul and the godlikeness of males and females grow and develop best in egalitarian and mutual sharing contexts. In these contexts each adult family member and marital partner takes full responsibility for himself or herself as well as creating an environment where all can grow into their full images of God.

4. Achieving liberated growth and the ethic of love within marriage and families is linked to the presence of God in human relationships bringing life, wholeness, and healing within community. Growth occurs best when marriages and families envisage themselves as members of the eschatological community because of the many spiritual and communal resources that are present for nurturing and care.

The implications of these four conclusions for pastoral counseling with African American marriages and families is that the uniqueness of each person and each person's participation in the marriage and family is essential. Helping marriages and families balance self-focus with other-focus is very crucial. The counselor needs to embrace each person as a relational whole who lives and interacts with others in interdependent ways. This means that pastoral counselors need to take the context in which people live and grow very seriously and help marriages and families to create caring environments. Pastoral counselors must take seriously the religious needs of each person recognizing that spirituality places a vital role in human development.

Pastoral counselors also need to challenge marriages and families where marital partners and family members live at the expense of others within the marriage and family. This includes propositional notions that seek to make one person's growth more significant than another's growth. Moreover, the biblical traditions that support egalitarian relationships can be discussed in the counseling session.

This chapter began with a case study of multigenerational abuse that was exposed because a mother refused to be silent any longer. The forces pushing her to confront the abuse openly related to a theological worldview that is at work in her life. This worldview embodies many of the themes that are explored in this chapter. Having themes in mind when doing pastoral counseling with African Americans can assist greatly the therapeutic process.

• • •

The Men's Movement and Pastoral Care of
African American Men[*]

The emasculating influences of racism and racial discrimination toward African American men have meant that the men's movement among African American men has taken a different direction than that among white men. The white men's movement is geared to helping men move beyond the stereotypical images of masculinity and femininity held out by wider society in order to develop new definitions of human wholeness that are liberating both to women and men. In contrast, the men's movement among African American men often imitates the dominant images of masculinity and femininity held out in wider society. The white men's movement is often perceived as a threat to African American men's sense of manhood, given the emasculating influences of racism in the United States. As a result, the African American men's movement is rooted in traditional and patriarchal understandings of what it means to be a man and a woman.

This chapter has several goals: first, to provide a sociopsychological context for understanding the pressures that African American men face in the United States as they try to develop into full maturity; second, to explore existing approaches of the African American men's movement as they appear in the literature; and finally, to present a narrative approach to the pastoral care and counseling of African American men along with the cultural resources needed to help them grow.[1]

The thesis of this chapter is that constructions of African American masculinity should be rooted fundamentally in the egalitarian, androgynous, and spiritual impulses that characterized African American maturity of the past. There is a long egalitarian and androgynous tradition of African Americans rooted deeply in Africa and in the black experience in the United States. African American women often embody these equalitarian and androgynous impulses; African American men need to cultivate the capacity to see the world through the eyes of African American women if they are to recover what has been lost from the past.

This chapter is intended for those who are engaged in ministries of care and education to African American boys and men. Its major purpose is to

---

[1] The narrative model on which this chapter is based can be found in Edward P. Wimberly, "Pastoral Counseling with African American Men," *Urban League Review* 16, no. 2 (1993): 77–84.

[*] This selection was previously published in *The Care of Men*, edited by Christie Cozad Neuger and James Newton Poling (Nashville: Abingdon, 1997), 104–21 and associated notes. © 1997, Abingdon Press. Used by permission. All rights reserved.

suggest one avenue for promoting wholeness, maturity, and hope in African American boys and men as well as for the African American community and society as a whole.

A Sociopsychological Context

The dominant sociopsychological images, rules, and expectations in society define what it means to become a man. There are at least two contradictory pressures that African American boys and men must face in growing up in the United States: the dominant images of masculinity held out for *all* men, and the sometimes subtle and often blatant pressures on African American boys and men to adopt alternative images of masculinity. The dominant images held out for all men to achieve are generally patriarchal, with the man as the center of the universe defining for all people what it means to be human. Becoming a man has meant having a sense of self and purpose, taking on the responsible roles of husband and father, and taking one's rightful place in society by defining one's own destiny.[2] However, white men have been given the privilege and authority to define what it means to be a man in the United States. This definitional privilege and assumption has been emasculating for African American men and has cut off the avenues for their achieving stereotypical images of manhood.

When the defining of manhood is restricted to a privileged set of men in a patriarchal system, entitled men take for granted their right to define the place and destiny of others, and others who are not so advantaged are expected to be passive and compliant in accepting their assigned role and place.

Within the psychological literature on identity formation, Romney Moseley has explored the roles and places in society that have been assigned to African Americans.[3] He posited that the wider society holds out a negative rather than a positive identity for African American youth.[4] Key to developing a positive identity is to become an active agent in meaning-making and to create one's own identity in interaction with others and the environment.

In forming a negative identity the self is passive in the meaning-making process. However, positive identity presupposes not only active participation in meaning-making activity, but also a positive cultural response to meaning-making. This cultural response involves the provision of viable

---

[2] For a definition of masculine values see Nathan Hare and Julia Hare, *Bringing the Black Boy to Manhood: The Passage* (San Francisco: Black Think Tank, 1985), 20.

[3] Romney M. Moseley, *Becoming a Self Before God* (Nashville: Abingdon, 1991).

[4] Moseley, *Becoming a Self*, 70.

roles, rituals, economic avenues, and job opportunities that concretely confirm and affirm the identities of meaning-makers.[5] However, in negative
identity, acquisition of positive roles and the provision of societal supports
for meaning-making are restricted.

One example of how society fosters and supports the formation of negative identity has been explored by the psychologist Erik Erikson. He has
pointed out that African American male youth are forced by social expectations to limit themselves to three historic roles in culture that often result
in a permanent loss of identity.[6] These historic roles are:

1. Mammy's oral-sensual "honey-child"—tender, expressive,
    rhythmical

2. the evil identity of the dirty, anal-sadistic, phallic-rapist "nigger"

3. the clean, anal-compulsive, restrained, friendly, but always sad
    "white man's Negro."[7]

Erikson went on to say that the only real identity allowed African Americans is that of the slave.

While Erikson's concept of negative identity is dated, there is evidence
that negative identity is still a viable way to explore African American
identity-formation today. This becomes evident when the narrative metaphors undergirding the formation of negative identity are explored. The
dreams of unlimited opportunity and self-actualization have been deep
metaphors undergirding the narrative tradition of positive male identity in
the U.S. However, there is an alternative narrative tradition undergirding
negative identity that I call the Sisyphus narrative.[8]

The Greek Sisyphus myth tells of a tragic figure who was condemned
"to repeatedly roll a stone up a hill only to have the stone roll back down
the hill just as it neared its destination."[9] Moreover, "the Sisyphus myth
is the fate held out by the wider society for African American males and
females. Covert and overt messages push and pull for African Americans
to adopt this role."[10]

The significance of negative identity and the Sisyphus mythology for
the growth and development of African Americans cannot be underesti-
mated [sic]. In fact, the high proportion of African American men that

---

[5] Erik Erikson describes the cultural role in meaning-making in *Childhood and Society*
(New York: W.W. Norton, 1963), 261.

[6] Erikson, *Childhood*, 241.

[7] Erikson, *Childhood*, 242.

[8] Wimberly, "Pastoral Counseling with African American Men," 78–79.

[9] Wimberly, "Pastoral Counseling with African American Men," 78.

[10] Wimberly, "Pastoral Counseling with African American Men," 78.

are incarcerated and involved in the criminal justice system, the spread of AIDS, growing drug abuse, and violence are all, in part, due to the sociopsychological factors associated with negative identity and the Sisyphus mythology for African American men. Negative identity and Sisyphus mythology push African American males into exaggerated masculine postures that often are acted out in violence.[11] Other contributing factors are undereducation and miseducation of youth, low teacher expectations, tracking in schools, placement in special education classes, and school dropout problems. The growing criminal population among African American young men is precisely a fulfillment of the negative identity. These young males often feel that the only viable identity open to them is that of criminal. This notion is reinforced by culture's distorted images of manhood for African American men in particular.

In response to the influences of negative identities held out to African Americans, there is recent literature that focuses on how negative identities can be turned into positive ones. Victor De La Cancela, for example, examines "cool pose" as such an act of transformation. It is

> defined as a ritualized masculinity entailing scripts, posturing, impression management and other carefully constructed performances that present the male as proud, strong and in control. "Cool pose" makes African American males visible and empowers them, yet it can also hide doubt, insecurity, rage and vulnerability, leaving males aloof from others and alienated from their deeper emotions.[12]

Cancela traces "cool pose" to practices in West African tribes as part of the rebellion against colonialization.[13] The positives of this legacy are seen in rap music, graffiti art, and break dancing. Such cultural transformation of the negative identities lend themselves to transcending poverty, correcting a lack of formal education, and creating new ways of expressing self. Often the transformation of negative identities into creative forms of self and community expression lead away from violence and into ways of participating constructively in society. They also serve to produce pride, dignity, and respect and provide rites of passage for males, group solidarity, and group identity.[14] However, there is also an underside to such cultural

---

[11] For a discussion of masculine reactions of African American males, see Dionne J. Jones, "African American Males: A Critical Link in the African American Family," *Urban League Review* 16 (1993): 3–7. See also Victor De La Cancela, "Coolin: The Psychosocial Communications of African and Latino Men," *Urban League Review* 16 (1993): 33–44.

[12] De La Cancela, "Coolin," 33.

[13] De La Cancela, "Coolin," 14.

[14] De La Cancela, "Coolin," 35.

expression that Cancela identifies as sexism, criminal activity, homophobia, and expressions of an antisocial nature.[15]

I have explored negative identity and Sisyphus mythology in order to describe the limited avenues for personality growth and development for African American boys and men. The implication for pastoral care and counseling with African American men is that developing selfhood means tapping into sources of personhood that transcend the negative images of masculinity and identity prescribed for them.[16] This means that the sources of positive identity must be found in other places. Historically, these sources are found by retrieving racial and archetypal images of African personhood in prehistory, attending to oral styles of relating, remembering stories and myths, using Scripture as an important source of personhood, seeing the world through the eyes of women, and attending to stirrings from within the spiritual core of persons.

Forms of the African American Men's Movement

Critiques of the White Men's Movement

Before exploring the sources of African American personhood and maturity beyond negative identity, it is important to examine the contemporary models of the African American men's movement. The first task is to explore why African American men have rejected the dominant men's movements. The second task is to present divergent approaches to the African American male maturity.

De La Cancela provides a critical understanding of why Latino men and African American men do not get involved in the white men's movement, especially the mythopoetic movement. He points to the class limitations of the movement as well as their appropriation of symbols belonging to ethnic groups. He says:

> The generally affluent urban Caucasian men's movement can examine how its concepts of experiencing the wild man within, dancing the warrior's dance, and other mythopoetic / metaphoric weekend gatherings may be failing Latino and African American men. Critical to this examination is how the movement could be "ripping off" the cultural myths, rituals and practices of indigenous peoples globally such as sweat lodges, dancing, drumming, and council fires, and dangerously fashioning them into some pop, ersatz masculinity. The movement has also ignored current social conditions such as the fact that the majority of homeless people

---

[15] De La Cancela, "Coolin," 35.
[16] Wimberly, "Pastoral Counseling with African American Men," 78.

are men and the perpetuation of police brutality and harassment against both men of color and gay men.[17]

He concludes that the Bly-influenced men's movement demonstrates some male emasculating tendencies and "men of color do not need to be further exposed to Caucasian males' unique form of male-bashing, racism, heterosexism and misogyny that has historically claimed that African American women castrate or feminize their men."[18]

Wayne Davis, another critic of the white men's movement suggests that it does not address racism and sexism, it does not deal with skin color as the major source of brokenness, and it reinforces black male invisibility and isolation.[19]

In an age where the academic emphasis for African Americans has been on cultural difference and uniqueness, it is not appropriate for them to seek salvation from copying the white men's movement. There are diverse cultural expressions among ethnic people, and these differences are not deviant nor inferior to what exists in the dominant culture. Given this emphasis on cultural uniqueness, it is easy to see why there are not too many African American men involved in the dominant men's movement.

The Alternative of the African American Men's Movement

There is, indeed, a contemporary African American men's movement in this country. Its genesis was in the Civil Rights movement, and it found philosophical and practical underpinnings in the Black Power movement. A more contemporary expression of this movement is the "boys to men movement," which seeks to mentor black boys into men and is an attempt to insure full participation and survival in wider culture. Most forms of this men's movement do not question dominant images of masculinity nor do they raise critical issues about patriarchy. Other more recent approaches assume that black males do not have access to fulfilling the normative images of masculinity, which is defined as autonomy over and mastery of one's environment and dominance in the nuclear family.[20] There are at least five approaches to enabling African American male maturity, and all but one assume a patriarchal view of manhood, along with dominant images of masculinity. These five approaches include:

[17] De La Cancela, "Coolin," 33.

[18] De La Cancela, "Coolin," 41–42.

[19] Wayne R. Davis, "An Examination into the Process of Grief as Experienced by African American Males" (Ph.D. diss., Southern Baptist Theological Seminary, 1994), 41–45.

[20] Robert Staples, *Black Masculinity: The Black Man's Role in American Society* (San Francisco: The Black Scholar Press, 1982), 1–2.

1. the Liberation, Civil Rights, and Anti-sexist form
2. the Evangelical Biblical form
3. the Full Participation/Integration form
4. the Humanistic Rites of Passage form
5. the Narrative form.

Each is explained briefly below.

The Liberation, Civil Rights, Anti-Sexist Form

This socio-political approach to the African American male movement focuses on being "cool" as a behavioral and attitudinal script.[21] It emphasizes responding to the social circumstances that African American men face and challenging the economic and political conditions that keep them and their communities oppressed. Its central focus is on all people of color courageously asserting their rights. It is critical of sexism, racism, selfish consumerism, hedonistic sexual attitudes, homophobia, and classism. Though with origins in the Civil Rights movement, it is critical of the sexual exclusiveness of the Civil Rights and Black Power movements. It is sensitive to the cultural rites of passage that assist both males and females to actualize their possibilities through modes of verbal expression and styles of dress, music, and dancing. It addresses the problems facing the African American community including AIDS, violence, teen pregnancy, and black on black crime.

From a mental health perspective this approach focuses on helping people explore the negative side of the cool pose. It helps people explore their positive individual and group histories, and lifts up the significance of perpetuating an oral history of the survival skills used by African Americans. The goal is to improve the mental health of men and to help them respect both themselves and women of color.

Evangelical Biblical Form

This form of the men's movement is built on the biblical understanding of men as heads of their homes (Ephesians 5), and of examples of males who were raised by their mothers and grandmothers (such as in 2 Timothy), coupled with providing positive models of leadership for other males.[22] In this biblical approach, the male head of the household accepts the patriarchal model of male leadership. However, from Ephesians 5 some evangelicals

---

[21] De La Cancela, "Coolin," 33–44.

[22] Clarence Walker, *Biblical Counseling with African Americans* (Grand Rapids: Zondervan, 1992), 26–27.

have interpreted male headship as a form of mutual leadership by both males and females rather than the lethal form of patriarchal leadership where the man dominates. Leadership of men is based on the principle of selfless love that was demonstrated by Jesus. However, some African American evangelical Christians, both male and female, take the traditional patriarchal interpretation as normative and attempt to live it out.

Full Participation/Integration Form

This approach envisages as normative full participation of African American men in wider society. It seeks to use the dominant institution of society, namely school, as the central means for facilitating this full participation. Full participation in every aspect of society is called integration, and this is not necessarily social integration. This form of integration means that each person has the opportunity to fulfill his or her full potential as a human being without being hindered by racial oppression or segregation. It is possible to live in racially homogeneous communities in this form of integration as long as these communities are completely voluntary and not legislated or coerced into existence. Unfortunately, integration has come to mean social integration, where even voluntary homogeneous communities are suspect. This full participation approach assumes that sufficient involvement in American society can be accomplished either by predominantly African American or socially integrated schools. The full involvement approach helps visualize how African American institutions such as the church, fraternities, African American colleges, and public and private schools serve the ends of full participation in society.

Perhaps the best representative of this full participation approach is Jawanza Kunjufu, who has written and lectured throughout the United States on black boys becoming men.[23] His particular model assumes the marginality of African American boys and men, particularly their systematic exclusion from full participation beginning in the fourth grade. He believes that by the fourth grade level black boys become threats to teachers because of teachers' fears of behavioral problems. He believes that teachers begin to lower their educational expectations at this point and become disinterested in their African American male students. This contributes to the boys feeling marginal and isolated. To counter this trend toward

---

[23] Jawanza Kunjufu's works include *Countering the Conspiracy to Destroy Black Boys*, 3 vols. (Chicago: African American Images, 1985); *The Black Peer Group* (Chicago: African American Images, 1988); and *Hip-Hop Vs. MAAT: A Psycho-Social Analysis of Values* (Chicago: African American Images, 1993). Another author in this school of thought who draws on Kunjufu's work is Mychal Wynn, *Empowering African-American Males to Succeed* (South Pasadena, Calif.: Rising Sun Publications, 1992).

marginality and exclusion, emphasis is placed on a holistic approach to the empowerment of black boys by including spirituality, understanding racism, improving time management, developing skills and talent development, paying attention to nutrition, diet, and physical fitness, creating an understanding of economics, being members of positive peer groups, and participating in service organizations.[24] Moreover, this approach focuses on the developmental needs of boys and the related psychological, emotional, social, and practical tasks that must be accomplished at each developmental stage.

Kunjufu also lifts up the central role that Sunday school and church have played within the African American community, citing studies that show that boys who are reared in Sunday school are less likely to go to prison. He concludes: "In the first barometer, we are in trouble if a large number of children, specifically male children, are not developing spiritually."[25] He feels that a relationship with God will reduce the self-hatred and destructive behaviors that exist within the African American community.

The Humanistic Rites of Passage Form

This approach focuses on rites of passage or ceremonies of transition from boyhood to manhood in African traditions. It views the loss of the "ceremonial of etiquette" evident in pre-European Africa as a major problem for African Americans.

Nathan and Julia Hare indicate that the function of rites of passage are to provide customs, traditions, rituals, and ceremonies for the socialization of boys into their roles and place in society.[26] They look to African culture for these traditions as well as to the boys' connectedness to family and community.

This Humanistic Rites approach highlights the significance of patriarchy. They say:

> There can be no viable race without a viable patriarch in a patriarchal society. In the patriarchal world of the past and the foreseeable future it is the male and his performance that constitute the missing link to family stability and racial survival.[27]

I contend that it is possible for African American men to grow and develop into mature manhood without becoming patriarchs whose growth might well come at the expense of African American women.

---

[24] Kunjufu, *Countering the Conspiracy*, 3:71.
[25] Kunjufu, 3:22.
[26] Hare and Hare, *Manhood*, 21.
[27] Hare and Hare, *Manhood*, 16.

The Narrative Form

This narrative form capitalizes on the role of Scripture as the vision-shaping force in the lives of many African American men. Na'im Akbar in *Visions for Black Men* points to the symbolic universality of biblical mythology and its potential for helping African American men to become mature.[28] He highlights the significance of Scripture and its history in providing a liberating vision for African Americans and suggests it holds out the same potential for African American men today.

This brief presentation of the literature is an attempt to show that African American men's movements exist. There is no one approach. There are many. Consequently, there are many attempts being made to address the needs that African American boys and men have.

A Narrative Approach to Pastoral Care

Pastoral care with African American men emphasizes a holistic understanding of the maturing process of selfhood rooted in the deepest inner feelings, values, intentions, and spirituality emerging from a man's life.[29]

> Through pastoral counseling, the African American male discovers his unique self, his emotions and feelings, his meaning and purpose for life, and his unique contribution and vocation to the world. He is able to engage in all aspects of life, including the formation of close and intimate relationships with significant others, while taking full responsibility for his own growth and development. Pastoral counseling identifies the sources of his manhood as including his African heritage, the African American tradition of equalitarian [sic] relationships and androgynous roles, the penchant for oral styles of communication, the use of Bible stories and characters, and the capacity to be empathic with African American women.[30]

One spiritual source of a man's sense of selfhood can be found in Genesis 1:26 where human worth is grounded in God's image and likeness. Within each person there is a push from within to realize this God-given image and the infinite worth and value of each person that is inherent in being God's creation. Pastoral care recognizes this divine urge in each human being and attempts to help African American men claim their creature roots and their innermost spiritual push toward selfhood. Pastoral counseling uses the counseling relationship between the evolving person,

---

[28] Na'im Akbar, *Visions for Black Men* (Nashville: Winston-Derek, 1991), 43–62.
[29] This definition represents a modification of the definition found in Wimberly, "Pastoral Counseling with African American Men," 77.
[30] Wimberly, "Pastoral Counseling with African American Men," 77.

the person's relationships with others, and the pastoral counselor to facilitate the emergence of the person's full identity and selfhood.

Not only are the spiritual roots of African American identity found in being created in the image of God, they are also rooted in the ongoing activity of God establishing God's reign on earth. God's reign has been characterized as the unfolding of a story to which Scripture points and to which persons are called. All human beings are visualized as being called to a significant work and a unique place in God's unfolding drama of salvation. When one embraces this call, one's life and community take on significance and meaning—the significance of God's narrative salvation—and personal identity is linked to participation in God's life and work. Each person, whether lay or clergy, has his or her special vocation in God's salvation drama. Pastoral care within this narrative context helps people to discover God's claim on their lives, how this call brings significance to their individual and collective lives, and how it should be carried out to bring personal meaning and fulfillment.

Being created in the image of God and finding personal significance and vocation in God's unfolding drama of salvation are the spiritual roots to becoming a mature person. Mature persons also grow in context as they participate with others, their sociocultural surroundings, and their historical roots. Consequently, there are contextual sources of the identity and maturity that must be explored along with the spiritual roots. Below are some of these contextual sources of African American male identity.[31]

Racial and Archetypal Sources of Personhood in Africa

Egypt and Africa avoided the split between matriarchy and patriarchy that dominated the rest of the world. According to Charles S. Finch there was a creative reconciliation between matriarchy and patriarchy in lower cultures of the Nile.[32] The archetypal and racial source of African American manhood is found in the creative tension between matriarchy and patriarchy. The racial and archetypal inheritance of African Americans is a creative synthesis between the masculine and feminine cultural dimensions. It is part of our African past.

There is an abundance of evidence that the creative reconciliation between the masculine and the feminine has survived in the United States. A review of the literature on black male and female sex role imagery reveals that equalitarian roles and androgynous learning of roles were very

---

[31] The resource for the sources of African American manhood in culture is Wimberly, "Pastoral Counseling with African American Men," 77.

[32] Charles S. Finch III, *Echoes of the Old Darkland: Theme from the African Eden* (Atlanta: Khenti, 1991), xiii.

common within the African American community.[33] From this alone, it is clear how helpful it is for pastoral counselors to be aware of the cultural heritage of African American males and to employ this awareness in pastoral counseling.

The Oral and Cultural Style of Communication

Emerging out of the creative synthesis between matriarchy and patriarchy is the African American male's inclination for storytelling. Historically, oral skills were highly prized in Africa and in the African American community.[34] This indigenous style of relating was comfortable for African American men and women. It is of immense importance when doing pastoral care with African American men and their families, for the men especially are more apt to participate when a style of relating is comfortable for them.

My discovery of the importance of oral styles of communication came when my wife and I did marital enrichment with African American couples. In the early 1980s many African American men were afraid of marital enrichment because they felt that this was women's turf, and they felt at a disadvantage in the area of intimacy. My wife and I tried a variety of things with the couples, but we were careful not to go straight into working on methods of intimacy. Much of what we did was modeling, where my wife and I shared information from our lives that we felt the couples needed to share with each other. In the process we told stories about our marital life, particularly stories about our meeting, our courtship, our marriage ceremony and related events, our ideal images or mate expectations, and our ideal images of marital life. We also shared how the ideal images had to be modified when encountering the real mate. The men seemed to be greatly interested in the stories we told and in the method of storytelling itself. From this we discovered the importance of storytelling as a major method of enabling African American men to participate in a nonthreatening way in marital enrichment, and, by extension, other forms of counseling.

Exploring the Stories that African American Men Use

Given the bent to use oral styles of communicating, it is critical to explore the stories that African American men tell. Are the plots tragic and

---

[33] Walter Allen, "The Search for Applicable Theories of Black Family Life," *Journal of Marriage and the Family* 40, no. 1 (1978): 117–29; Diane Lewis, "The Black Family Socialization and Sex Roles," *Phylon* 36 (1975): 221–37; Bernadette Gray-Little, "Marital Quality and Power Processes Among Black Couples," *Journal of Marriage and the Family* 44, no. 3 (1982): 633–46; and Leland J. Axelson, "The Working Wife: Differences in Perception Among Negro and White Males," *Journal of Marriage and the Family* 42, no. 2 (1980): 457–64.

[34] Edward P. Wimberly, *African American Pastoral Care* (Nashville: Abingdon, 1991).

growth-hindering (akin to the Sisyphus story) or hopeful and growth facilitating? Offering alternative stories that challenge existing negative or tragic stories is essential in pastoral counseling.

An example is instructive. A young African American male actually referred to his life as resembling that of Sisyphus.[35] This young man was bright. Though he was college and seminary trained, he saw his life as a life of tragedy and dead ends. From him I learned that counselees often see their lives in terms of central stories. In fact, many not only identify with the characters in these stories, they also mimic or imitate the plot that lies behind the story and find it hard to embrace any alternative plot for their lives.

This young man was not an isolated case. Many African American males between the ages of sixteen and twenty-six are finding themselves caught up in the Sisyphus myth with no way out. Pastoral counseling with African American males must identify and explore in depth the stories that undergird their lives, for example, by imagining how the plot will unravel if they continue to follow it. Another goal is to help them discover alternative stories that are growth-producing.

Editing Stories of African American Males

Pastoral counseling with African American males means providing a context for them to edit their personal stories in light of divine Scriptures. Scriptural stories in the Old and New Testaments provide a vision and future hope for many African American males.[36] It is important to explore with them the biblical characters and stories with which they have identified. Bible stories and characters still permeate the lives of African Americans, and they are important resources for pastoral care.

The narrative story that undergirds Scripture challenges such stories with tragic plots like the myth of Sisyphus. The goal of pastoral counseling is to help African American men find a deeper reason for living meaningful lives in the present rooted in a hopeful Scriptural vision of the future.

By helping African American males in counseling to compare their own personal stories with that of the larger vision of biblical stories, one can help them to edit or reauthor their stories in light of a larger vision of reality. The case of a homeless African American man is a good example of this. The man was in his early thirties and the oldest of several children. At fifteen he had had to go to work as a crane operator to support his five

[35] Edward P. Wimberly, "Spiritual Formation in Theological Education," in *Clergy Assessment and Career Development*, ed. Richard A. Hunt et al. (Nashville: Abingdon, 1990), 27–31.

[36] Wimberly, "Pastoral Counseling with African American Men," 81–82.

younger brothers and sisters. His parents had both died, and there were no relatives for him to fall back on for support. Consequently, he raised his younger brothers and sisters himself.

When I explored with him his homeless situation, he said that he had made his contribution to society by successfully providing for his brothers and sisters. He was proud of the fact that he had only lost one brother to crime; the rest were living productive lives. However, he also felt that it was time for someone to take care of him for a change and that, although it was a hard life, being homeless was a way to be taken care of and supported.

The scriptural story that made the most sense to him in our counseling time was told in a movie he saw. He pointed out that in the movie there was a small boy who followed Jesus, but Jesus would not let him join up with him, saying he should go home and mature some more. The counselee felt like the little boy; he was not ready for life but had some growing left to do.

This story was very instructive to me because it told me that he needed to be in a community where he could be nurtured; it pointed to the possibilities of what he might become if he found that nurturing community. The movie was a beacon in his life pointing to what his future could be like as a follower of Jesus. It was a metaphor and hope to which we returned in counseling as we struggled with his homeless situation.

Developing the Capacity to See the World Through the Eyes of African American Women

In addition to helping African American males edit the stories of their lives in light of the larger spiritual vision of the faith tradition, pastoral counseling also needs to help African American men to be more empathic with the world perceived by African American women. Masculinity in the wider culture connotes the separation from the influence of mothers and the relational culture that the mother represents, as well as becoming free from external control. African American boys and men develop these pushes toward autonomy in an exaggerated sense because of the emasculation they experience due to the legacy of slavery and reality of racism. Therefore, African American males have less access to masculinity-conforming settings than many white males.[37] Consequently, compulsive masculinity is a result of the psychological push for autonomy and for mastery of self by separation from the control of others. Compulsive masculinity is defined as masculine behavior characterized by toughness, sexual conquest, manipulation, and

---

[37] William Oliver, *The Violent Social World of Black Men* (New York: Lexington Books, 1994), 19.

thrill-seeking.[38] It is "the belief that toughness—physical prowess, emotional detachment, and willingness to resort to violence to resolve interpersonal conflicts—is an omnipresent characteristic of masculinity."[39]

While the emphasis in the above definition is on lower-class black men, no African American male escapes these influences. Added to this masculine orientation is the idea of being a "player of women," in short, of the sexual, emotional, and economic exploitation of females.[40] In other words, the end result of compulsive masculinity is complete alienation from women and the cultural connectedness needed to survive in a hostile society.

In pastoral counseling one remedy for this alienation is assisting African American males to have more empathy by seeing the world through the eyes of African American women. Beyond increasing empathy, this also helps to keep black males connected to their cross-generational roots. Womanist theologians have indicated that African American women are concerned with relational and cultural roots of their personhood, and men could benefit greatly from learning this perspective of black women.[41] The capacity for empathy with African American women does not make a man less masculine but helps him to tap into the inner resources of his manhood rooted deeply in his racial and cultural heritage.

Many African American males fear getting too close to the world experienced by African American females. For some of us it exposes our own vulnerability. Yet, African American men feel better about themselves if they allow themselves to feel what their female partners feel.

One African American male was terrified at his wife's fear of abandonment. He was a problem solver, and he didn't know how to make her feel better. He would stay home, but this did not seem to work, so he gave up and started to distance himself from her. Their relationship worsened.

From watching my responses to her in pastoral counseling, he learned that his wife seemed satisfied by my attention to her feelings and to her view of reality. He began to see that his attention to her seemed to reduce his wife's anxiety, and so he began to abandon the problem-solving approach. He learned to be more emotionally present, and he also began to realize that attending to the feelings was not as frightening as he thought. He began to feel better about himself and his marriage.

[38] Oliver, *Violent Social World*, 11. For more information on masculinity, see Richard Majors and Janet Mancini Billson, *Cool Pose: The Dilemmas of Black Manhood in America* (New York: Lexington Books, 1992).

[39] Oliver, *Violent Social World*, 23.

[40] Oliver, *Violent Social World*, 25.

[41] For the trend describing the cultural connectedness of African American women, see Katie G. Cannon, *Black Womanist Ethics* (Atlanta: Scholars Press, 1988), 87–88.

Cross-Generational Connectedness

Closely related to seeing the world through the relational eyes of women is the notion of cross-generational relatedness. This means being connected to at least three generations of extended family members. Masculinity in the culture of the United States usually means cutting off generational roots for the sake of competition and advancement. Consequently, all men, whether African American or not, have difficulty maintaining cross-generational roots. Therefore, assisting men to return to extended family roots is a major function of pastoral counseling. This is especially the case when marital and family discord seems to stem from unresolved family-of-origin issues. Learning to do family-of-origin work with African American males and teaching them to reconnect with the extended family are efforts crucial to their ability to survive and develop creative lives.

An example of this diagnostic and creative work is found in Byron. As he felt like he was being controlled by his wife, he would withdraw from her emotionally and go into his own world. He was raised by an overprotective mother who frequently intruded on his life and relationships. He responded by distancing himself from his mother. Consequently, he and his wife were having severe marital problems as he repeated the distancing strategy with her.

As a result of counseling, Byron established more frequent contact with his mother as a means to learn to be less intimidated by her intrusiveness. He worked on controlling his anxiety while he was with his mother, and he also worked on not overreacting by running to or giving in to his mother. As time went on, the relationship between him and his wife began to improve because he was dealing successfully with a pattern that he developed when he was very young.

Attending to Hurt Feelings

Violence associated with compulsive masculinity makes it especially important that pastoral counselors attend to the feelings of hurt and shame of African American males. Violence always masks feelings associated with being less than a man and having one's vulnerability exposed. Showing empathy and sensitivity in this area by helping African American men examine these feelings is essential for the pastoral counselor.

Peter was very volatile. When arguing with his wife, he felt as if she undermined his manhood. Neither knew how to express anger in constructive ways. In counseling Peter would shut down and refuse to participate if his wife became too critical of him. Gently, I helped him to express what he was feeling. Slowly, he became more articulate about what he was feeling and this increased articulateness seemed to make him less threatened by what his wife said. I also helped his wife to explore what was behind her anger toward him. This helped to reduce some of the anxiety between them. As his wife explored some of her own feelings and as his ability to constructively express his feelings increased there was a decrease in the explosive volatility of their relationship.

Immediacy

Attending to feelings of hurt is important, and attending to the relationship between counselor and counselee is also vital. Immediacy means attending to the feelings and the relationships that exist between the pastoral counselor and the counselee at any particular moment in the counseling process. It is important here because of the cultural values placed on the relational style in the African American community.[42] This means that many African Americans are people-oriented and prefer direct styles of relating. This is especially important when counseling with African American males.

In counseling this means dealing with the moment no matter how explosive and difficult it may seem. Dealing with how people feel about the counselor is vital in a particular moment of counseling. Equally, exploring the counselee's feelings about the counselor is vital to developing a working counseling relationship and a healthy outcome of counseling.

Conclusion

The African American men's movement has taken many forms. These forms have been reviewed here, and a narrative model of pastoral counseling with men has been presented as a means of addressing the needs of African American men. Rather than drawing on wider cultural images of masculinity that have led to negative identity and compulsive masculinity, the model presented here focuses on indigenous sources of personhood rooted in African American spirituality, culture, and history. An important link to this rich heritage is reconnecting with African American women who are relational carriers of the African tradition.

---

[42] Janice Hale, *Black Children: Their Roots, Culture, and Learning Styles* (Provo, Utah: Brigham Young University Press, 1982), 69.

3

Narrative Care for Spiritual Renewal (1997)

In these chapters from one of Edward Wimberly's impressive and lasting books, *Recalling Our Own Stories*,* Wimberly introduces narrative therapy as a resource for the spiritual renewal of caregivers. Here Wimberly expands his audience so as to include, along with African American pastors, a multicultural readership. At the same time, Wimberly writes in a way that is firmly rooted in his own story and the stories he remembers his father, the Reverend Edgar Wimberly, telling about his own call to ministry.

The use of the word "recalling" in Wimberly's book title is a play on words, suggesting more than simply remembering one's story, but actually being called anew. Wimberly explains how weary caregivers can challenge the personal, familial, or cultural myths that restrict their self-understandings and pastoral imaginations. Using narrative therapy principles, Wimberly offers exercises that invite caregivers to be re-called into spiritually vital lives. The key explanatory chapters reprinted here set the stage for case material found in the latter part of the book that demonstrates the impact of narrative pastoral care.

Edward Wimberly's pioneering work in narrative pastoral care, along with Christie Cozad Neuger's critical contributions, anticipated the current

---

* Edward P. Wimberly, "To Be Called Anew: Finding Spiritual Replenishment in Our Own Stories," *Recalling Our Own Stories: Spiritual Renewal for Religious Caregivers* (San Francisco: Jossey-Bass, 1997), 1–13; Wimberly, "Personal Myths: Stories that Empower Us or Leave Us Vulnerable," *Recalling Our Own Stories*, 14–33; Wimberly, "The Possibility of Change: Reauthoring the Myths that Bind Us," *Recalling Our Own Stories*, 73–88.

surge of interest in this approach.* As pastoral theologians seek to integrate critical (postmodern, postcolonial, and decolonial) theories into models of care, narrative approaches, which have been a part of African American pastoral care, are gaining traction in the field.† Wimberly saw narrative care as a particularly useful tool in honoring the cultural knowledges of African Americans, women, and members of other marginalized groups. Just as an individual's spiritual testimony invites the whole community to experience a spiritual truth, narrative models move pastoral care beyond individualism to engage the fullness of personal, communal, spiritual, and political dimensions of human stories.

Further Reading

Wimberly, Edward P. "A Narrative Approach to Pastoral Care in an Intercultural Setting." In *Knowledge, Attitude and Experience: Ministry in the Cross-Cultural Context*, edited by Young-Il Kim, 84–103. Nashville: Abingdon, 1992.

Wimberly, Edward P. *Recalling Our Own Stories: Spiritual Renewal for Religious Caregivers*. With a new foreword by Tapiwa N. Mucherera. Fortress Edition. Minneapolis: Fortress, 2019.

• • •

---

* See in particular, Christie Cozad Neuger, *Counseling Women: A Narrative, Pastoral Approach* (Minneapolis: Fortress, 2001).

† See, for example: Carrie Doehring, *The Practice of Pastoral Care: A Postmodern Approach*, rev. ed. (Louisville: Westminster John Knox, 2015); Duane R. Bidwell, *Empowering Couples: A Narrative Approach to Spiritual Care* (Minneapolis: Fortress, 2013); Karen D. Scheib, *Pastoral Care: Telling the Stories of Our Lives* (Nashville: Abingdon, 2016); Tapiwa N. Mucherera, *Meet Me at the Palaver: Narrative Pastoral Counseling in Postcolonial Contexts* (Eugene, Ore.: Wipf & Stock, 2009); and Tapiwa N. Mucherera, *Glimmers of Hope: Toward the Healing of Painful Life Experiences through Narrative Counseling* (Eugene, Ore.: Wipf & Stock, 2013). As noted in the introduction to this volume, Tapiwa N. Mucherera is a former student of Edward Wimberly. He has also written the foreword to the 2019 edition of *Recalling Our Own Stories: Spiritual Renewal for Religious Caregivers*, Fortress Edition (Minneapolis: Fortress, 2019).

To Be Called Anew: Finding Spiritual Replenishment in Our Own Stories*

I have been asked to do a number of spiritual renewal retreats. Those of us who are engaged in caring for others who are in ministry have seen firsthand how people need spiritual replenishment in their professions. The need is ongoing because many of us regularly feel we are running out of energy and gas. More than once, we have faced burnout. I believe we have all felt the need to refuel, to tap the sources of renewal that reside in our faith community.

Original Motivation: Our Call

In seeking spiritual renewal, we can take up the neglected tradition of reconnecting with our original motivation for ministry. In the Judeo-Christian tradition, that motivation is often referred to as "the call"; it was our first awareness that a form of ministry would be our life's work. Generally, most of us in ministry can identify the point in our lives at which we can say we made a commitment to ministry. Some of us came to our call after a period of growth and development in which we came to recognize our own gifts of ministry, gifts that others might have recognized, confirmed, and affirmed for us. Some of us had a more dramatic call: something sensational happened to bring our calling abruptly to awareness. Whether our awareness came suddenly or over time, a chance to reconnect with our original call is often the beginning of spiritual renewal.

As a boy, I learned from my dad how he went about finding renewal and meaning in life. He is a retired African American minister in the Methodist tradition. Once a year or so, he would rehearse from the pulpit his call to ministry. I can't say at what point in his life's journey I first heard him tell his story, but I do remember several things from hearing those rehearsals.

First, he would tell how he had finished a black college and returned to his home in Florida to teach. This was in the early 1930s, a time of full segregation. Before my father left Lincoln University in Oxford, Pennsylvania, one of the administrators recognized his proclivity for ministry; Dad had not seen it. The administrator told him that he could have a scholarship to seminary if he decided to enter the ministry. My dad thanked the administrator for his kind and generous offer but said he was not ready for such an endeavor at that time in his life.

---

* This selection was previously published in Edward P. Wimberly, *Recalling Our Own Stories: Spiritual Renewal for Religious Caregivers* (San Francisco: Jossey-Bass, 1997), 1–13. Used by permission.

Dad taught school for several years. Then, to his surprise, what the college administrator discerned several years earlier began to manifest itself. One uneventful evening, he lay sprawled across his bed, not anticipating anything but sleep since he was very tired from a long day's work at school. He was not asleep; he was in a semiwakened state. Suddenly a vision appeared that would alter his life. Dad's voice would grow excited every time he retold what transpired. He vividly saw himself in front of a congregation, preaching the gospel. A small group of people were sitting before him, on the stairs on which he was standing. He slowly moved backwards up the stairs while he expounded on the word of God. When he reached the top of the stairs, the vision disappeared as suddenly as it had come.

My dad attributed religious significance to the vision; it was his call to ministry. He knew, he said, that he had to begin preparing himself for a new life's work. Instantly, the college administrator's offer of several years earlier came to mind. The next morning, Dad contacted the administrator and discovered that the invitation and scholarship to seminary remained open. He made plans to attend seminary the following autumn.

The second thing I remember about my dad's rehearsal of his call was that for him it was a form of spiritual renewal. It appeared to bring a new perspective to his life. Of course, this is my conclusion looking retrospectively on what I saw on those occasions. No doubt he intended his testimony to contribute to the growth and development of his audience. But he seemed to derive new meaning for his own life from his excursus back to his original call.

One reason I so boldly interpret the effect of his rehearsing the call relates to what he often said following his recitation. He would use another story to interpret his call. In Acts 25:13–26:32, Paul defended himself after being arrested by telling King Agrippa the story of his own call on the Damascus Road. My father would recount the story of Paul's testimony, concluding with Paul's famous words in Acts 26:19, "Wherefor, O King Agrippa, I was not disobedient to the heavenly vision" (Note: all citations are from *The New Oxford Annotated Bible*, edited in 1977 by May and Metzger). I conclude from what my dad offered in interpretation that he drew some measure of focus and new life from recounting the two stories.

Paul found himself in hostile circumstances, as did many of the Christians in the early church. He periodically derived a sense of renewal from returning to his reasons for arriving in the predicament. Likewise, I surmise that my dad found similar renewal for his ministry by also returning to his memory of his own call.

From my dad and from this episode in the life of Paul, I conclude that a model of spiritual renewal exists in Scripture. It is many centuries old, but it informs what is needed in spiritual renewal today. Such a model helps us as religious caregivers to return routinely to our original motivation for ministry as a means of renewal. The model of spiritual renewal that I point to comes from African American spirituality, which has a strongly biblical character.[1] It also has a dimension of confession and self-disclosure to it.[2] Telling stories about one's call to ministry dates back to the slave narrative tradition.[3] This tradition of spirituality has shaped both my father's and my own way of doing and conceptualizing spirituality.

I have found that this biblical tradition of spiritual renewal appeals to more than just African American religious caregivers. I have used it for many years with different ethnic and racial groups; they have all found it helpful and timely in their own spiritual renewal. It is one among many approaches to renewing the vitality of our ministry.

A third thing I learned about spiritual renewal from my father is that it requires not only reflecting on the call but also rehearsing and recounting the story in a community or public setting. My dad chose the pulpit, and Paul had to use the courtroom. Spiritual renewal is greatly enhanced when it is done with others present.

Reviewing our call in a community of caring people, especially a community of colleagues, has much significance. Time out with colleagues, as in a retreat from the daily routines of ministry, enhances the quality of spiritual renewal. When we use this particular model in the presence of many, we are grateful not to be a one in the wilderness of ministry. We feel less vulnerable to isolation and are encouraged to risk more of ourselves in the process. I hear people report that the companionship gives them courage to face the edge of their personal growth that would be hard to face alone. Some have found that this form of group spiritual renewal hastens emotional and interpersonal maturity along with spiritual renewal.

Renewing our motivation by reconnecting to our original call allows us to visualize again how God has decisively acted in our lives at crucial junctures. It reminds us that God has been intricately involved in our lives. The routine duties of ministry and life take on new meaning when looked at in light of the call.

---

[1] Jamie Phelps, "Black Spirituality," in *Spiritual Traditions for the Contemporary Church*, ed. Robin Maas and Gabriel O'Donnell (Nashville: Abingdon, 1990), 332–52.

[2] William H. Myers, *God's Yes Was Louder than My No: Rethinking African American Call to Ministry* (Grand Rapids: Eerdmans, 1994).

[3] Edward P. Wimberly and Anne Streaty Wimberly, *Liberation and Human Wholeness: The Conversion Experiences of Black People in Slavery and Freedom* (Nashville: Abingdon, 1986).

But spiritual renewal involves more than returning to our original motivation for entering ministry. It also examines past and present experiences and issues in our lives that are related to ministry. For example, recovery from burnout—or its extreme case, a sudden and public "flameout," as some call it—involves recalling our motivation for entering the ministry and examining the issues of burnout in light of our call. The call is a marker event that we must return to periodically to examine where we are in life, and to alter our way of believing and doing.

Spiritual renewal is finding a fresh, novel, and creative way of allowing the call to reorient our present lives so as to bring replenishment and hope. Spiritual renewal is a process of connecting with our original motivation for ministry, and then moving systematically into examining areas of our lives in light of that call.

Mythology

In the spiritual renewal process that I propose in this book, the concept of mythology is immensely helpful. By *mythology*, I mean *the beliefs and convictions that people have about themselves, their relationships with others, their roles in life, and their ministry*. As used here, myth refers to the way beliefs and convictions are constructed and how these constructions shape our lives and our behavior.

Beliefs and convictions are represented by certain repetitive themes that appear in the stories we tell. At times, I may use the words *myth* and *theme* synonymously, although they are different. Myths are the stories we tell, while themes reflect the beliefs and convictions in the stories.

The Project of Existence

The call constitutes the "project of existence."[4] The project of existence is an overarching framework in an individual's life that gives meaning and shape to everything that goes on. It is a vocational umbrella, or window, through which we look at all of what we do. It is the dominant, self-understood purpose for which we have been born. It tells us what to do daily in our ministry, and it informs how we execute our roles and functions. It serves as a kind of road map in fulfilling our call.

Narrative Story

Supporting this project of existence is a worldview, or narrative story, that gives shape and meaning to the roles we execute in ministry. It "relates" (in the sense of telling) to us what our role is. We find in our lives a dominant

---

[4] Adrian Van Kaam, *Religion and Personality* (Garden City, N.Y.: Image Books, 1964), 20.

story or myth out of which we come, while the other stories or myths in our lives become submyths or secondary myths. The dominant myth, the project of existence, gives meaning and shape to our lives. For example, one person's dominant story may be that she is always an embattled hero working valiantly against great odds, while another's dominant story may be one of awe and gratitude in the face of surprising gifts over which he has little instrumental control.

The project of existence has at its core the call coming from God. For my father and the apostle Paul, renewal came because the source of the call was outside themselves. God provided the call, the power to fulfill the call, and the historic meaning for the call. What people who are called have done historically, then, is orient themselves and their personality, relationships, and ministry in terms of the call from God. Spiritual renewal is a reorientation process of allowing the original call and its ongoing nature to continually transform our lives in the present.

A basic assumption in spiritual renewal is that the call is ongoing. Consequently, the project of existence—the dominant story of our lives—is being renewed by God each day. Connecting with this transcendent activity brings renewal into our lives.

The Problem of Submyths

Lesser stories—our submyths—often take center stage in our lives. When this happens, we suffer loss of meaning and direction. The submyths or lesser myths of our lives emerge from our experiences as human beings. They function best when they are in line with our project of existence or our call, when they are being renewed daily by the ongoing call of our lives. However, sometimes the submyths of our lives are so powerful that they block the influence of the ongoing call.

When the lesser myths block the working of the call in our lives, spiritual renewal becomes the removing of the blocks that are in the way of our call. Spiritual renewal is an attempt to bring our submyths back in line with the ongoing call or project of existence. Consequently, it is important to identify the submyths at work in our lives and bring them into connection with the ongoing call in our lives.

The Problem of Perfection

One of the lesser myths that block the call in our lives is the cultural myth of "perfection." The myth of perfection relates to the domination of the therapeutic model that greatly influences ministry today.

Since the turn of the century, a psychological model has been at the center of our understanding of the pastor's relationship with parishioners.[5] In some minds, the increasing influence of psychology and counseling psychology has secularized pastoral conversation. That is, psychological language has slowly replaced religious language in pastoral dialogue during this century.

Empathy

A major theme in much of our pastoral conversation today is the perfection of empathy. In the history of modern pastoral counseling, for example, empathy was not seen as just a skill. Rather, it was a way of approaching life and caring that yielded an engaged stance, a relational posture, where human beings connected with each other.[6] Growing out of the humanistic philosophical tradition, empathy entails several assumptions: human beings are innately good and worthwhile; they tend toward actualizing themselves by unfolding from within; their growth comes from evolving and interacting; human relationships are essential to the unfolding of human possibilities; and empathy, or entering into another's internal world, is essential to a person's growth, development, and self-actualization.[7] Thus empathy became a comprehensive perspective for viewing all human relationships, and for viewing what all human beings needed to become true persons. Empathy became all-encompassing for the pastoral counseling movement and has continued to influence the way pastors have been trained since the 1940s. The ability to be empathic has thus been considered the most critical element for effective caregiving. It has achieved the level of a practical mythology as a theme that is centrally emphasized in pastoral relationships.

In the myth of empathy, it is possible to achieve perfect empathy or reach complete positive regard for another person, without flaw. Entering another's internal frame of reference and viewing the world through his or her eyes is not only achievable but perfectible. To be perfect in demonstrating empathy means the caregiver takes on the other's point of view so completely that the caregiver's own interests, attitudes, concerns, and problems are prevented from interfering with those of the other person. In general, textbooks in pastoral care assume this expectation of achieving complete empathy. The result is that many pastoral counselors enter counseling relationships believing that it is possible to achieve self-sacrificing empathy.

[5] E. Brooks Holifield, *A History of Pastoral Care in America: From Salvation to Self-Realization* (Nashville: Abingdon, 1983).
[6] Howard Clinebell, *Basic Types of Pastoral Counseling* (Nashville: Abingdon, 1984).
[7] Rodney J. Hunter, ed., *Dictionary of Pastoral Care and Counseling* (Nashville: Abingdon, 1990).

Carrie Doehring, the author of *Taking Care: Monitoring Power Dynamics and Relational Boundaries in Pastoral Care and Counseling*, talks about the social context of the perfection of empathy: "In a culture in which attunement may be greatly lacking in many relational contexts (in the community, in work relationships, and in the corporate world) there may be a demand for 'perfect attunement' in dyadic healing and nurturing relationships. The parent, the minister, the counselor, or the teacher is expected to be an expert at attunement and empathy."[8]

The emphasis on perfection has led people to describe the effort to achieve empathy as having "sucked the life out of the caregiver," and as having "the potential to contaminate" us as caregivers if we have no place to turn to for emotional and spiritual renewal. How to renew and sustain our vital spiritual and emotional life as religious and professional caregivers, and thus replenish our energy, remains a crucial need in the face of the demand for perfect empathy.

The myth of perfection dominates North American professional circles in caregiving. Beneath this myth is a superheroic narrative; it supports the caregiver's effort to sacrifice self regardless of whether that self is regularly renewed or not.[9] The theme that supports the notion of perfection is that we caregiving practitioners desire and expect to be flawless in connecting empathically with those needing our care. The theme also implies that we be free from personal hang-ups, and perfectly available and approachable for the person in need of care. It calls for denial and repression of our humanness: "To achieve perfection in any of its classical senses, as so many perfectibilists have admitted, it would first be necessary to cease to be human, to become godlike, to rise above the human condition. But a god knows nothing of love, or science, or art, or craft, of family and friends, of discovery, of pride in work."[10]

To be a superheroic empathizer, we must deny all aspects of our own humanness. Doing so cuts us off from the human family. It also leads to us to deny our own needs for spiritual, emotional, and interpersonal renewal. It sets the stage for burnout and failure in ministry. It makes us vulnerable. As Doehring points out, it leads to neglecting ourselves as well as those for

---

[8] Carrie Doehring, *Taking Care: Monitoring Power Dynamics and Relational Boundaries in Pastoral Care and Counseling* (Nashville: Abingdon, 1995), 80.

[9] Richard K. Fenn, *The Dream of the Perfect Act: An Inquiry into the Gate of Religion in a Secular World* (New York: Tavistock, 1987); Robert Jewett, *Saint Paul at the Movies: The Apostle's Dialogue with American Culture* (Louisville: Westminster John Knox, 1993); Robert Jewett and John Shelton Lawrence, *The American Monomyth* (Lanham, Md.: University Press of America, 1988); Donald E. Messer, *Contemporary Images of Christian Ministry* (Nashville: Abingdon, 1989); John Arthur Passmore, *The Perfectibility of Man* (London: Gerald Duckworth, 1970).

[10] Passmore, *Perfectibility of Man*, 326.

whom we care—especially when we lack the expertise we need to carry out empathy well.[11]

"Good Enough" Empathy

Our expectation of achieving perfect empathy is unreasonable. It is unrealistic to expect that we can execute empathy without flaw. But it *is* realistic to expect from us "good enough" empathy. Good enough empathy is not flawless. Good enough empathy is rooted in an awareness that although we are wounded and hurting, we have taken time to tend to the wounds. Healing our own wounds means they can be a source of healing for those whose wounds are similar to ours. Good enough empathy means we have had our wounds transformed from sources of personal weakness to reservoirs of strength for those in need. This presupposes that we spend time in spiritual renewal, time in spiritual retreat.

Throughout this book, I draw a subtle contrast between realism and perfection. *Perfection* refers to flawless performance. *Realism* refers to performance that is permeated with a grace-filled acceptance of our limitations and flaws (and our strengths). Grace-filled realism enables us to make significant—but not unflawed—contributions to the lives of others. It is not driven by fear of falling short of an impossible external standard, or law, or expectation. Rather, grace-filled realism is caregiving nurtured by a transcendent love that motivates and energizes.

A Case of Disappointed Perfection

It is not easy for religious caregivers to move beyond the perfectionistic impulse to awareness of the need for spiritual renewal and retreat. Perfectionistic thinking is so strong that we deny our own need for healing and resist the efforts of others to help us see our vulnerability and suffering.

I met a pastor at the grocery store. He had just left a group of other pastors in a hospital, engaging in what is called clinical pastoral education (CPE, an interpersonal training program for ministers and chaplains located primarily in hospitals).

The pastor looked very tired, and somewhat perplexed. He sighed: "I wish someone had warned me about this CPE. I'm tired. I have four weeks to go. I get so tired of discovering how many inadequacies I have. It's embarrassing for others to see just how inadequate I am. I try to hide my vulnerabilities, but others find them out. I wish they would give me some breathing space."

Part of this minister's self-expectation was perfection. Rather than seeing CPE as an opportunity to grow and improve his interpersonal skills for

[11] Doehring, *Taking Care*, 80.

ministry, he wanted the CPE experience to affirm his perfect ministerial skills. He was so tired because he was expending so much effort trying to keep his imperfections hidden from himself and others.

This illustration is typical of many who experience CPE. The myth of perfection dominates; it is hard for us to consider becoming wounded healers. Some of us feel that our call to ministry bestowed upon us all the grace and gifts needed for ministry, and therefore training is not required. CPE helps us ministers get in touch with our vulnerabilities so we can learn to care for ourselves and our own needs.

Transformation of the Walking Wounded

The myth of perfection has engendered many other metaphors and myths about ministry. For example, Henri Nouwen coined the metaphor of the "wounded healer" as a response to the perfectionistic myth.[12] Rather than deny our wounds and vulnerability, Nouwen emphasized the need to embrace one's woundedness and tend to it by seeking spiritual direction and therapy.

A colleague of mine, Calvin Morris, offered the metaphor "walking wounded" as another reply to the perfectionistic myth. He uses the term to characterize those of us who deny our vulnerability and woundedness and who, consequently, walk around as wounded people seeking to help others. Instead of achieving good enough empathy, we become dangerous to ourselves and to those we seek to care for. We cannot temporarily set our own needs aside or keep them out of the way in our caring effort. Sometimes as walking wounded, we use our caring relationships to *receive* care ourselves by reversing roles with those who are actually in need of pastoral conversation.

Early in my own ministry, I often shared stories from my life that I thought would help my parishioners while I was counseling them. Ordinarily, this would work. But there was one elderly woman with whom I would share my stories—and she would inevitably end up ministering to me! She sensed that I was new in ministry and that I needed motherly attention. Although she had her own needs as well, in our conversations I found myself sharing more from my life and connecting less with her needs.

I began training for pastoral counseling very early in my ministry. In the training I presented cases to a consultant, who identified my tendency to take the focus away from my counselee. He suggested that I go into therapy

---

[12] Henri Nouwen, *The Wounded Healer* (New York: Doubleday, 1972); Messer, *Contemporary Images*.

for myself and not use my counselees to receive counseling. I was one of the walking wounded.

My perfectionism was influential in that reversing of roles whereby I sought to receive counseling from my counselees. Because of the influence of the myth of perfection, I could not acknowledge my own needs for care. My needs went underground, but they surfaced in my attempts to care for others.

Sometimes as walking wounded we find ourselves in conflict with parishioners, with very little control over the conflict. James was such a person. There was a particular man in the church who continually challenged James' decisions and ideas. He was greatly frustrated. He spent many sleepless nights thinking about it.

James is African American. He grew up in a culture where peers made fun of others' physical stature; since childhood, he had been teased because he was short. He was a victim of what is called "sounding" or "woofing," in which someone protects his or her own identity by ridiculing another.[13] Usually, anyone who takes the brunt of constant woofing finds his or her identity devastated. So when James was called to ministry, he began to receive a level of respect that he had never known. He promised himself that he would never again be disrespected. But his feelings from childhood were close to the emotional surface. Thus, when the parishioner in James' church challenged him, he felt disrespected and deeply angry. He became so preoccupied with dealing with this man that the conflict eventually led to James' losing the church.

The walking wounded have a certain personal style that prevents receiving nurture and care. Zelda's mother was very young when Zelda was born, and she felt she could not raise her daughter. Consequently, Zelda grew up as an only child, in a home with her aging Jamaican grandparents. She was a very obedient, very responsible child. Zelda made a lot of the decisions and seemed to become an adult before her time. People came to her for advice even while she was a child. She received a lot of rewards for being adultlike and taking responsibility for her grandparents. The culture in which she grew up emphasized the traditional African value of care for aging elders.[14]

Zelda accepted her call to ministry in her mid-forties and started her own independent church. She found herself playing the role of minister similarly to the role she had played as a child. She was very responsible,

---

[13] William Oliver, *The Violent Social World of Black Men* (San Francisco: New Lexington Press, 1994).

[14] Anne E. Streaty Wimberly, *Honoring African American Elders: A Ministry in the Soul Community* (San Francisco: Jossey-Bass, 1997).

and people brought their problems to her. However, she grew resentful and found she did not have the energy needed to continually care for others. She felt she was giving generously but receiving very little. She began to avoid her parishioners and not answer her calls. Eventually, she was hospitalized for complete exhaustion. Medical personnel advised her to learn how to take better care of herself. She, too, was one of the walking wounded in need of care.

Something keeps us walking wounded from working on our own needs. Sometimes it is related to images of perfection. At other times, we lack recognition of our own need for care and nurture. We don't feel we have permission to take time to care for our own needs. So we never learn to transform our own woundedness into a resource to be used in caring. As walking wounded and wounded healers, we need times of retreat and care to tend to our own needs so that we can return to the caring task of providing good enough empathy.

A Theological Base for Wounded Healers

A detrimental aspect of the myth of perfection is that it blinds us to the meaning of the call to ministry. The biblical and theological roots of the call go back to the prophetic tradition of Israel, yet they influence our understanding of the call today. This prophetic image of the call is not rooted in perfection. It is based on God's transformation of the ordinary person into a servant of God. Thus, the origin of ministry is in God—not in the caregiver.

The call of Isaiah illustrates what the call means for the wounded healer. In Isaiah 6:1-13, the prophet's call includes his announcing his woundedness and vulnerability, to which an angel of the Lord attends. The prophet declares of himself: "And I said: 'Woe is me! For I am lost: for I am a man of unclean lips, and I dwell in the midst of a people of unclean lips; for my eyes have seen the King, the Lord of hosts!'" (Isa 6:5)

The same is true in Jeremiah 1:4-9, where Jeremiah felt unfit to be a prophet because as a youth with little experience he felt vulnerable. In verse 6, he says: "Ah, Lord God! Behold, I do not know how to speak, for I am only a youth." The prophet Moses was also viewed as wounded and vulnerable in the book of Exodus. In being called, Moses found that God gave him words to equip him for the task.

In Isaiah chapters 41 to 43, we have a fuller picture of the call and its implications for carrying out ministry. God promises companionship to these servants as they execute God's call (41:10). God promises to uphold them, strengthen them, and enable them in their work; God promises to give them God's spirit so that they can carry out their given tasks (43:1). Moreover, God is portrayed as redeeming those who are called from their past sins and vulnerabilities.

Jesus' understanding of his own call is also grounded in the prophetic tradition of the Old Testament. While the Gospel writers do not portray him as having to be cleansed, he is baptized and otherwise seen as a human being (this is evident in his experience in the wilderness) and in need of empowerment by God's Spirit following baptism.

The call tradition that I have emphasized so far is male-oriented. This does not mean that women are excluded from God's call. I do indeed envision women as being under the same prophetic tradition of the call as men. Narrative understandings of Scripture and women's participation in interpreting Scripture have allowed us to discern women's inclusive participation as disciples in the ministry of God. For example, Elisabeth Schüssler Fiorenza's *In Memory of Her: A Feminist Reconstruction of Christian Origins* helps us place women's stories in the stories of Jesus; she discovers also that women were called disciples and had roles equal to those of men. She concludes (and I concur) that "Only when we place the Jesus stories about women into the overall story of Jesus and his movement in Palestine are we able to recognize their subversive character. In the discipleship of equals the 'role' of women is not peripheral or trivial, but at the center, and thus of utmost importance to the praxis of 'solidarity from below.'"[15]

Analysis of the call centrally emphasizes God's call of those who were not perfect, but inadequate. Fiorenza also emphasizes that women were included in the call as themselves being ordinary and imperfect: "The Jesus movement articulates a quite different understanding of God because it had experienced in the praxis of Jesus a God who called not Israel's righteous and pious but its religiously deficient and its social underdogs. In the ministry of Jesus God is experienced as all-inclusive love, letting the sun shine and the rain fall equally on the righteous and on sinners."[16]

To spell out the import of these examples from the Old and New Testament prophets, first of all salvation is something that God does. Human beings are called by God to assist in this process. Second, God equips those called and makes them ready by whatever means are necessary. Third, God becomes a companion to the called; they are not in it by themselves. Fourth, perfection is not a requirement for the call. Finally, the lead and the energy for executing the call come from God.

---

[15] Elizabeth Schüssler Fiorenza, *In Memory of Her: A Feminist Reconstruction of Christian Origins* (New York: Crossroad, 1992), 152.

[16] Fiorenza, *In Memory*, 130.

The problem with the myth of perfection is that it contradicts the understanding of the call that is found in the prophetic tradition. The perfectionistic myth is anchored in a form of "works righteousness" that puts the focus on the minister's effort and leaves God out. Moreover, the perfectionist myth joins with another myth, "narcissistic individualism," that denies God's companionship along the way in ministry.[17] In addition, the perfectionistic myth forces its adherents to buy into the myth of "triumphalism," which denies the reality of suffering and vulnerability. In all these ways, the perfectionistic myth denies the need for God and God's involvement in our ministries.

As the walking wounded, we make biblical and theological understanding of the call to ministry secondary. We deny our need to be redeemed. We seek the power for ministry from within ourselves. We see no need, or deny the need, for God to be our companion.

Given both the pervasive influence of the perfectionistic myth and our tendency to deny our woundedness, spiritual renewal is essential. The approach of this book is to reconnect us with our call and examine it in light of whether or not we are wounded healers, the walking wounded. We also try to clarify the things in our lives that prevent our call from transforming us into wounded healers. The key idea is to be aware first that we must update our call regularly, and second that it requires spiritual retreat and renewal.

A Model for Reauthoring Mythologies

Our task is to reedit, or reauthor, our own mythologies where they make it difficult to carry out our call. In reauthoring the myths in our lives, we assume that the call from God is ongoing. God's call is like an unfolding drama in which new meaning is disclosed daily, and as the called we are invited to participate in these new meanings and possibilities.

Several related theoretical concepts give shape to how this unfolding of the call influences the lives of those called. One important concept is liminality. The term *liminality* suggests a threshold of perception. I use it to describe a period of retreat wherein we must suspend the ordinary routine of life so as to have time to regroup. The intention in such a liminal period is to allow the call to resurface. It is an "in-between" time when new models of reality are disclosed.[18] Amid the suspension of routine, the call is an action story, a "deep narrative of the soul," where God's intentions for our

---

[17] Messer, *Contemporary Images*, 81.
[18] Doehring, *Taking Care*, 143.

lives can be made clear, to give focus and shape to our experiences.[19] The call is a shaping story that creates new meanings so that our lives and ministry regain freshness and are renewed. During the liminal period, the call crosses a threshold of perception and brings new meaning, a new world, a new self, and a new future.

The walking wounded who are called confront a problem: the moments of liminality are easily obscured, and new possibilities and breakthroughs are easily frustrated. Spiritual renewal helps attend to what is blocking our awareness so that it is no longer an obstacle to renewed meaning in life.

The process of editing the various myths so as to foster liminality follows several steps and poses important questions as we proceed. First, we identify the themes that inform our lives; can we see effects of the personal, marital, family, and ministerial myths? Step two is assess whether these themes or the related myths are producing growth in ourselves and others; or are they contributing to our remaining wounded? Step three discerns the ongoing, continuously unfolding nature of our call; what is it doing to bring renewal to the life themes and myths at work in our lives? Finally, step four sets goals; can we make plans to alter our myths and bring them in line with our continuing call?

• • •

---

[19] Doehring, *Taking Care*, 142.

Personal Myths: Stories That Empower Us or Leave Us Vulnerable*

Religious caregiving can be hazardous to your health. It is important for all religious caregivers to hear what the authors of *The Psychology of Clergy* say about the hazards inherent in the ministry:

> Ministry is just as much a hazardous occupation as that of high-rise window washing or stunt car driving. In fact, all of the "helping professions" are hazardous in the sense that they include a high danger of burnout and a high risk of fallout. Burnout can be seen in those who become fatigued, discouraged, and overwhelmed. Fallout can be seen in those who leave one vocation and enter another. While it is not likely that clergy will plunge ten stories to their deaths, as those perched near the top of skyscrapers might, still, they are constantly exposed to dangers that could threaten their mental health, their judgment, and their motivation.[1]

We do, indeed, face hazards in ministry and caregiving. We face temptations, whether to be sexually indiscreet or to misuse our role and power to fulfill some personal need at the expense of others' needs. We face role conflicts, when as willing caregivers we spend more time in the roles that are demanded of us than in the ones we would prefer. And we face our own unresolved family-of-origin issues, as they are aggravated by the expectations of those who receive our care.

Then there is the inability to allow ourselves to be human and in need of care; the dysfunctional myths we cling to in our personal, marital, family, and ministerial lives; and denial of our need for the support of others. Regardless of the specific problem that arises, our personal beliefs and convictions—about ourselves, about our relationships with others, and about our world—play a crucial part in how we manage the hazards of religious caregiving.

Clarity about four kinds of myth—personal, marital, family, and ministerial—is essential. We need to understand the myths so as to "reauthor" them. Failure to find clarity and to reauthor the myths leaves us completely vulnerable to the hazards and the stresses related to them. We must identify and assess the myths before we can decide to alter our

---

[1] H. Newton Malony and Richard A. Hunt, *The Psychology of Clergy* (Harrisburg, Pa.: Morehouse, 1991), 33.

* This selection was previously published in Edward P. Wimberly, *Recalling Our Own Stories: Spiritual Renewal for Religious Caregivers* (San Francisco: Jossey-Bass, 1997), 14–33. Used by permission.

responses; only then can we facilitate our personal and professional growth as caregivers.

This chapter presents common myths from these four areas of our lives and work. Because they are so common, we must lift them up for scrutiny. They suffuse our ingrained convictions and beliefs about ourselves, others, and the ministry. Such deep convictions and beliefs are intrinsic to the fact of hazard in our profession.

Origins of Personal Myths

A personal mythology is made up of the convictions and beliefs that we hold about ourselves. It is made up of specific themes, including:

Early memories

Whether or not we feel welcomed and wanted

Our birth order in relationship to other siblings

Gender

Name and nickname

Peer and sibling relationships

Roles we played (or still play) in our family of origin

Parental discipline in our family of origin and in school

How our parents relate(d) to each other

The stories with which we identify[2]

As we see from the list, these themes have their genesis in our family of origin and our early childhood experiences. They are symbolic in nature and laden with affect (which is defined as "the conscious subjective aspect of an emotion considered apart from bodily changes"). The themes have several components, notably the internalized and externalized relationships that we have with significant others early in our lives and how the self interprets experience. They form a basic narrative, an overarching frame of reference that governs our feelings about ourselves, our relationships with others, and how we behave in the world. Lifelong interpretations and narratives become permanent parts of our self; we act to perpetuate them, which is why we confront change reluctantly. They assist us in developing a lifestyle or a pattern of existence that affects every situation we face. This thematic narrative is formative, and once formed it is difficult to change.

---

[2] Dennis Bagarozzi and Stephen A. Anderson, *Personal, Marital, and Family Myths: Theoretical Formulations and Clinical Strategies* (New York: Norton, 1989).

Personal myths have their roots in the way we cognitively organize our thinking as we interpret reality. They also have theoretical roots: in object relations theory, self-psychology, and family systems theories.[3]

The first two of these theories offers a perspective from depth psychology. Object relations theory focuses on how we as individuals internalized the positives and negatives we saw in significant others, and how we then go on to form a structure of the self that interprets reality from this basis. Self-psychology focuses on how we as individuals respond empathically to our externalized relationships with significant others, and how the responses impact our sense of self positively or negatively.

Family systems theory deals with how the interactions of marital and family members influence the growth of others. Later chapters say more specifically about family systems theories; this chapter largely stays in the depth psychological dimensions of the personal myth.

As we easily suspect, perfectionism is an important factor in how the themes of our narrative play out. The empathic responses of our significant others have great impact on how we interpret reality and form our personal myths. For instance, according to self-psychology theory, if significant others fail to show us empathy early in childhood, we will interpret ourselves as being worthless and without regard. Such an interpretation might lead us to seek to be perfect, or perform perfectly, to gain from the significant other the regard that we hunger for.[4]

Personal myths are significant because they form the basis of all our interactions and experience with others. They improve or lessen the quality of our interactions and our ability to interpret our experience. If our personal myths are healthy and we feel positive about ourselves, then our interactions and experiences with others are enhanced. The reverse is also true. Those of us who believe we are called and who have good self-esteem generally treat hostility received from others as part of the job, and we do not take criticism personally. Those of us who have negative convictions about ourselves often take criticism as an attack upon ourselves, and we experience a deflation of our self-esteem. Good personal myths help us deal positively with the potential for self-sabotage; negative myths make us more vulnerable.

---

[3] Bagarozzi and Anderson, *Personal, Marital, and Family Myths*; Glen O. Gabbard, *Psychodynamic Psychiatry in Clinical Practice: The DSM-IV Edition* (Washington, D.C.: American Psychiatric Publishing, 1994).

[4] Gabbard, *Psychodynamic Psychiatry*.

Common Personal Myths

I have encountered certain personal myths in retreats, in classes, and in my counseling with others. My selection of certain myths here is not exhaustive; there are many possible types. In fact, your own mythologies may be quite different. Yours may incorporate elements and themes of some of these myths but not of others. I intend only to spark your thinking about your own mythology by giving you a range of vivid examples I have observed with religious caregivers. I use the same rationale for presenting the other three types of myths—marital, family, and ministerial—in chapters three and four.

The Myth of Rejection

A common myth that I have noted among religious caregivers is the myth of rejection. In any workshop or class, at least one or two people are convinced that they are rejected and unwanted by their significant others.

The myth of rejection is the belief that you are unwanted, even unwelcome, in life. It often stems from childhood experiences in the family of origin; sometimes it originates in the "womb or birth mythologies." These are stories told to us by significant others about our conception, the time in the womb, our birth, and the first six to twelve months of our existence.[5] The stories are significant because we read into them clues as to how we were welcomed to the world. They also give us our earliest sense of who God is. How we are welcomed into the world initially lays the groundwork for our experience of graceful acceptance from God as we grow up.

The myth of rejection makes us highly vulnerable to the myth of perfection. When we feel unwanted and unacceptable, we respond by trying to win love and affection from others. If those who withhold the possibility of being loved have high expectations around our performance in life, then we who feel rejected may go on to try to meet these demanding expectations.

Fran is a middle-age white woman who came to a spiritual retreat for chaplains. She discussed what she had found out about the circumstances surrounding her birth. Because she was adopted, she had a great need to put together a phantom genealogy, a make-believe heritage of her own. The need came from a deep feeling that she was wanted by neither her biological nor her adoptive family.

She worked hard to find out about her biological parents. A cooperative social worker at an adoption agency found a letter from her birth mother that filled in some of the reasons she had been given up for adoption. The

---

[5] Ana-Maria Rizzuto, *The Birth of the Living God* (Chicago: University of Chicago Press, 1979).

letter showed that Fran was actually wanted by her biological mother, but the circumstances of her conception and birth were very difficult. At the time, her mother was nineteen and Catholic; because her father was Protestant, Fran's mother's parents had the marriage annulled for religious reasons and forced her birth mother to put Fran up for adoption.

A genogram is a written- or drawn-out structure of three or more generations of a family. Fran developed a phantom genogram, based on her adopted family and what she could find out about her biological family. Piecing together more information from the adoption records and from answers to questions she asked her adoptive parents, Fran filled in the gaps of her early life. Where there was no information, she supplied it with her imagination. Motivating it all was a gnawing sense of not being wanted. (Often in such cases of feared rejection, the person has to search for the truth before any inner peace will come.)

Fran's feeling of not being wanted was dually based. She knew she had been adopted, but she felt she really did not fit with her adoptive family either. The feeling grew that something was missing in her life; it was deepened by the discovery that she had actually been welcomed into the world by her biological mother. Believing that her real name was Hilda (as she discovered when she obtained her adoption records) permitted her to imagine that Hilda was mature, self-assured, and self-assertive, just the opposite of Fran.

Fran's need to fill in the gaps and give herself a phantom history is the need of all human beings to sense a reason for being born. This in turn is basic to our experience of who we are in life, and feelings that we are not wanted powerfully influence how we feel about ourselves and our significance in this world. Fran's myth of rejection made her vulnerable to a variety of hazards in the ministry. She desired to belong, to be part of a family. If left unattended to or unmet, her desire could cause her call to caregiving to become instead a search for a family. She might inappropriately turn the concerns of her ministry primarily to herself and her own needs, rather than to those who are entrusted to her care.

The Myth of Powerlessness

Another myth I often encounter among caregivers is powerlessness. This myth is not as obvious since we often hide our feelings of powerlessness, from ourselves and others. Facing a difficulty or crisis could make us quite aware of being powerless.

The myth of powerlessness is the conviction that we have no real power or agency to impact our lives and the lives of others, our environment, and our world. We see other people as having more power and control over our lives than we do. We feel that things happen to us, that we have no real choice or decision. We may feel victimized by others, helpless to respond to what is being done "to us." We may become overly vigilant, seeking to identify potential perpetrators before they can abuse us.

The danger of perfectionism is that we might see ourselves unrealistically as imperfect or flawed. In our expectations of perfection, there is no possibility for grace-filled self-acceptance. The others whom we envisage as perfect have all the power.

In ministering, it is essential to claim power.[6] We learn to feel confident in our ministerial identity, functioning and affirming our gifts for ministry. "Affirming our power" does not mean power over anyone or the power to dominate; it means being empowered to do what God has called us to do. If we are to be effective in ministry, we need to learn to claim the power that we have.

A sense of powerlessness hinders our ability to be in ministry. Feelings of powerlessness come mainly from our experiences in our family of origin. There are also racial and gender factors that make it difficult for women and African Americans to claim their power.

Miriam Anne Glover-Wetherington, a professor at Duke University Divinity School, points out how difficult it is for women to claim their power. She writes that women are socialized to act vulnerable, passive, tender, gentle, supportive, and powerless; they hide their strength because to display it is taken as being unfeminine. The result is that women's strengths, abilities, perceptions, and opinions are often not affirmed.[7]

Historically, African Americans have also been prevented from claiming power in the wider culture. This sense of powerlessness in the majority culture is often accompanied by resort to negative power within the African American community. The sexism among African American men toward African American women is often an attempt to affirm the power that is denied in the larger culture. Violence against other African Americans is also a compensatory, but distorted, understanding of power.[8]

It is my experience that cultural images of what it means to be powerful and powerless are mediated through family relationships; thus, family-of-origin issues cannot be neglected. Minner, who is white and in his late twenties, has what he calls his "dining room table memory":

[6] Miriam Anne Glover-Wetherington, "Pastoral Care and Counseling with Women Entering Ministry," in *Through the Eyes of Women: Insights for Pastoral Care*, ed. Jeanne Stevenson-Moessner (Minneapolis: Fortress, 1996).

[7] Glover-Wetherington, "Women Entering Ministry."

[8] William Oliver, *The Violent Social World of Black Men* (San Francisco: New Lexington Press, 1994).

This memory involves a rectangular table, with me at about age six sitting at the end of the table (at the position many people might say the head of the table sits) with my parents on each side of me. And as I remember the scene, my parents turn to me and ask me which one of them I love the most. Having asked my parents about the memory, and them having no recollection of the scene, I have come to realize that whether the episode actually happened or not matters little. What matters is that memory represents some very valid feelings I have had growing up in my family of origin. I have felt many times as if I were trapped between my mom and dad. And this theme has run throughout my life. It has manifest[ed] itself in trying to take responsibility for others, trying to please others, and feeling a deep sense of guilt and shame when I try to claim my own power or boundaries. I feel like my parents abused me and took advantage of me unfairly.

This early childhood memory definitely gives a clue to the reality behind the helplessness that Minner feels today. He was trapped, not old enough to have any impact on what he felt his parents were doing to him. Feelings of powerlessness begin with being abused by significant others in life; there are real bases for feeling victimized and trapped.[9]

While the basis of the myth of powerlessness is real, we who were victimized are responsible for *how* we remember the early experiences and *how* we form beliefs about ourselves and others.[10] We may have been victimized, but we do not have to form a victim mythology or a myth of powerlessness. We are responsible for forming a myth, with its beliefs about our own impotence and ineffectiveness—as well as our own inability to confront what power we actually have.

A mythology of victimization or powerlessness can have a very negative impact on our caregiving. If we view those who seek our care as similar in any way to the abusers, it will be very difficult to respond positively to their legitimate needs. We might distance or disengage from the careseeker, to prevent being victimized again. We might rationalize the distancing by telling ourselves consciously that we don't want to be walked on again like a doormat.

We who feel powerless cannot ignore the fear of being victimized again. Yet the victim mythology may prevent us from responding to someone's genuine needs, for fear of disengaging or becoming combative with a parishioner or careseeker. We need to edit our victim mythology so that

[9] James Poling, *Deliver Us from Evil: Resisting Racial and Gender Oppression* (Minneapolis: Fortress, 1996).

[10] Rollo May, *Power and Innocence: A Search for the Sources of Violence* (New York: Norton, 1972).

we can distinguish potentially real victimization from our own projection of victimization, that is, projection when there is no substantial threat of being victimized.

Minner has explored the themes at work in his myth of powerlessness in the hope of being able to distinguish real victimization from projected victimization. Exploring early memories and mapping their influence on his life helped him to identify the themes. As a religious caregiver himself, Minner faces the hazard of "finding" perpetrators of abuse where there are none. Clearly, the impact on his ministry is potentially devastating. We can also see the importance of not ignoring or excusing real abuse at the hands of parishioners or those for whom we care. When real abuse occurs, an appropriate response is very important for our spiritual and mental health. Recognition of our myth of powerlessness and victimization is the first step in learning to distinguish between real victimization and projected victimization.

The Myth of the Loner

Some ministers prefer to go it alone in ministry, for any of a variety of reasons. Some of these become apparent as I explore the meaning of the myth of the loner.

A person who perceives himself or herself to be a loner distrusts the world. The loner fears getting emotionally close, fears being hurt or disappointed. He or she desires closeness, but intimacy is threatening. The loner believes he or she is alone in the world; indeed, this person prefers working alone and prizes and protects privacy.

This fear of closeness is accompanied by a belief that we are unrealistically flawed and imperfect. Isolation from close relationships helps us handle the overwhelming sense of imperfection. But wishing to be perfect is still deeply rooted in our sense of self, and so we loners are often preoccupied with perfection, especially when relationships hamper our efforts.

My own birth mythology reveals a loner mythology. I never knew my birth mythology until my mother told my wife, and my wife told me. After I learned it from my wife, both my father and my mother talked about it as well.

My parents were married in 1939. They believed that it was important not to let marriage and children interfere with achieving individual goals for education and professional development. Consequently, they waited two years after being married to consider having children. But they were rushed into it before they were ready.

According to the story they tell, my dad was pastoring a church some eighty miles from where they lived. He also worked during the week for the government in a factory that made cloth goods for the military. Because World War II was beginning, Dad was expected to give priority to his job; he was expected to work even on the weekends. He told his supervisor that he could not work on Sunday because he was pastoring a church and had duties there. His supervisor said, "Either work or fight." He realized the consequences, but my dad went to church that Sunday, and the following week he was told to report for military service. When the bishop realized what was happening, he acted to intervene with the selective service. In the meantime, my parents had decided to have children, thinking that if Dad had to go into the military he might be killed and there would be no children born to their union. My brother was born in November 1942, and I was born eleven months later, on October 22, 1943. The bishop's intervention succeeded, and Dad continued to pastor and work for the government.

The birth narrative continued, with my mother suffering from what is today called postpartum depression. She was exhausted from the first pregnancy, and becoming pregnant two months after the birth of her first child was too much. Shortly after I got home I had to be put back into the hospital so that my mother could get rest.

I speculate that my propensity for being a loner stems from this event. I often prefer to be alone—and I also detest being in the way. I will do anything not to be a burden to anyone. These themes in my birth mythology help me identify the themes that operate in my life today. For example, I have a hard time relaxing and not working. In December 1994 I had heart bypass surgery. Following this emergency, I have really looked at my own personal mythology and have gone back to participating in my own personal therapy as a result. My pastoral counselor says that my life was spared so that I could learn to love and be loved. I interpret this to mean that my theme of being a loner has caused some deficit in my being able to give love as well as to receive love. This deficit appears to have originated in my birth mythology. My coming to this world caused a problem for my mother, and my life has been spent trying not to be a problem for others—not to be close to others.

The danger of the loner mythology for the ministry is our being disengaged and isolated from the people for whom we have caring responsibility. We often view them as intruders into our time and as threats to our privacy. This can lead parishioners to feel neglected and uncared for. My own style of relating to people is either to pastor small churches or to have counseling appointments. I have difficulty seeing people who just stop by without appointments; I vigorously protect my free time from what I feel are intrusions. This is how I accommodate my awareness of my personal mythology. The older I get, the more I am able to allow other people close to me. However, there is much room for improvement.

The Myth of the Good Girl

Many women who pursue the ministry bring with them a conventional understanding of what it means to be "nice girls." Although ministry is a nontraditional undertaking for women, stereotypical images of femininity are always lurking in the background. Even the feminist and "womanist" impulses of many women do not keep traditional images of what it means to be female from emerging. And early expectations in the home can have a lasting impact, as an African American pastor in her late twenties reveals:

> I was always told to be a "good girl," and it seems I was determined to do just that. My mother referred to being a good girl as respecting authority, listening, and doing what I was told. I was always told to pay attention to those in authority and listen to my elders. Good girls are rewarded, I was told.

The myth of the good girl is the conviction that you must be good and gracious at all costs. It is rooted in feelings that you cannot be angry or upset because this will make others uncomfortable. The goal is perfect goodness.

The pastor quoted above learned to suppress her feelings about her abuse at the hands of authority figures. This also concealed an entire aspect of her personality and silenced an important part of who she was. To be an effective minister, she had to rediscover what was silent and give it voice. It was essential to recover her anger toward abusive authority figures in order to develop responses to authority that went beyond "good girl."

Working to reclaim her voice was hard. As long as she tried to meet the good-girl expectations, she remained depressed and could not provide appropriate care for her parishioners. The good girl was always silent, when she needed to speak up.

This person suffered from what Beth Erickson calls the "goodness code."[11] She points out that, from many centuries of socialization, this code of overresponsibility makes the care of relationships primarily an assignment given to women. Women are the relational experts; they have the capacity for sensitive, intuitive, generous, nurturing, and genuine comforting. Sometimes this capacity is overdone and leads to self-sacrifice and burnout. The goodness code can lead women caregivers to take full responsibility for the success of relationships at all costs, for overconcern about the

---

[11] Beth M. Erickson, *Helping Men Change: The Role of the Female Therapist* (Thousand Oaks, Calif.: Sage Publications, 1993).

approval of others, and for the very lives of others. This theme of goodness at all costs needs editing if the person is to gain any effectiveness in ministry.

The goodness code crosses racial lines. African American girls and women feel the same pressures to be good girls; they, too, make decisions about being silent or speaking up. However, evidence suggests that the socialization of African American girls is less stereotypical than for white middle- and upper-class girls.[12] While African American girls are raised to assume traditional female roles of nurturing and child care, evidence also suggests they are encouraged to be self-sufficient, to stand up for themselves, and to fight back. However, my experience with clients and others is that in the case of abuse, especially sexual abuse, silence is the norm.

The Myth of Invulnerability

The myth of invulnerability is a major theme in the lives of most ministers. I have found it the most prevalent myth in my teaching in seminary. Even in retreats, ministers seem to need permission from the leader and others to be open about their vulnerability. In a competitive and success-oriented culture being vulnerable is a liability. Not recognizing our vulnerability and using it appropriately is a liability as well.

Many students come to talk to me about clinical pastoral education. Some call it "ministry through navel gazing." These are people who have difficulty letting others see their mistakes and hang-ups, that is, being vulnerable.

Some of us were taught that vulnerability and weakness—signs of human imperfection—are disastrous and must be avoided at all costs. We who have learned stereotypical male and female roles characteristically find it hard to deal with our vulnerable side, by which I mean we are told that just having certain feelings (fear, tenderness, warmth, anxiety, and others) is a sign of weakness. For us men, these are inappropriate, unmasculine feelings that should be avoided; for women, these feelings are risky and could lead to harm.[13] To deny feelings of vulnerability is to embrace the myth of invulnerability.

Being in touch with our feelings of vulnerability is essential for the caring ministry. They help us empathize with others. Denying the feelings takes away some of our humanness and makes it difficult to connect, care for, and be intimate with others. The effective caregiver in ministry moves beyond the stereotypical images of what it means to be male and female, so we can be more human and more responsive to the needs of others.

[12] Jill McLean Taylor, Carol Gilligan, and Amy M. Sullivan, *Between Voice and Silence: Women and Girls, Race, and Relationship* (Cambridge, Mass.: Harvard University Press, 1995).

[13] Taylor, Gilligan, and Sullivan, *Between Voice and Silence.*

It is important to realize the gender issues related to being vulnerable. Because women are taught to be vulnerable,[14] it is important to recognize that claiming vulnerability for women has its limitations. Women need to balance affirming their strengths with recognizing their limitations and vulnerabilities.[15] A "code of masculinity" also deserves attention. The code prescribes that men must dread, abhor, and deny feeling vulnerable, weak, or helpless.[16] Consequently, we male caregivers are often out of touch with our feelings; we find it hard to be aware of them. Even though our family-of-origin experiences have prepared us well to be caregivers, we often seek to be carers in characteristic ways that prevent us from getting too close emotionally. We often maintain emotional distance from those for whom we care. The more we men caregivers are in touch with our nurturing and tender sides, the more effective we can be. We may prefer to be problem solvers because we have difficulty being emotionally present or available to those with problems who need our care.

The Myth of Sole Responsibility

Ministers of both genders may suffer from an overblown sense of responsibility. The myth of sole responsibility relates to the conviction that what happens in life depends solely on us. It is a heavy burden, accompanied by the feeling that because no one else can carry the responsibility we are left all alone to do so. We often feel drained and tired; burnout is always a prospect. The feeling comes from early childhood, from prematurely taking on adult responsibilities, hence from trying to be perfect in meeting unrealistic expectations. We often recognize a loss of childhood, and a feeling that one is doomed to a life of being burdened. Having tried to be perfect in meeting the expectations of premature adult responsibility as a child, we find that a sense of unconscious futility persists into adulthood.

Self-abuse is a hazard of the myth of sole responsibility. Some of us had parents who were substance abusers. Or our parents reversed roles with us children. Both of Edna's parents were alcoholics and ineffectual as parents. Edna is white, the oldest child; she was assigned the role of caring for her younger brothers and sisters. In her ministry, she entered fully into caring for others, but she often felt resentful about it. It got to the point where she could not hide her resentment, and she had difficulty functioning. While the resentment was strong, she could not release herself from the role, because

---

[14] Glover-Wetherington, "Women Entering Ministry."
[15] Theresa E. Snorton, "The Legacy of the African-American Matriarch: New Perspectives for Pastoral Care" in *Eyes of Women*.
[16] Erickson, *Helping Men Change*.

she believed that she was the only person who could make a difference in the lives of others. She felt that only she could solve the problems of others.

The Myth of Self-Sacrifice or Unlovability

This myth is not as common as the preceding myths. Yet occasionally I run across people in ministry who sacrifice themselves because they feel unloved and hope to gain the love of others.

This myth relates to the belief that we will only be loved if we hide our true selves. The love we received as children was often conditional, based on performing up to others' expectations, to the detriment of self. A major theme in this myth is unrequited or unreturned love. We hide our real selves, burying deeply our anger about having to sacrifice selfhood. One woman pastor of my acquaintance said she feared that if she allowed her real self to be known, people would not like her. Therefore, she hid her self and tried to keep certain aspects of her personality under wraps.

Self-sacrifice has a gender component. Pointing out that women are socialized to sacrifice themselves, Brita Gill-Austern draws some important conclusions.[17] First, women are raised to consider and take care of the needs of others, especially men and children. Second, women must sacrifice themselves and their needs in order to remain connected and maintain relationships. Third, structural inequities exist in society, and economic and social dependence reinforce self-sacrifice. And fourth, self-abnegation, self-doubt, and false guilt often motivate self-sacrifice; such a view of love prevents women from claiming the voice that they have.

Gill-Austern identifies the devastating influences of women's self-sacrifice: loss of a sense of self and of voice, loss of connection with their own needs and desires, feelings of anger and resentment for being victimized, overfunctioning with regard to others, underfunctioning on behalf of self, undermining their capacity for genuine mutuality and intimacy, and abdication of using publicly all of their God-given gifts.

Parishioners and those for whom we care may feel grateful for having persons around who are invariably pleasant. Yet how many of us are dying inside, because we don't dare let our true selves be known? We are intimidated by feeling that we could not possibly be loved for ourselves.

The Myth of the Savior

Given our childhood and family-of-origin experiences, the myth of the savior is one to which many ministers are prone. We are prime candidates for

[17] Brita Gill-Austern, "Love Understood as Self-Sacrifice and Self-Denial: What Does It Do to Women?" in *Eyes of Women*.

developing this myth because of the sometimes limitless hopes that others bring to us.

The myth of the savior is the conviction that our role in life remains to bring stability and peace to the "family." This role can be negative or positive, depending on whether we have received the nurturing and support we need in order to grow. More precisely, a family can provide an emotional atmosphere where we are each encouraged to grow into a unique person. A family environment in which we are sidetracked, if we want to be accepted, into taking on a designated family role or expectations that stifle growth is debilitating to our personal growth.

Michael was the oldest son of a family living in the Caribbean. He was born after his mother had a series of miscarriages. Because her pregnancy with him went smoothly, his parents felt he was special. Therefore, while he was a child they dedicated him to God, feeling that God had brought him into the world for a special reason. When his parents told him the circumstances of his birth, he too accepted his specialness and sought to fulfill their expectations through ministry. Family members responded to him as if he were a savior to them.

George was also special to his family. However, he was born while his parents were having tremendous marital conflict. His mother had had an affair several years before her pregnancy and kept it hidden from her husband. George's father found out and was going to leave his wife, when she told him she was pregnant. He suspended his plans to leave when the pregnancy proved difficult. Following George's birth, his father stayed on. His mother felt that George had saved the marriage.

George's mother told him this story often; she relied on him for many things. He felt she was constantly expecting him to perform the role of savior of the family; he had no life of his own. Others in George's life, too, saw him as someone who could rescue them from pain and suffering. Although he was intimidated by these expectations, he felt very bad when he could not deliver people from their pain. Anxiety about not being what others wanted him to be led to health problems. He was often very sick, and parishioners were upset when he was not available to them. But by being sick, he found the only way he could relax.

The Myth of Aloofness

The loner is convinced of his or her ineptness in close relationships. In the myth of aloofness, we believe that emotional closeness is dangerous. We must stay disengaged or disconnected from relationships in order to be a self. As aloof persons, we fear being swallowed up in relationships. We are intimidated and overwhelmed by the perfectionistic expectations of others, so we must remain aloof in order to survive emotionally.

Most often, aloof persons experienced a blurring of the role boundaries between children and adults. There might have been a reversal of roles, with the children expected to become the parent for the younger children in the family (or for the parents). Another blurring of boundaries is when the parent relates to the child as a peer and confidant; the child is expected to be the emotional companion to the parent, and the child has no opportunities to develop other relationships with peers. Sometimes the child feels threatened, afraid of being taken over and smothered. The child learns to survive by distancing from others.

The myth of aloofness is not common among ministers, in my experience. I include it here as a myth that exists; with growing numbers of clergy addicted sexually and relying on fantasy to motivate them, it is important to include this myth here. Indeed, some people sexualize relationships or turn to fantasy as protection against intimacy or emotional closeness.

Melton was reared in a family where he became very close to his mother. She relied on him, especially when his father was emotionally unavailable. While their relationship never crossed any sexual boundaries, she was often partially undressed in his presence. Melton always felt that there was a sexual quality to their relationship that he found very threatening. He developed an interest in pornography early in adolescence, which was his way of distancing himself from his mother.

Later, Melton developed dating patterns that were a series of one-night stands. He also frequented adult bookstores. He often worried that he might get caught in his activities and disgraced in the eyes of his parishioners. He made many unexpected trips out of town to satisfy his sexual needs and interests. He made up intricate lies to maintain his secret lifestyle, all the while avoiding dealing with his fears of being too close that stemmed from an overly close relationship to his mother. As much as he desired to be in relationships with others, it was too awkward for him emotionally.

Summary

Personal myths are the focus in this chapter. They foster our convictions and beliefs about ourselves and the world; they inform everything we do. Personal myths invariably have their origin in early childhood experiences.

The myths presented here are drawn from the lives of people whom I have encountered over the years in caregivers' retreats, in counseling, and in the classroom. The myths narrate the struggles in persons I have known; they are ones to which caregivers are prone because of their personalities and background experience. The selection of myths here is representative, but not exhaustive. Other myths are the subjects of the next few chapters.

Each myth connects with the myth of perfection. To win favor or love, those of us who are convinced of our unacceptableness seek to please others perfectly. Or we may be convinced of our own personal flaws and are therefore intimidated by others' expectations.

The myth of perfection is the well from which most of us as religious caregivers draw in developing our personal and ministerial myths. Not only is perfectionism the result of attempts to win favor and love despite our unacceptableness; we are urged by cultural expectations to be perfect. As religious caregivers, our lives are grounded in the Puritan heritage, whose perfectionistic expectations are nonnegotiable. We are to be exemplary in every way; we are to be almost godlike. Such expectations make religious caregivers particularly susceptible to certain myths.

I suggest that to reauthor our myths as religious caregivers, we must look consciously for a connection to the myth of perfection. In doing this, we find a great measure of freedom to be ourselves, as well as to respond to the needs of our careseekers.

Exercises

You may now want to identify some of the personal myths that are at work in your own life. Below are some exercises designed to help you do just that. For example, the first exercise deals with your earliest memory. Often, exploring the earliest memory reveals some of the themes that are currently at work in your life. The other exercises are designed to help you identify some of the myths that are at work and how they impact your life today, positively as well as negatively. Your birth myth, for instance, may be one that is very positive, and those exercises are designed to help you to get in touch with how your birth myth is working in your life today.

I recommended that you not try to do these exercises totally alone. It is good to have others accompany you on the journey. This not only provides companionship, but it is a good source of feedback on what you might find. If you decide to go it alone, be sure to have someone you can call so as to talk about what you are discovering. Journeying alone may increase a sense of isolation and continue to promote negative myths.

Personal myths deal with different areas of our early life; the questionnaire focuses on those areas.

Personal Mythology Questionnaire

Exercise I: Earliest Memory

1. What is your earliest memory of your family of origin?

2. After thinking about it, write down a few things you remember.

3. What themes do you see that were operating then?

4. In what ways are the same themes present in your life today?

5. How do these themes contribute to or take away from your present way of doing ministry?

6. How do these themes relate to your ability to discern God's presence in your life and ministry?

Exercise II: Birth Mythology

1. What circumstances, beliefs, and values do you think played a part in your parents' decision to have you?

2. What were your parents' reactions to discovering that your mother was pregnant with you?

3. What were your parents' reactions on seeing you for the first time?

4. Write down a few of your discoveries in recalling this information.

5. How do you feel that your welcome into this world influences your way of doing ministry today?

6. How does your welcome into the world influence your discerning God's presence in your life and in the church?

Exercise III: Birth Order

1. Where were you born in the family birth order?

2. Specifically, were you the first, second, last, or only child?

3. What does this mean in terms of your self-understanding now?

4. Pick a concrete example to illustrate your self-understanding.

Exercise IV: Gender and Sex

1. How do you think your mother felt about your sex?

2. How do you think your father felt about your sex?

3. How have their feelings contributed to your ministry today?

4. How have their feelings contributed to your sense that God is present in your life and in your ministry?

Exercise V: Names and Nicknames

1. Who named you?

2. Why were you given the name you have?

3. What roles are implied in your name?

4. What is your nickname?

5. Why were you given that nickname?

6. What roles are implied by it?

7. How has your name contributed to your ministry?

8. How has your name helped you to see God at work in you or in your ministry?

9. How has your nickname contributed to your ministry?

10. How has your nickname helped you to see God at work in you or in your ministry?

Exercise VI: Peer and Sibling Relationships

1. How would you characterize your relationship with siblings (brothers and sisters) and peers?

2. Pick an example of what you feel has been most characteristic of your sibling and peer relationships.

Exercise VII: Roles

1. What roles were you expected to play in your family of origin?

2. What roles did you actually play?

3. What were the costs (in love and affection) involved in not playing the role you were expected to play?

4. What were the payoffs from playing the role?

5. How do the roles that you played in your family of origin influence you today?

6. How have these roles contributed to or detracted from your ministry?

7. How have these roles enabled you to discern God's presence in your ministry?

Exercise VIII: Parental/School Discipline

1. Typically, how were you disciplined as a child at home and at school?

2. What impact do you feel this had on you?

3. Give a specific example of discipline in your home and in your school.

Exercise IX: Parents' Relationship

1. What role were you expected to play when your parents had marital conflict? Were you expected to mediate or take sides, or did your parents resolve their differences without drawing you into their conflict?

2. How do you think your parents' expectations toward you and their marital relationship influence your ministry today?

3. How do you think your parents' expectations toward you and their marital relationship influence your ability to discern God at work in your life and ministry?

Exercise X: Story Identification

1. What is your favorite fairy tale, book, short story, play, movie, TV show, et cetera? Select only one or two examples.

2. Who is your favorite character, and why?

3. What happens to your favorite character throughout the story?

4. What happens to the character at the end?

5. What character do you dislike the most, and why?

6. What happens to the disliked character throughout the story?

7. What happens to the disliked character at the end?

8. How does your identification with these stories relate to your present ministry?

9. How do these identifications enable you to discern God's presence in your life and ministry?

Assessment I

1. Given the above exercises and categories, what is the dominant theme that you see running through your life?

2. What are some of the lesser or subthemes running through your life?

3. What is the major conviction or belief that you have about your life and existence? For example, do you feel loved, worthwhile, accepted? Do you feel you have to prove yourself to somebody? What do you think you have to prove?

4. Trace the cross-generational legacy of these themes. Can you see these themes present in your parents' lives, your grandparents' lives, and your great-grandparents' lives?

5. Can you see these themes at work in your offspring? (Answer if applicable.)

Assessment II

1. Can you discern God at work seeking to transform the themes into growth opportunities?

2. What plans do you need to make to transform these themes into possibilities for growth?

• • •

The Possibility of Change: Reauthoring the Myths that Bind Us *

Reauthoring is about change in the personal, marital-family, and ministry myths. We can transform the beliefs and convictions we have long held about our sense of self, ourselves in relation to others, and how we engage in the activity of caring. Reauthoring recognizes that change in convictions and beliefs is possible; we are not totally at the mercy of our early child-hood experiences, unconscious processes, and cultural conventions. While altering our myths is a slow process with much struggle and resistance, reauthoring moves forward as our resolve grows that we are neither totally passive in creating and formulating myths nor acquiescent in living out the stories that myths entail.

Myths are not just handed down. We play an active part in developing the myths that inform our lives. We have the capacity to interpret events and give them meaning and significance. As White and Epston put it, "In regard to family therapy . . . rather than proposing that some underlying structure or dysfunction in the family determines the behavior and interactions of family members, [the interpretive method] would propose that it is the meaning that members attribute to events that determines their behavior."[1] Myth making, then, assumes that we are not powerless, not without agency in shaping the myths that inform our lives. We are participants in "meaning making" and story creating. Within realistic limits, it is possible to take responsibility for how we interpret reality and give meaning to it. Therefore, to some degree it is possible to alter the stories and myths that inform our behavior.

This chapter is about the possibility of changing personal, marital-family, and ministry myths. First, I identify the phases of the reauthoring process. I present a description of each phase, along with some idea of the personal work involved, what the experience of modifying myth is like at each phase, how difficult transformation is, the length of time change takes, how we move from one phase to the next, and how the process might have an impact on our lives and our ministry.

---

[1] Michael White and David Epston, *Narrative Means to Therapeutic Ends* (New York: Norton, 1990), 3.

* This chapter was previously published in Edward P. Wimberly, *Recalling Our Own Stories: Spiritual Renewal for Religious Caregivers* (San Francisco: Jossey-Bass, 1997), 73–88. Used by permission.

Some Assumptions about Reauthoring

Several significant assumptions underlie the reauthoring process:

1. Reality is socially constructed.

2. Transformation is possible, but not easy.

3. Change occurs normally throughout life cycle transitions, as well as at less predictable moments such as a sudden upheaval or trauma.

4. Innovation is facilitated when we can envisage our own role in creating our own myths.

5. Re-storying or discovering novel dimensions of our own stories facilitates transformation.

6. Bringing new perspectives to past experience helps create new story possibilities.

Transformation is Possible

Myths can change, because they are inherently social constructions or social attributions.[2] Attribution assigns meanings to experience; attribution is shared as well as private. As we participate in life, we engage in attributing or assigning meaning, which gives significance to our experience. Early in our childhood, we must rely on publicly shared attributions common to our family and community. As we mature and grow older, however, we discover that unique and personal attributions are not only possible but can be different from those shared by others. Ultimately, as adults we combine shared and private attributions to shape our understanding of reality and experience.

Personal, marital-family, and ministerial myths are shared and private attributions in a storied formulation, a mythical pattern. They develop socially and personally, based on interactions with others as we participate in life. As social creations, myths are not just socially inherited or passed on to others without being personally modified. In fact, we make subtle shifts in them as we develop our own private attributions. All of this is to say that attributions that make up myths can be altered; they are modifiable in their evolution.

---

[2] Peter Berger and Thomas Luckmann, *The Social Construction of Reality: A Treatise in the Sociology of Knowledge* (New York: Doubleday, 1966).

Transformation of Myths is Difficult

While transformation is inherent to the formulation of myths, it is not always easy. Myths function to interpret reality and events that take place throughout life. In the early process of myth formulation, our experiences in the family of origin and with significant others are very influential—so influential that the myths evolved from them seem unalterably resistant to change. They seem to be part of an indelible, genetic blueprint, non-malleable by any environmental influences.

The nature of myths is to appear fixed and unchangeable. Yet if we understand how myths evolve and see how we participate in their creation, we can discern the possibility of transformation. In the actual process of editing myths, we are surprised to discover that what was once considered closed and permanently fossilized in our being is not only changeable but actually *awaiting* transformation.

Life Transitions and Crises Precipitate Transformation

Attribution, or assigning meaning to life experiences, is the result of our encounters with life transitions and traumatic events. Myths are formed from attributions that help us make sense of things. Life transitions and traumas such as accidents challenge our existing, attributed structure of meaning. Existing attributions are often inadequate in helping us respond to new challenges; they need to be modified to "explain" the new situational demands.[3] Failure to alter existing attributions in the face of new situational and transitional challenges hampers our ability to respond. Our emotional, interpersonal, and spiritual well-being is at stake.

Envisioning Our Role in Reauthoring Eases Transformation

Life will always present us with transitional and situational challenges. Existing attributions and myths need modifying, as a result. As we face challenges to our existing mythic formulations and interpretations of reality, not all of us will do the necessary editing and updating. Some of us resist changing them, feeling secure with what we already have done regarding our beliefs. Others of us, however, readily welcome the challenges and grow as a result. We see the new challenges as opportunities rather than dangers. What distinguishes those of us who envisage challenge as opportunity is what I call the "Columbus risk."

---

[3] G. Lloyd Rediger, "A Primer on Pastoral Spirituality," *The Clergy Journal* (January 1996): 17–20.

Christopher Columbus did not know with utter certainty that the world was not flat. He had to risk falling off the edge of the world in order to explore the future. The result was new discoveries—of a *preexistent* world, we should note. New attributions and myths about the nature of the world and the universe also resulted. Similarly, those of willing to modify our existing myths need to be adventurous and risk-taking, as Columbus was. If we can risk going beyond what we can see with our own two eyes, we can bring about new horizons in our lives. Better self-understanding and new growth await us as we sail beyond our current horizons.

The Columbus risk comes with our understanding that part of our task is to modify the existing mythic structures that are informing (and limiting) our lives. In the reauthoring process, we must discern that our existing myths are alterable.

Re-storying is Possible

Re-storying is possible when we discern new dimensions in our existing stories. Sometimes there is hidden meaning in existing stories; it remains obscure until we actually risk editing the existing attributions. White and Epston call these hidden possibilities "historical unique outcomes."[4] This refers to new possibilities that result when, in reediting our stories, we encounter new information from the past that contradicts the way information had been organized. Such discoveries can precipitate new meanings and attributions, which in turn assist in the re-storying process.

Transformation Means a New Perspective on Things

Change can come when we are able to reframe our experience. Reframing refers to putting experience into a different perspective, or framework, and thus envisioning new possibilities for life that were not initially evident. It can be said that reframing is not really change, because it shifts only the perspective and not the actual facts of the experience. Facts are interpreted so as to bring meaning to them; while there is merit in the argument that nothing has changed, nevertheless behavior generally follows changes in beliefs and convictions. Consequently, changing convictions and beliefs is a prerequisite for transforming behavior.

The Phases in Reauthoring Personal Myths

There are several stages in the reauthoring of personal myths:

1. Identify the themes that make up our personal myth.

---

[4] White and Epston, *Narrative Means*, 56.

2. Assess the influence of these themes on our lives over a period of time. This assessment determines if the themes are growth-facilitating or growth-inhibiting, and whether they contribute to our being wounded healers rather than remaining walking wounded.

3. Attempt to discern God's presence or a spiritual force at work in transforming these themes into themes of a wounded healer.

4. Make plans to alter the themes of the personal myth in order to increase our growth possibilities.

Establishing the Environment for Reauthoring

Prior to identifying the themes and subthemes of personal myths, we who seek to reauthor our myths must attend to several conditions conducive to successful reauthoring.

The most important one is to set a *proper environment or context* for the reauthoring process. The environmental context must be favorable to the reauthoring process: we need to give some attention to making sure that the atmosphere is safe, warm, and open. If we involve others in our reauthoring process, we must ensure that they are supportive and care about us. We must be sure that we discuss all expectations and goals. If we choose professional assistance, we need to do this based on the person's skills, training, and experience. We have to select a place for doing the reauthoring that is free from interruptions. We need to be relaxed and focused to get the most from the experience.

Creating a comfortable environment is essential, because reauthoring can be very threatening. Many of us have very debilitating and unhealthy myths at work in our lives. Changing these myths, although necessary, can provoke great anxiety because the existing myths and related behavior are known dimensions; they are predictable and bring a measure of security to our believing we know the future. Changing our beliefs and convictions threatens what is familiar and consistent. We will resist. We need to be aware of this reality and keep it in mind at all times.

Identifying Themes

You have already been given a series of questions designed to help you identify the themes in your personal mythologies. These questions, in the exercises at the end of chapters two, three, and four, are carefully designed to create an appropriately safe environment for your reauthoring process. I encourage you to use relaxation exercises if they will further your feeling of being at ease in this process. If you are undertaking the reauthoring process in a group, or with the direction of a leader, then another important aid in making the environment safe is self-disclosure by the leader. In self-disclosure, the leader shares aspects of her own early memories, birth myth, naming process, and other things that help bring participants on board in the process. As participants, we can envisage from the leader's self-disclosure how we might begin engaging in the reauthoring process ourselves; and of course disclosure helps reduce the anxiety of not knowing what to expect. It gives us some idea of what the process of reauthoring involves as well as insights and clues to what we need to do.

In my experience, most people are readily able to do the first exercise, exploring our earliest memories. Its purpose is to help us identify themes that are at work in our contemporary lives.[5] Generally, this opening exercise is nonthreatening; we usually identify only those themes we are emotionally ready to explore. Consequently, early memories are a good starting point for helping us identify the themes that make up our personal myth.

The second exercise, exploring our birth mythology, can be more anxiety-provoking for some people. Birth mythologies are the stories that significant others tell or told us about our conception, time in the womb, birth, and the first six months after birth.[6] They are significant because they deal with themes related to how we were welcomed into this world. I have seen people get up and leave the room when doing this part of the exercise. When I inquire, they indicate that the memories of what they found out about the circumstances of their birth are too painful; they don't want to feel the pain that comes with recollection. I try to warn people that there might be some pain in exploring birth mythologies. If it becomes too much for you, just stop the exercise. Don't feel obligated to finish it. Feel free to wait for a less-threatening exercise. In the reauthoring sessions that I conduct, I encourage people to approach me to discuss what it felt like to do the exercise. Most of them can then continue, and confront their feelings in small groups where they share what they felt in doing the exercise.

As we proceed through the other exercises related to personal myths, the themes unfold. We write them down; we are then ready to move to the next phase of the reauthoring process.

Mapping and Assessing

The second phase is mapping and assessing the impact of the personal myths on our lives. The myth we create is related to how we carry out our

---

[5] Dennis Bagarozzi and Stephen A. Anderson, *Personal, Marital, and Family Myths: Theoretical Formulations and Clinical Strategies* (New York: Norton, 1989).

[6] Ana-Maria Rizzuto, *The Birth of the Living God* (Chicago: University of Chicago Press, 1979).

lives and live in our relationships. We begin tracing the themes of our personal myths: how they are associated with experiences we had early in our lives. We begin to correlate our current behavior with our interpretation of those early experiences. For example, one person traced a contemporary pattern in how she dealt with the men in her life to certain convictions she had come to regarding family-of-origin experiences; specifically, she felt that in order to be accepted she must always please those who had the potential to accept her. Other people seek a link between early-childhood assumption of responsibility and myths about their adult patterns and roles.

In assessing and mapping, we expect as an outcome that we will begin to envisage obstacles to our growth and happiness. These obstacles are caused by the myths that we created in response to the early experiences of our lives. We hope not only to visualize the problems encountered in our present functioning, but also to discover alternative ways to interpret the past as well as unique (but unnoticed) facts that might alter our present life scenarios.[7] Often, current myths prevent us from discerning new meanings and different attributions. However, by identifying the myths at work in our lives in the present and mapping their influence, we find it easier to revise our notions of the past in light of new discoveries about it. Some reauthorers remember other events and experiences in their lives that challenge their original interpretation of the events, and they can then revise or reedit their long-standing beliefs and convictions.

I recall an example of a young African American adult. He was considering whether to answer a call to ministry but felt he could not because of his conviction that he had been deliberately abandoned by his mother. He felt that her deserting him had paralyzed his ability to care.

He had been raised by his grandparents but always wondered why his mother had not raised him. His conclusion was that he was not wanted. One day, he received the courage to sit down with his mother and explore why she had left him with his grandparents. She told him about the abusive relationship she was in after he was born, how she did not have the money for a refrigerator, and how she had to put his milk outside in the cold to keep it from spoiling. His mother confided that she had felt like an emotional wreck and for that reason thought her child would be better off with his grandparents. His mother's revelation was enough to help him revise his personal myth about being unwanted and abandoned.

The second stage in reauthoring helps us assess the impact of the myth on our lives. Sometimes the impact is both positive and negative.

---

[7] White and Epston, *Narrative Means*.

Mapping it gives those of us having negative myths the opportunity to begin revising them.

Discernment

The third stage of the reauthoring process is that of discerning the transforming forces at work, seeking to make the personal myths growth-facilitating. Identifying God's presence and work in our lives is a process unique to each of us. How we discern depends on a variety of things relating to how we carry out our spiritual discipline. Some of us use prayer to discern God's presence and help in our revising of our personal myths. An appropriate prayer of petition is to ask where God is working to bring healing to past relationships, and how God is helping us edit the beliefs and convictions we use to interpret life. Others turn to reading spiritual books, including the Bible. This approach focuses on discerning patterns of how God worked in the lives of biblical persons, in the belief that God continues to work in similar ways in the present and future. Some people identify with biblical characters, knowing that there are similarities in their own lives.

Or we may find God at work in our lives as we attempt to edit our personal myths, beginning with our work on the questionnaires that lead us to the themes of our personal myths. It may happen as we begin to review our call and its continued work in our lives. We may see God working through a slow process as we examine our lives in segments, in the different periods of time.

Just as we are able to map the influence of our personal myths on our lives, so too we are able to chart God's influence as challenges to the construction of our myths arise. Once we do this, we are ready to begin making plans.

Making Plans

The goal of reauthoring personal myths is to revise the story that runs through our personal behavior, to heal wounds and transform them into sources of strength in service to others. The identification, assessment, and discerning phases of the reauthoring process are all essential components to altering personal myths. Making plans is the final phase, wherein we outline the specific steps that will modify the myth.

The plans vary as widely as the individuals who make them. Some people contract with spiritual guides to explore in more depth their various mythologies. Some commit to doing research on their favorite biblical character, to learn more about how that person lived out his life. Some choose to enter personal counseling, while others seek accountability groups of peers to help them care for themselves better. Many choose the path of continuing education focused on spiritual disciplines. Some choose to be coached in how to go home, to work on family-of-origin issues.

Returning Home

This dimension of the reauthoring process is meant to gather information to fill in the gaps in our understanding of personal myths. Monica McGoldrick emphasizes that life patterns are multigenerational, and so it is important to trace the themes of the personal myths across several generations.[8]

Preston used a unique method to trace the legacy of his personal myth. He was interested in his own myth, but he also felt that knowing his father's personal myth might provide some clues into his own. He asked to interview his father, who agreed. Preston received a rare gift from reconnecting with his father in an extraordinary way. After the interview, Preston began writing up the results; he could clearly see the impact of previous generations on his life.

Preston took a great personal risk in approaching his father. He might have dredged up all the past hurts that he had felt at one time or another. He was at a point in his life, however, where he felt the risk was worth it, that he stood to gain more than he might lose. Although he approached his father fearfully, the result was that the pieces of his life fit together with new meaning.

Some people do not have the choice to return home. A woman approached me about a sermon I had just preached. She had spent many years in therapy working on her personal mythology, which centered around being sexually abused by her father. She had not been able to let go of her anger toward her father and hence had not revised her myth. But the sermon brought back a recollection: her father had approached her before he died and confessed his sin to her. She had not then been able to accept his confession, nor forgive him. In fact, she told me, she really did not believe he had actually admitted doing such a horrible thing. It was during the sermon, she said, that she fully recalled his confession of sorrow for his act. He had died several years earlier, but she said the Holy Spirit brought back his words so clearly that she could no longer distort what he said so as to go on protecting herself from pain. She was finally able to accept his apology from the past; she could forgive him. This breakthrough event enabled her to move on, to form a new myth for her life.

We can see that reauthoring personal myths has no specific timetable. It varies with each person, depending on the level of maturity, the severity

---

[8] Monica McGoldrick, *You Can Go Home Again: Reconnecting with Your Family* (New York: Norton, 1994).

of the problems involved, and other complex factors. Some people are able to revise their myths in a weekend retreat, while others may need much longer.

Reauthoring Marital and Family Myths

We can reauthor our marital myths as well, including both ideal-mate and ideal-marriage myths. This is true, too, with revising the family myths: ideal-child images and ideal-family images.

Revising marital and family myths follows the same phases as reediting personal myths. There comes a point in time where there must be a *symbolic* divorce and remarriage (to the same person) if the marriage is to grow and develop. There are times in marriage and family life when the old beliefs about men and women, children, marriage, and family life must be changed to meet the realities that people are facing. Such times of change may be moments in which individuals, marriages, and families face life-cycle transitions; when they face threats from outside the marriage and family, such as discrimination, unemployment, economic hardship, dislocation, and others; and when the myths that govern marital and family life are no longer adequate to meet the needs of those involved. When myths are no longer adequate, the family has an opportunity to change the myths, for the individuals, the marriage, and the family.

Change in marriage and family life can be "first order" or "second order" change.[9] First-order change is returning the marriage or family system to the original dynamic state that existed prior to the impetus for change. In this form of change, the marital and family myths remain intact. Second-order change refers to actually reauthoring (editing) the marital and family myths so that the original myths are altered considerably and the behavior of those involved is substantially affected. In some cases, marriages and families experience both first-order and second-order changes, depending on what the precipitating events are.

Editing marital myths means altering ideal images of our mate and what our marriage should be. I often do pastoral counseling with people whose lives are disrupted because one or both spouses are in seminary. Seminary is often a triggering factor in facing marital partners with the need to revise or reedit personal myths. Most often, changing the marital myth begins with identifying the marital difficulty and the family-of-origin patterns that influence the problem. We explore ideal-mate and ideal-marriage images as part of the family-of-origin influences.

[9] William C. Nichols and Craig A. Everett, *Systemic Family Therapy: An Integrative Approach* (New York: Guilford, 1986), 130.

Depending on the level of pain in the marriage and the level of reactivity between the spouses, this identification step can take one session or as many as are needed for the spouses to recognize the sources of their ideal images. Reactivity stems from our emotional attachment to our own family of origin and the degree to which we feel we must resist changing that attachment.[10] Spouses who have a good measure of self-distinction from the family of origin can explore the source of the ideal-mate images in the family of origin with some dispatch. Those who are more attached have more difficulty. In the latter case, many counseling sessions might be needed before moving to the next phase of the reauthoring process.

The seminary experience often triggers marital and family difficulties for students. There are two quite common causes: the student has to commit emotional energy to the seminary experience, or the curriculum work precipitates his or her personal growth. In the first instance, the seminary experience challenges the student's assumptions about life and how life should be lived in light of faith. This is often a traumatic experience, and the student often withdraws emotional energy from marriage and family relationships in order to invest it in dealing with the challenges to her or his way of viewing life and faith. When this withdrawing and reinvesting is taking place, the marital partner and children know immediately. Feelings of being abandoned often result along with marital stress. In the second instance, the pace of personal growth accelerates because of new and intense experiences that the student undergoes with peers, in the classroom, and in supervised ministerial encounters. These experiences also upset the seminary student's marital and family stability. They exert severe pressure on marriage and family, and marital adjustment is often necessary. For some, a marital crisis results, and intervention is needed.

I have found that couples with good enough separation from their families of origin can respond to a retreat model of reediting. They are often emotionally free from the roles and dynamics that they endured in the family of origin such that they can invest that energy in the reauthoring. They have the requisite ego-strength to identify ideal-mate and ideal-marriage themes, map the influence such themes have on their marriage, discern God's work in helping them change, and make plans to follow through on the changes once they leave the retreat. I have also found, however, that persons with less-than-optimal separation from family-of-origin roles and dynamics need marital counseling or personal counseling before they can begin to approach the reauthoring process. That is, some persons don't have the necessary emotional freedom or energy to devote to their own

[10] Philip J. Guerin, Jr., et al., *The Evaluation and Treatment of Marital Conflict: A Four-Stage Approach* (New York: Basic Books, 1987).

growth. They need to become a self in the family of origin before they can commit themselves to the work of reauthoring.

Distinguishing oneself from family-of-origin roles and dynamics is known as self-differentiation; it is vital to reediting our marital and family myths. People with relatively good self-distinction can engage in the reauthoring process of their ideal-child, ideal-parent, and ideal-family myths in a retreat format. Others with less self-distinction need marital and family counseling.

The Singletons and Houstons, whom we met in chapter three, are examples of parents who had clear ideal-child expectations. In both cases, they had to alter the expectations for each child to some extent, differently depending on the child and the family's circumstances. Moreover, each of these four parents had an ideal-parenting expectation for himself and herself that also became part of the family mythology.

Their reauthoring process followed the same process we have already identified. Each parent had to examine his or her ideal images of child and parenting. Each also had to assess whether such images helped him or her deal with the real child and the real situation. In the case of the Singletons, Mitchell had good self-differentiation and was willing to alter his ideal expectations, or at least suspend them. Nicky, however, was tied too closely to the parenting expectations of her family of origin and lacked the necessary self-differentiation to begin the reauthoring process. Consequently, she could not change her ideal-child expectations or deal with the fact that she might not be the ideal parent. This produced too much anxiety for her; she undertook family counseling but withdrew. She also withdrew emotionally from her son Clarence as a result. Mitchell and Clarence continued family counseling, and the father took on all the responsibility for dealing with his son as he (the father) proceeded to modify his ideal-child expectations.

The Houstons were very different. Each of the parents had good self-differentiation. When they assessed their own ideal-parenting expectations, they discovered that the images were not working. Their expectations regarding Brittany's maturity were not consistent with her age, and as parents they were not responding to their child's real needs. This embarrassed them, temporarily. But they had the necessary ego-strength to admit their mistakes, and they began to alter their style of relating to Brittany to correspond to her developmental needs.

Both the Singletons and the Houstons were part of my counseling load. The counseling with the Singletons took many sessions, mainly because of Nicky's low level of self-differentiation. In the case of the Houstons, however, the intervention was very brief—three sessions, in fact. This was because each parent had a high level of self-differentiation. The lower the level of self-differentiation, the more threatening is the reauthoring process. The reverse is also true, with greater self-differentiation being less of a threat.

Both the Singletons and the Houstons were religious; both fathers were religious caregivers. Both felt that creating an environment for the growth and development of each child was important in the sight of God. Therefore, it was important to them how they lived as family members and raised their children. Annette Houston also felt the same way. Nicky Singleton, however, was angry that God had given her such a recalcitrant son and wondered why he could not have been more like her daughter, Grace, who fully met her ideal.

Let us not view Nicky as the bad apple here. In fact, she epitomizes what the experience of reauthoring is often like. For most people, the process raises anxiety because change can disrupt secure ways of thinking and behaving. It is safe, and prudent, to expect moments of anger and pain during the process—moments when it would be more comfortable to stop.

Reauthoring Ministerial Mythologies

Identifying ministerial myths, assessing or mapping their influence on the caregiver's life, discerning God's presence in the work to alter the myths, and making plans to change them are the phases in reauthoring ministerial myths as well. Here, I want to focus primarily on phase three: the role of the call (whether ongoing or subsequent to beginning this work) in the process of reediting ministerial myths. The emphasis here is on discerning God's presence in the reauthoring process.

God's Presence

In chapter one, I suggested that the etiology of spiritual renewal is in recalling our original motivation for ministry. I described my father's rehearsing his call as an example of a traditional model for spiritual renewal. In that introductory model, I said very little about my understanding of the period of liminality, the "in-between time" (following the original call) that leads to a subsequent call or renewal. The period of liminality is one in which our call is renewed daily; because it is often during a retreat, the liminal time deepens our call and our commitment to religious vocation. Liminality or in-between time is when new models or visions of reality are disclosed; it is when we begin to envision or imagine new possibilities for our lives. The subsequent call, as a moment of liminality, renews, reignites, and reawakens old passions and directions for ministry. The in-between time period continues to remove old blocks to our meaningful commitment to ministry;

it continues to reauthor and revitalize lesser myths. It puts God's imagination in our heads, and new possibilities for our ministry surface.

The subsequent call of God at moments of liminality is a work of God as was the original call. Because the call is ongoing, it is possible to discern God's presence again as we find our call renewed in moments of liminality.

A Personal Story of Reauthoring

Permit me to narrate my own renewing and updating of my ministerial mythology, that is, my own experience with a second call in a moment of liminality. In February 1992 I began to be aware of chest pain about eight minutes into my regular jogging routine. I also discovered that the pain abated when I stopped exercising. When I first felt the pain, I went to my primary physician, who then sent me to a cardiologist. The cardiologist gave me a stress test and a treadmill examination to check my heart. The stress test registered normal; I experienced no pain when doing the examination, and the cardiologist pronounced me fit from a cardiovascular point of view.

I continued to have chest pain when exercising, however. My primary physician sent me back to the same cardiologist who told me that in his experience as a heart specialist, my treadmill results meant that I had heart problems. He then attributed my problems to exercise-induced asthma. I spent several months getting checked out for this new diagnosis. When asthma was ruled out, the doctors settled on esophageal reflux, since the pain was in the esophagus area of my chest. The pain persisted, and in early December 1994 I changed primary physicians. I was immediately diagnosed as having angina. During testing, I went into heart distress during heart catheterization and had to have immediate surgery. On December 8, I had quadruple bypass surgery—after two years of complaining about chest pain. During bypass surgery, the doctors discovered that my left main artery was more than 99 percent closed. The medical people said they couldn't understand why I had not had a massive heart attack. They said this kind of artery disease was a "widow maker." While some physicians marveled at my good fortune, other physicians attributed my miraculous survival to God.

This miracle of surviving arterial disease without any heart damage at all was only the physical side of my story. There is another. It is about renewal and the reauthoring of my ministerial mythology.

During the two-year period of failed diagnosis, I was depressed. I was depressed about my failing physical health because of my inability to exercise, and I was also worried about what to do for my aging parents, who had reached the point where they were unable to care for themselves any longer. They were resisting all efforts by others to help or intervene in their lives, and I didn't know what to do. My wife noticed that I really seemed no longer to care if I lived or died. It was at that point that we decided to find a way for my parents to come to live with us. (They have now been living with us since December 1993.) My parents' coming to live with us released me from one aspect of my depression considerably.

After my surgery, and during my recovery period in the hospital, I had a moment of liminality. The still, small voice of God came to me almost inaudibly. Suddenly, a question came to my mind. It was clear. It was, "Do you accept what I have done for you?" My mental response was, "What do you mean?" But what I said in response was, "Of course." Then the thought came to me: accepting God's miracle in my life means accepting a new purpose and focus for my life. I believe the voice was trying to tell me that my work on earth is not done; God intervened to make sure that I stay around to complete the work that has been given to me. At that moment, I realized that the remaining years of my life are to be driven by a deeper sense of calling and purpose than I had prior to my surgery.

The reauthoring of my ministerial mythology has a key element: reaffirmation that I cannot do ministry as a loner any longer. My personal mythology, marital mythology, and ministry mythology all rested on the theme of being a loner. It has become clear to me that my ministry is God's ministry, not "mine," and that God has become a companion to me and provided me with others to be in partnership with me as I carry out ministerial tasks. I have a renewed sense of God's intent for me and God's presence at work in my life. I know that I was given new life by God for a particular purpose. I was given a second chance to live my life differently.

Since my surgery and spiritual moment of liminality, I have become a vegetarian and begun to live in ways that take better care of my whole self. I have a better balance between work, recreation, spirituality, and nurturing relationships. I seek more mutual relationships than I once did. I tend not to overfunction, as I once did. I no longer see ministry and my life as a pilgrimage isolated from other people.

At the time of writing, it has been two years since my heart surgery. The major impact of the surgery on my ministry seems to be in the way people now respond to me. I seem to be regarded as one of the elders who are in charge of the faith traditions that must be preserved and passed on to the next generations. I turned fifty just prior to the surgery; at that time I saw myself as a disciple, still learning the traditions of caring and of faith. I did not consciously see myself as one of the elders, as a steward or guardian of the mysteries of the faith. However, following my surgery, it has become very clear to me that I was promoted: from the ranks of a disciple to the ranks of a steward.

From a developmental point of view, moving from disciple to steward means that I have reoriented my life from being based on external societal standards to a more inner and spiritual orientation.[11] Wisdom has taken center stage, and I seem to be less driven by meeting external standards of success. I am not as intimidated as I once was by meeting expectations of perfection. I seem to be living more on grace and less by the demands or expectations of others. I seem to be more at peace with myself and happy with what I have done and am currently doing. I can accept what I have and that I have not achieved better. I am more comfortable with my spontaneous life in that I can express more of my feelings, and I can tolerate intimacy better. I seem to be more emotionally available to others than prior to my surgery. Finally, I think I am more in touch with the unfolding of God's story in my life, and I can allow myself to better cooperate with what God is doing in my life. In the words of my therapist, I am learning to love and be loved.

Spiritual renewal of caregivers rests on renewal of our original call. The original call is renewed by a subsequent call or calls, which take place at key moments of our lives. These key moments are not unlike those original moments when we were sure God was calling us. The subsequent calls can come at any time and at any point in our lives. They can come during spiritual retreats, spiritual guidance, pastoral counseling, or ordinary moments of our everyday existence. At these times, our lives suddenly come into clear focus, and a new awareness dawns on us.

Summary

The reediting process involves:

1. identifying the themes at work in the various mythologies in our lives

2. mapping or charting the influence that these themes have had on us and our ministry

3. discerning where God's renewing influence is as we come to grips with these themes and their influences

4. making plans that will aid us in changing some of the themes.

As we mature toward knowing ourselves apart from our family-of-origin patterns, we can enter the reauthoring process with relative ease and

---

[11] C.G. Jung, *Modern Man in Search of a Soul* (Orlando: Harcourt Brace, 1933).

profit more from reauthoring. Those of us less able to distinguish ourselves from our family of origin, however, have difficulty reauthoring our myths. We need a therapeutic environment, and ongoing spiritual direction, where we can work through our resistance and anxiety about change.

4

Relational Refugees (2000)

In 1998 Edward Wimberly and his wife, Anne Streaty Wimberly, had the opportunity to spend a sabbatical at Africa University in Mutare, Zimbabwe. There they found a caring network of colleagues who embraced them and swiftly incorporated them into a community of caring relationship. Edward Wimberly noticed how different it was to live in a village-based community that fostered close connections, in contrast to his usual life in the United States, where they had felt isolated at times. For Wimberly, this experience validated narrative theory's claims about the centrality of cultural stories to human identity and wellbeing.

After reflecting on this experience and reading an important new book by his colleague and friend, Archie Smith, Jr.,* Wimberly sat down to write *Relational Refugees: Alienation and Reincorporation in African American Churches and Communities.†* Wimberly defines relational refugees as people struggling to live in an alienating, consumerist culture who become isolated, separated from nurturing and positive relationships. He points out that for African Americans, racism and sexism can induce self-hatred, thereby increasing the sense of alienation. In order to challenge such self-hatred that "is caught

---

* Archie Smith, Jr. *Navigating the Deep River: Spirituality in African American Families* (Cleveland: United Church Press, 1997). Here Smith, Jr. develops a concept of "spiritual refugees."

† Edward P. Wimberly, "Adolescence and the Relational Refugee," *Relational Refugees: Alienation and Reincorporation in African American Churches and Communities* (Nashville: Abingdon, 2000), 63–73; Wimberly, "Poverty, Prosperity, and the Relational Refugee," *Relational Refugees*, 75–84.

like a disease" (132), Wimberly cites a need for affirming mentors and supportive social networks.

In the first essay, Wimberly addresses African American adolescents' identity formation. He engages African American works of fiction and drama, using these stories as case material. For example, Toni Morrison's *The Bluest Eye* is used to illustrate how racism can wound black adolescents and interfere with a healthy sense of self and other. In the second essay, Wimberly focusses on poverty and its insidious effects on relationships, which he illustrates with stories from Lorraine Hansberry's famous play, *A Raisin in the Sun*. Wimberly notes that economic relational refugees suffer from despair and low self-esteem, and need support systems and models that do more than mimic the competitive values of the marketplace.

Wimberly notes that "God's liberation is never a call to join the ranks of the oppressors or to benefit from their spoils. Rather, our liberation is a call to service and social transformation" (136). These words appear prescient today as pastoral theologians recognize the challenge of offering life-giving pastoral care in a neoliberal age that supports and sustains oppression in the name of Christian evangelicalism. Pastoral and practical theologians are addressing the challenge of caregiving in religious and other relational contexts marked by social isolation, racial and intersectional violence, and gross economic inequalities.[*]

Further Reading

Wimberly, Edward P. "Reestablishing the Village: The Task of Pastoral Counseling." *Journeys* (Summer–Fall 1999): 5.

Wimberly, Edward P. "The Family Context of Development: African American Families." In *Human Development and Faith: Life-Cycle Stages of Body, Mind, and Soul,* edited by Felicity Kelcourse, 111–25. St. Louis: Chalice Press, 2004.

• • •

---

[*] See Cedric Johnson, *Race, Religion, and Resilience in the Neoliberal Age* (New York: Palgrave Macmillan, 2016); Bruce Rogers-Vaughn, *Caring for Souls in a Neoliberal Age* (New York: Palgrave Macmillan, 2016); Nancy J. Ramsay, "Resisting Asymmetries of Power: Intersectionality as a Resource for Practices of Care," *Journal of Pastoral Theology* 27, no. 2 (2017): 83–97.

Adolescence and the Relational Refugee[*]

Human identity is formed in a matrix of relationships. We discover ourselves in and through our encounters with others. Our sense of "me" is
dependent on the existence of a "you." We can only see our own eyes in
the reflection of another's. Human identity is also not a possession but a
process. We come to discover ourselves more fully throughout our lifetimes.
Adolescence, a stage betwixt and between, involves substantial physical and
emotional changes. Raging hormones affect adolescents' moods as well as
bodies. The drive to be independent is matched only by the great emotional
neediness of the period. It is a time when many are at risk of becoming
relational refugees.

Young men and women attempt to discover themselves but are dependent on how others treat them in this process. Some are strong enough to
resist experiences of harm or neglect but others are not. Those at risk of
becoming relational refugees are those who believe that they are worthless
and that they must pretend to be someone else in order to be considered
valuable. Adolescents sort through a jumble of messages, both internal and
external, as they arrive at some sort of self-understanding. Parents, the
church, peers, and teachers all send cues to young people suggesting what
they should believe and who they should be. Many young people come to
believe that what they think is really of no great consequence. Some get
the idea that to be of significance, they have to be someone other than
themselves. They strive for affirmation by fitting themselves into someone
else's prescribed set of expectations that are often alien to who they truly
are. Those who insist on defining themselves by the standards of others will
become relational refugees.

In this chapter I explore black adolescent identity formation, particularly, the importance of receiving confirmation of one's own sense of self for
healthy identity development, from one's environment and from significant
others. Adolescents especially need consistent affirmation by others who
provide positive plots, roles, scenes, and attitudes on which the young persons can draw for their behavioral choices and worldview.

The eminent developmental psychologist Erik Erikson has pointed
out that healthy self-identity is very difficult for young African Americans
to develop in a society that communicates only negative attitudes toward

* This chapter was previously published in Edward P. Wimberly, *Relational Refugees:
  Alienation and Reincorporation in African American Churches and Communities* (Nashville:
  Abingdon, 2000), 63–73 and associated notes. © 2000, Abingdon Press. Used by per-
  mission. All rights reserved.

African Americans.[1] Toni Morrison explores these same issues in her novel *The Bluest Eye*. In the previous chapter, I discussed the relationship between Cholly and Mrs. Breedlove from this same narrative. Here, I look at the experience of their daughter, Pecola, a young black woman growing up in the United States during the pre-Civil Rights era of the 1940s. Pecola serves as a model for my reflections on mentoring African American young people through the rough terrain of adolescence in a land of racism.

The Bluest Eye

This book is Toni Morrison's account of a young African American girl, who is growing up in a family, a community, and a world in which black means ugly. The book depicts, in graphic detail, the process through which Pecola learns to hate and despise what she sees in the mirror. Hating the way one looks, one's physical appearance and one's color, has to be carefully taught, and Morrison takes the time to narrative the learning of self-hatred.

Pecola comes to believe that she would be acceptable to herself and others if she had blue eyes. The world values blue eyes. They are often a symbol of the superiority of whiteness. Pecola's fixation with acquiring blue eyes contributes to her demise. She undergoes a psychotic break with reality. Everyone around her confirms that she is ugly rather than help her see that beauty is only skin deep. Abandoned by those who should provide her with support, Pecola becomes a relational refugee.

Self-Hatred is Caught like a Disease

Pecola's sense of self-worth is attacked on two major fronts: the racist, classist, and sexist standards of beauty of the larger society, and the stubborn convictions of her own dysfunctional family. This combined attack proved irresistible, especially because she had so few allies, so few resources to preserve her self-esteem.

Pecola succumbs to the standards of her culture, just as many of us do, because the messages are so powerful, constant, and inescapable. Morrison reminds so many of her readers of how we come to hate ourselves:

> Adults, older girls, shops, magazines, newspapers, window signs—all the world had agreed that a blue-eyed, yellow-haired, pink-skinned doll was what every girl child treasured. "Here," they said, "this is beautiful, and if you are on this day 'worthy' you may have it."[2]

[1] For a discussion of black identity and negative identity formation in the work of Erik Erikson, see Edward P. Wimberly, *Counseling African American Marriages and Families* (Louisville: Westminster John Knox, 1997), 54.

[2] Toni Morrison, *The Bluest Eye* (New York: Plume, 1994), 20.

These values of the wider culture sank deeply and unimpeded into Pecola's psyche.

Pecola could not resist the many voices that told her that she was ugly and that blond haired, blue-eyed dolls were pretty. However, the standards of beauty were not the sole cause of Pecola's self-hatred. Pecola did not just think that she was not beautiful, she was convinced that she was ugly. This sense of ugliness was profound and had roots not outside in the world, but deep within her own home.

Morrison helps us to see that learning ugliness can be a part of a family legacy, carefully passed on from one generation to the next. Morrison describes Pecola's heritage:

> The Breedloves did not live in a storefront because they were having temporary difficulty adjusting to the cutbacks at the plant. They lived there because they were poor and black, and they stayed there because they believed they were ugly. Although their poverty was traditional and stultifying, it was not unique. But their ugliness was unique. No one could have convinced them that they were not relentlessly and aggressively ugly. Except for the father, Cholly, whose ugliness (the result of despair, dissipation, and violence directed toward petty things and weak people) was behavior, the rest of the family—Mrs. Breedlove, Sammy Breedlove, and Pecola Breedlove wore their ugliness, put it on, so to speak, although it did not belong to them.[3]

In another passage, Morrison continues, "You looked at them and wondered why they were so ugly; you looked closely and could not find the source. Then you realized that it came from conviction, their conviction."[4] The family defined itself by the standards of the world, standards that defined them as hopelessly inferior. They internalized the wider cultural attitude, then passed it on to their children, as if it were the simple truth. As we saw in the previous chapter, Cholly and Mrs. Breedlove are trapped in an endless maze of destructive relational patterns. Their relationship as husband and wife is a breeding ground for self-hatred. They agree not to kill each other physically, settling instead for dying a slow emotional and spiritual death by denying daily each other's value and worth.

Pecola is a victim of her parents' dysfunction over and over again. Her father commits the ultimate act of emotional destruction by raping her. Her mother emotionally abandons her to serve her white employers. In scene after scene, Pecola's legacy of self-hatred is reinforced. Without alternatives, she internalizes the attitudes of those around her. At every level,

---

[3] Morrison, *Bluest Eye*, 38.
[4] Morrison, *Bluest Eye*, 29.

her self-esteem is eroded. In this sick relational environment, Pecola could hardly avoid becoming a relational refugee.

At one point in the novel, Morrison has Pecola compare herself to a dandelion.[5] Pecola wonders why people do not like dandelions. She notes that people use dandelions to make soups and wine and yet work hard to keep them out of their gardens and yards. Pecola feels like a dandelion, available to be used but kept out of sight, exploited yet disdained.

Pecola might have escaped her tragic fate if she had some support, some person or persons who could confirm her beauty and self-worth. Pecola is taken in by a family that includes the narrator, a girl who speaks in Morrison's voice, who has rejected the standards of beauty that her culture values, who thinks blonde-haired, blue-eyed dolls are ugly. This character, Morrison, and her sister, Frieda, are portrayed as Pecola's only friends, but their friendship with her is not enough to kill the weeds of self-hatred planted in her life. Though Frieda and Morrison adored Pecola, the crack in the dam of her self-esteem continues to widen.

Mentoring

Pecola is an adolescent girl. Morrison makes clear that black women suffer the violence of sexism, as well as racism. To form a healthy self-identity, black girls contend against these interlocking structures of oppression. As womanist scholars have made clear, African American women survive and thrive despite multiple levels of persecution.[6] African American adolescent girls need support to fight the attacks on their self-esteem on these various levels. Pecola had to search for an alternative to the blue-eyed standards of beauty but also needed to heal from the betrayal of trust by her parents, especially from her father's sexual violence.

The process of identity formation for young black men is no less difficult than that of young black women. Black men contend with racial oppression but have access to sexist privilege, nonetheless, suffering is not a matter of comparison by simple addition. The long traditions of Western racism makes the search for self-esteem difficult for all those not born with white skin.[7] I highlight the female example here to affirm the multiple attacks on their self-worth but I proceed in my discussion of pastoral responses, concentrating primarily on the obstacles placed before young people by racism.

[5] Morrison, *Bluest Eye*, 47.
[6] See, as an example, Emilie Townes, *A Troubling in My Soul: Womanist Perspectives on Evil and Suffering* (Maryknoll, N.Y.: Orbis Books, 1993), 1–9.
[7] On the historical development of racism in the West, see Cornel West, *Prophetic Fragments* (Grand Rapids: Eerdmans, 1998), 97–108.

Mentors who become involved in supporting young people in their struggle to find and sustain a healthy self-identity must begin by affirming the irrevocable value of all people that is foundational to our spiritual traditions. Ultimately, one's true value comes from one's relationship with God. The world around you may dismiss you as inferior. Your family may hurt rather than support you. You may not believe you are worth much. But, our traditions say, "you are a child of God." Thus, no one, not the abandoned, raped, dark-skinned, "ugly" girl, nor any other human being, is an orphan. We belong to the family of God. This must be the starting point for anyone who hopes to rescue adolescent relational refugees.

As a consequence, the mentor might continue, we must treat others as equals for they too are God's children. To harm, shame, or neglect another member of the family of God is a sin. Moreover, to accept images abroad in the wider society that denigrate the self is a form of idolatry, because it obscures God's validation. African Americans have proved skillful at revaluing the self. Devalued by the society in which we live, we look to God for affirmation. Enslaved, we found in God freedom promised and fulfilled. We might have been forced to live in bondage, but we did not regard ourselves as slaves.

For many African Americans, the black church, the black family, and the black institutions of higher education have been the countercultural training ground where the message of worth and value could be heard and internalized. These sanctuaries of affirmation in a culture of discrimination provided a place to contend with the demons of racism. Yet, self-hatred rooted in the internalization of racist and sexist ideologies could not be completely eradicated by these institutions. Not only do African Americans have to move across the thresholds of these sanctuaries and out into a hostile culture at various times, the ideologies of the larger world permeate these supposedly safe havens, as well. The internalization of racism and sexism is ethically and morally unacceptable. The question, then, is how do we strategically intervene in the process of African American adolescent personality development to support young people in their journeys toward self-acceptance and liberated growth?

Strategic Intervention

In *Paradise*, a more recent example of Morrison's work, she tells the story of an African American town in Oklahoma after the Civil Rights revolution of the 1960s. The scars from this community's long battle for freedom from oppression and injustice are so deep that there is no energy left with which to nurture the emerging personalities of the town's youth. Morrison narrates the failure of the first post-Civil Rights generation of parents and grandparents to support the growth and development of their children.

Morrison simply tells the tale of these families. She does not analyze the reasons for the inadequate parenting that occurred. However, some possibilities exist in my mind. First, post-Civil Rights parents, like the children of Israel following the exodus from bondage in Egypt, may simply have concluded that the battle of oppression was over, that children growing up after the hard-won passage of Civil Rights laws did not need as much support at home. Perhaps, we assumed that the end of segregation ended as well the assault on black self-esteem so that our young people would just fall automatically into line. Second, the first post-Civil Rights generation shifted their energies from the struggle for equality to pursuing careers and material wealth in the newly accessible arenas of the mainstream corporate world. Our well-intentioned efforts to escape poverty or otherwise offer our children a better start than we had may have resulted in a neglect of other needs. We simply may have become too busy to raise our own children.

Archie Smith has noted that in this period many African Americans made a drastic shift in strategy. If in the Civil Rights era we had worked for the overthrow of the systems of inequality, afterwards we sought to become middle class, to join and benefit from capitalist economic structures. For Smith, the economic system itself functions to maintain rather than alleviate inequality. He makes the further claim that entering into market-based relationships spiritually impoverishes the participants. For black people, the destruction of supportive networks in favor of consumerist models of community is especially damaging.[8] In our effort to get our piece of the American pie, we have forgotten our responsibility to nurture the next generation. We have been deceived into thinking that all was well. Our children's self-esteem is therefore very much at risk. God's liberation is never a call to join the ranks of the oppressors or to benefit from their spoils. Rather, our liberation is a call to service and social transformation. "We have come over a way that with tears has been watered."[9]

The African American faith community must reclaim its prominence in nurturing the next generation of leaders. The church has been the training ground for most of the great leaders in our history. But today, for the first time, African American young people can conceive of the possibility of not being members of the faith community. Whereas we must accept the pluralism of the current age and the suspicion of all institutions, including

---

[8] Archie Smith, Jr., *Navigating the Deep River: Spirituality in African American Families* (Cleveland: United Church Press, 1997), 23.

[9] Hymn lyrics from James Weldon Johnson, "Lift Every Voice and Sing" (Edward B. Marks Music Company, 1921).

religious ones, that now pervades our society, we must all reassert the power of the church in the continuing struggle for equality and justice, for social and personal transformation.

In the next few pages, I offer some reflections on how parents and community leaders, who indeed accept their vocation to raise the next generation, can encourage the healthy development or young people today. The first point to recognize is that personal transformation and social transformation are intricately linked. Smith, drawing on the work of Vincent Harding, outlines the following process of growth that bridges the two spheres. First an individual must tap or rediscover a sense of meaning. This results in a discovery of personal agency. When accompanied by the development of a critical perspective on the status quo, the individual is ready to take some action for change. Commitment to sustain such action is based in the discovery of a vocation of service. In this way, the effort to humanize the world is linked to personal renewal.[10]

Thirty years after the Kerner Commission Report on the state of the various racial/ethnic groups in the United States, there was a follow-up study.[11] The conclusions of this report include observations that America's neighborhoods and schools are resegregating and the number of children who live in poverty has increased 20 percent since the 1980s. Although the economic and social situation of African Americans, as a group, has improved during this period, things have become worse for many individual families. For instance, black youths remain disproportionately likely to be unemployed or imprisoned. On a more personal level, I observe this generation of parents has too often abdicated the responsibility of raising its offspring so that grandparents must fill the gap. At this time, it is critical that adults reclaim their role as mentors for young people, especially youth at risk.

The Ecumenical Families Alive Project is an important example of programs that address the needs of young people. Funded by the Robert Wood Johnson Foundation and staffed by Anne Streaty Wimberly, other members of the Interdenominational Theological Center faculty, and community leaders, the program provides assistance to grandparents raising grandchildren and to other families with troubled youth. Through visits, telephone hot lines, support groups, referrals, and advocacy, the volunteers support the primary caregivers and serve as role models for the youth.

Adolescents need a variety of resources to help them grow and flourish. They need stories of heroes and heroines to inspire them. They need

[10] Smith, *Deep River*, 24.
[11] Jonathan Karl and Kevin Smith, "30 years after Kerner report, some say racial divide wider," *CNN U.S. News*, March 1, 1998.

traditions that testify to God's presence in the struggle to become a mature human being who lives responsibly in community. They need mentors who provide listening ears and other types of support. They need hope that the constraints on their lives are not the deepest reality, that the limitations of racism, for instance, do not have the last word on their future.

For stories, let us follow Archie Smith's suggestions that we engage in "reflexivity," in a reexamination of the past for valuable lessons which can stimulate imagination for new possibilities and new outcomes.[12] Looking back allows us to tap the deep spiritual resources that ignited the Civil Rights movements and other black liberation movements and which still sustain the black family and extended family. Looking back we encounter the loving and transforming God of history who acts for justice and peace still. Looking back we join in a hermeneutics of engagement, an identification of God's active presence in the past, that fuels our movement with God into the future.

The story of Mary McLeod Bethune is one story that I find empowering. I recommend it to those who are engaged in ministries with young people. My father went to Bethune Cookman College, which she helped found, and often told me of her and how she had inspired his own ministry. Bethune was born in 1875. Her mother worked as a domestic. When Mary was little she accompanied her mother to the house of the white family for whom she worked. One day Mary wandered about the neighborhood and came upon two little girls who were playing in their playhouse. The playhouse seemed larger and nicer than the shack that was Mary's home, but nonetheless she ventured in and began to play. The white girls gave Mary their dolls to care for. They were just imitating the realities of their world in which black women cared for white children, but the implication that Mary could play with them only if she took a subservient role was clear. Later, Mary spotted a book in the playhouse and attempted to read. Her playmates scolded her, reminding her that black children were not supposed to learn to read. They put her out of the house as well.

Bethune told this story often, noting how her first experience of white racism was also her first recognition of her desire to learn to read. Her powerful connection to books and learning stems from what on the surface was a negative experience. Her ability to reinterpret her encounter with the white girls stems from her positive self-image that was cultivated among a supportive family and community.

Bethune was not known for her external beauty. She found the necessary spiritual resources from God, her family, and community to recognize

[12] Smith, *Deep River*, 26–27.

her internal beauty instead. Her firm belief in her own worth gave her the confidence and courage to help others, not the least through the establishment of her school. Bethune's story highlights the significance of supportive networks in the healthy development of black youth.

Young people need adults who can teach, through precept and example, proactive responses that our youth can use when they are devalued. We must show them how to stop the erosion of their self-esteem from relationships or experiences that communicate any sense of inferiority. We must help them speak up and speak out when they are devalued. We must help them to assert themselves respectfully and appropriately so that they do not put themselves or others at risk in a confrontation with authority.

Parents are the most important role models for adolescents. But parents are also the primary authorities against which adolescents must rebel as they come to accept and grow into their own authority. As parents, we must be both supportive and accepting. Our children face many obstacles as they grow into adulthood. We must affirm their aspirations and be available to them when they need support. But we must also allow them to define themselves, avoiding the extremes of being overcontrolling on the one hand and abdicating our responsibility on the other. We need to be aware that parenting youth is a process that necessarily involves tension. There is no easy way around the problems of adolescent identity formation. There is also no blueprint or road map. Our adolescent children need to have the assurance that we will always be there for them, that we respect them and the choices they are learning to make, even as we maintain enough limits to keep them safe, and that they can trust us as role models on which to build their own lives. These things will provide a secure home from which they can fly on their own.

Adolescents, especially those who belong to so-called minority communities, need a sense of hope that they can make their biggest dreams come true. Despite all the negative reports about black adolescent unemployment and the incarceration of our black youth, there is some good news as well. Where conformity to the standards of the majority culture used to be a prerequisite for success in the job market, the increasing diversity of our nation and the globalization of the economy means that young people who are skilled in crossing boundaries of culture are now considered assets. The owner of the Carolina Panthers, Jerry Richardson, predicts that the global economy will require a racially diverse workforce in the future. Those who can work together with people of different races and cultures are becoming highly sought after. In Mutare, Zimbabwe, where I wrote this book, I met hopeful black and white youth who have learned to work together for a common, bright future.

Whereas a bright future beckons, the process of identity formation has become no easier for adolescents today. Whether a relational refugee, like Pecola, or a girl blessed with a supportive family despite the racist and sexist culture that surrounded her, like Mary McLeod Bethune, our children all must fight against the demons of self-doubt and shame as they take their places beside us in the making of a better world. As their mentors, parents, and pastors, we must offer them our love and support, modeling for them wholesome and responsible ways of living. They require much of us, but this is our role and we have stories, role models, and each other to rely on as resources for our work with them. We all need to create or strengthen networks of mutually sustaining relationships in which our young people can thrive. Adolescents can so easily be lost. Without close-knit families, school communities, neighborhoods, and churches, they will be spiritually and emotionally impoverished. We were not liberated to become middle class, to accumulate wealth, or to fulfill our own selfish desires. We were liberated to participate in God's transformation of the world, and each of us has a particular calling to fulfill in this regard.

• • •

Poverty, Prosperity, and the Relational Refugee[*]

Lorraine Hansberry's play *A Raisin in the Sun* confronts its audience with the tension between community values and economic opportunity.[1] As I discussed in the previous chapter, the Civil Rights laws gave African Americans access to greater economic opportunity. Many have taken advantage of the legal protections from job and housing discrimination to pursue the American dream of prosperity. At the same time, this pursuit has undermined some of the basic values and commitments that African Americans have historically cultivated. For me, the play raises a fundamental question: at what price should the American dream of economic prosperity be bought?

I certainly understand that everyone must make a living. And I know of no alternative to the capitalist system that could sustain me, or others, materially. But I am concerned that we recognize the discontinuities between our economic behavior and the values of our heritage and do what we can to foster the latter even if it means curtailing the former. African Americans must make a living and at the same time resist the consumerist values of the market culture. It is my firm conviction that wholesale adoption of the values of market capitalism separates us into autonomous consumers who compete with each other to collect and devour products and services. The market disconnects us from each other and encourages us to act selfishly. It fosters a sense of rootlessness in us. It loosens our hold on the meaning of life. The market rewards homeless minds, relational refugees.

A Raisin in the Sun tells the story of an African American family who lives on the south side of Chicago. Three generations share a crowded apartment. They all dream of owning their own home where each family member has her or his own room, where children have a place to play, and where Moma, the matriarch, can have a garden. As the play opens the family awaits impatiently $10,000 of life insurance money. The money is coming because Big Walter, the patriarch, has died.

They all want a better place to live, but there are several other individual dreams as well. Moma and Big Walter have two children, Walter Lee and Berneatha. Walter Lee wants to use some of the money to start

---

[1] Lorraine Hansberry, *A Raisin in the Sun* (New York: Vintage Books, 1994).

[*] This chapter was previously published in Edward P. Wimberly, *Relational Refugees: Alienation and Reincorporation in African American Churches and Communities* (Nashville: Abingdon, 2000), 75–84 and associated notes. © 2000, Abingdon Press. Used by permission. All rights reserved.

a business. Berneatha wants some of the money to be set aside for her to go to medical school. Walter Lee's wife, Ruth, and their son, Travis, also live in the apartment. Ruth agrees with Moma that a house is the priority. Travis just wants everyone to be happy. When the money comes, Moma puts $3,500 down on a house in the white suburbs, and gives the rest of the money to Walter Lee. He promises to save some for Berneatha's education and to invest the rest, but instead invests the entire $6,500. Unfortunately, Walter Lee's partner turns out to be a con man and Walter Lee loses everything.

Walter Lee's dreams are dashed before they even take shape, and because of his selfishness, so are the dreams of his sister. Walter Lee experiences a clash of values, economic and material on one hand, spiritual and relational on the other hand. In the end, he chooses to embrace his family, finding a new sense of self-worth not dependent on the amount of money or things he has accumulated.

Hansberry's play is about a family that seems to gain the entire world but lose its soul. It is also a story about the possibility of finding hope again when dreams are stolen. Hansberry shows her audience how meaning can be found in the midst of disappointment and suffering. She explodes the false myth that money can solve all human problems.

The play also stresses the importance of maintaining relationships across generations and the value of multigenerational narratives of racial pride. It presents an important response to the yearnings of relational refugees in that it shows that it is possible for a household of three generations to work together and maintain harmonious relationships despite setbacks and betrayals.

Practical theological reflection on this play focuses on the tension between the pursuit of economic prosperity and the maintenance of a family's values. My intention is to provide insight about the ways African Americans can participate fully in the American dream and, at the same time, sustain their religious and cultural heritage.

A Clash of Cultures

None of the characters in Hansberry's play are relational refugees. Despite all of the conflict over the money, the family maintains itself and no one is lost, no one walks away; the characters remain in relationship. The play concerns the temptation to disconnect oneself from one's family in order to fulfill one's own dreams.

Walter Lee and Berneatha are most at risk for becoming relational refugees. Walter Lee is at risk because of his greed and his dependence on money for a sense of his own value. Berneatha rebels against the traditions that sustain her mother, most significantly, she asserts that she does not need Christian faith. Neither of these two follow through on their tendencies toward refugee status, but their choices reveal the strength of such temptations and show ways that temptations can be resisted.

Walter Lee is not easy to get along with. He thinks of himself first. He asserts his primacy as "man of the house" and expects the women in his life to sacrifice their dreams for his. He is devoted to his son but only in terms of being a provider for Travis' material needs and wants. His poverty threatens his sense of himself as a father. He believes money will prop up his fragile self-esteem. As the date the check is due to arrive nears, Walter Lee becomes pleasant to be around. His motto is "I got a dream." The money is, for him, the path toward fulfillment of this dream. Its approach makes him happy, but also puts him at risk for the scam that pulls the rug out from under him.

Moma, representative of the rich family legacy of racial pride, saves Walter Lee from his own foolishness. She, along with the now deceased Big Walter, were concerned not only with material well-being but emotional and spiritual well-being also. Moma tries to remind her children that Big Walter left them much more than $10,000. He left them a heritage, an identity, a model of one who, despite poverty, found self-acceptance and lived with pride. When Walter Lee loses the majority of their money, Moma does not attack him. The family is nearly defeated but she allows him a chance at redemption. Walter Lee is offered money by a white homeowner who is willing to pay him if he will agree not to move his family to a predominantly white neighborhood. Moma lets him decide what to do. He is torn between the values of the culture and the values of his family. This time he chooses to let the money go and choose a better life for his family, a life that also contributes to the welfare of his entire community. Moma is a model parent and mentor here. She provides guidance for Walter Lee but then allows him to learn from his mistakes and have the power to choose again.

Moma serves as a model parent and mentor in relation to Berneatha as well. In contrast to her brother, Berneatha rejected the values of the dominant culture and looked to Africa for her identity. She left the church and other central aspects of African American life because she felt they were too closely connected to the culture of the oppressors. By embracing African traditions, she asserted her individual identity and resisted the pressure to assimilate. Moma accepted her daughter's need to take a different path but modeled a middle way. Moma both preserved her racial dignity and participated fully in the wider culture.

Walter Lee's and Berneatha's decisions represent the two poles of the many choices facing African Americans as they find a way to live in a racist culture. Walter Lee, for a variety of reasons having to do with his sense of himself as a man, a father, and a poor black, struggled mightily to choose between get-rich-quick schemes and the rich legacy of values of his family. His temptation was to assimilate and accept the values of the market over the good of his family. Berneatha sought to express herself, to leave behind the trappings of America for her personal interpretation of African culture. Her temptation was to reject assimilation in a way that reflected modern individualism. Both were tempted to abandon their heritage for different reasons and in opposite directions. Morna's enduring values bridged the two spheres of realities.

Moma embraced what Andrew Billingsley would call bicultural or double consciousness. Bicultural consciousness is the ability to be both black and American simultaneously.[2] Full assimilation into wider society is not ideal for African American families, according to Billingsley. Rather, the African American genius has been the ability to maintain enduring, distinct, cultural kinship patterns, religious values, and a strong work ethic while participating in the socioeconomic structures of the wider culture. This stubborn strength to hold a self together when it is pulled in two directions has engendered whatever success African Americans have achieved. Moma and Big Walter embodied these values, this alternative to assimilation and individualism.

Values of the Religious and Social Legacy

One key value of the African American faith tradition is the ability to find hope and meaning in the midst of tragedy and difficulty. This has been a mainstay of our tradition.[3] African American faith traditions, like the biblical texts on which they are based, include many stories of people of faith enduring tough times, wilderness wanderings. And, as in the Bible, the testimonies, the stories of martyrs and saints, tell us over and over again that God's active presence was encountered on those stony roads. In situations of poverty, God sustains until the rains come or the check clears. In situations of shattered, deferred, or exploding dreams, God appears and a word of hope is heard one more time.

Hansberry wrote *A Raisin in the Sun* when the Civil Rights revolution was in full swing. It was a time of great hope and anticipation that new

---

[2] Andrew Billingsley, *Climbing Jacob's Ladder: The Enduring Legacy of African-American Families* (New York: Simon & Schuster, 1992), 224.

[3] Edward P. Wimberly, *African American Pastoral Care* (Nashville: Abingdon, 1991), 12–17; Henry Mitchell and Nicholas Lewter, *Soul Theology* (New York: Harper & Row, 1986), 11; Archie Smith, Jr., *Navigating the Deep River: Spirituality in African American Families* (Cleveland: United Church Press, 1997), 94.

and better economic horizons were dawning. The play acknowledges how limited actual opportunities were, however. The housing discrimination patterns were breaking down, and African Americans could buy homes in white neighborhoods. Whereas white racism still haunted these sales, they could not stop them. In the case of the Younger family, other obstacles existed. It was Walter Lee's behavior that threatened the family's hopes and dreams. He squandered their money on a get-rich-quick scam. The play shows that threats to economic security exist within the African American community, as well as from outside it. African American leaders have debated the value of self-help in reversing the economic situation of the community. Poor people must learn by example and precept about economic structures and the ways in which they can organize and discipline themselves to contribute to the well-being of the entire community.

The play stresses the importance of grounding masculine identity not in the exploitative values of the marketplace, but in a commitment to the needs of the next generation. Moma offers Big Walter as an example for Walter Lee to emulate. Big Walter's manhood rested in his contribution to a five-generation-long legacy of racial pride and to the growth and development of the next generation. It was difficult for Walter Lee to accept his father's model of masculinity, but he came to see its strength and authenticity.

The play also offers insight into values of parenting, of helping a son become a man and helping a daughter learn to love. I have already mentioned Moma's skill in enabling Walter Lee to redeem himself when he was offered money to not move into the white neighborhood. In another scene, after Walter Lee lost the $6,500, Berneatha wanted to disown him. In response, Moma preached a sermon to Berneatha about love. She asked her daughter when did she think it was appropriate to love? Then she answered her own question: "It's when he's at his lowest and can't believe in hisself 'cause the world done whipped him so!"[4] Thus, Moma gave her daughter the secret to facilitating manhood, to love men regardless, but especially when they are down. Such love is not a weak love that does not challenge a man to stand up when he falls. Such love abides and takes the risk of offering the man another opportunity to try. Withdrawing love from persons when they are at their lowest point can seal their self-destruction. Moma, however, never withdrew her love from Walter Lee, and he was able to internalize it and use it for his own growth, as well as for the growth of others.

---

[4] Hansberry, *Raisin in the Sun*, 145.

In the end, family members were able to embrace Moma's double consciousness, able to move toward a future of full participation in American society, without losing their footing in their own heritage. The blind embrace of the values of the marketplace leads ultimately to the destruction of families. Incorporating one's commitment to self, family, community, and village into one's attitude toward money and work keeps one in balance. This, at least, is my interpretation of Hansberry's lesson for how we as African Americans are supposed to relate to the market economy in the latter part of the twentieth century and into the twenty-first century.

Strategic Intervention

Postindustrial capitalism strains human relationships on many levels. Competitive models appear to encourage productivity and inventiveness, but where there are winners there are also losers. The values of the market—self-reliance, materialism, and consumerism—promote unbalanced ways of relating to others and relegate those without the skills that the market values to underemployment or poverty. For so-called minority groups, the pressure to adopt the values of the dominant culture is a double-edged sword. If African Americans and others do not participate in the larger economy, they will remain impoverished. If they assimilate completely, they lose themselves.

Hansberry's play provides a model of a middle way, a way in which people can preserve their identity while attending to their material needs. Through Moma, Hansberry promotes the strategy of double consciousness, a way of relating to the economic structures that avoids the pitfalls of total assimilation but maintains the individualism of the relational refugee. Such strategies require, but also enable, African Americans to affirm their faith and racial-ethnic heritage while participating fully in the pursuit of the American dream. By adopting a double consciousness, African Americans avoid the loss of identity entailed in assimilation by affirming what Archie Smith calls black history and culture, while still making a living in the capitalist economic system.[5]

The balancing act of double consciousness is both an unavoidable reality of African American experience and a skill that can be learned and honed. Those who would help African Americans as well as others whose attitude toward the market threatens them with alienation from their truest selves, need to mentor their charges in double consciousness.

The first task of the mentor is to facilitate critical reflection on the nature of the market economy and the economic problems facing African

[5] Smith, *Deep River*, 20.

American people in particular. The values of consumer capitalism need to be clearly articulated and compared with the values of the community's heritage. Archie Smith writes:

> The mainstream with its materialistic and utilitarian values is a central part of the problem we must address on the path to any reordering of our personal and institutional lives. It is, therefore, necessary to interpret personal and family difficulties in the light of an interpretation of how United States society as a whole works. It is the workings of this mainstream as a whole and our responses to it that give meaning to our experience. The deepening of meaning or purpose in life is the goal.[6]

The spiritual resources of African American traditions limit the extent to which we can participate in mainstream society by counter-balancing society's lure of self-interest. We must participate in the larger economy if we are going to survive, but we do not participate without a critical consciousness, an abiding loyalty to our family, race, and heritage.

The mentor also needs to set the clash in values in its larger context, in the fundamental differences in worldview that exist between the community's spiritual heritage and the market's materialism. Prosperity at any cost is a message to be rejected. We have large claims upon us that direct our economic values:

> Do not store up for yourselves treasures on earth, where moth and rust consume and where thieves break in and steal; but store up for yourselves treasures in heaven, where neither moth nor rust consumes and where thieves do not break in and steal. For where your treasure is, there your heart will be also. (Matt 6:19-21)

On the practical level, the mentor must support those who are learning the skills of double consciousness in several ways. First, support systems must be established for men and women like Walter Lee, who have suffered defeat and humiliation in the economic sphere whether because of their own naïveté or the vagaries of the market. Second, the mentor should create forums where people learn about the structures of the economy and learn skills they will need to evaluate their career plans. Third, the mentor needs to publicize, in a variety of media, stories of people who have successfully handled the balancing act of double consciousness in the economic sphere and in other spheres of life. Finally, those who embark on the life of double consciousness in the marketplace will need resources to support them in this exhausting but rewarding task.

---

[6] Smith, *Deep River*, 20.

Of special significance are the needs of men like Walter Lee, who pursue get-rich-quick schemes that result only in further impoverishment. William Oliver has described the circumstances that lead to such self-defeating strategies and has named the trap "the philosophy of compulsive masculinity."[7] Marginalized men have organized ruthless and, for the most part, hopeless economic strategies because of their unfamiliarity with mainstream structures and opportunities. These men need contact with other mainstream people, especially other males, so that they can develop realistic and sustainable strategies for supporting themselves. Unemployed or underemployed men are at great risk of becoming relational refugees in the current economic situation and need special attention by mentors and others in the community who can help them remain full participants in community.

Again, on the practical level, mentors might create forums in which successful African Americans help others who want to invest what money they have in meaningful ways. There are many legitimate financial planners and business investment guides that can help people like Walter Lee invest their money in appropriate ways. The practical theologian can help make this happen.

Of special concern are those who are the truly disadvantaged, who are not only on the fringes of the mainstream, but are also beaten down. I speak here of those on the "unemployable" lists. They do not have the requisite resources that they need emotionally or educationally to do well in society. Mentors must identify and reach out to the endemically poor. There are programs that exist that actually work very well with these persons. One such program that has survived the federal budget cuts of the 1970s and 1980s is Reverend Leon Sullivan's program. Sullivan's Opportunities Industrialization Centers, a network of community-based skills training programs, has helped more than 1.5 million people in one hundred cities and eighteen countries find productive employment. In this age of limited welfare benefits, such programs are becoming even more critical to create, strengthen, and sustain.

Economic relational refugees suffer universally from low self-esteem and despair. People who have been counted out need a great deal of emotional and support system help. They need to be surrounded by people who care and want them to succeed in what they are doing. Mentors must provide positive experiences that reinforce the relational refugee's sense of self, in addition to teaching the skills that will enable them to negotiate the

---

[7] William Oliver, *The Violent Social World of Black Men* (New York: Lexington Books, 1994), 10.

mainstream work world. The practical theologian needs to make sure these kinds of programs exist.

Conclusion

This chapter explored the economic factors that encourage people to become relational refugees. Both those who are most successful and those defeated by the market are at great risk. The double consciousness of African Americans is a helpful strategy for all those who want to preserve their truest identity and communal heritage while earning a meaningful living. Those who fail to develop double consciousness are vulnerable to becoming relational refugees. Those who remain grounded in their particular traditions of faith and culture can instead function as pilgrims, true to their God, true to their native land.

5

Politics, Oppression, and Empowerment (2006)

In *African American Pastoral Care and Counseling: The Politics of Oppression and Empowerment*, we see how Edward Wimberly's ideas are deepening and expanding on ways to interpret and confront the socio-cultural malaise experienced by African Americans.* Advocating for African Americans' liberation from the oppression of racism, he makes explicit the connections between personal, social, and political conditions for empowerment and transformation. He argues that the goals of individual empowerment and personal agency are not enough: pastoral caregivers must also be public theologians and cultural critics who influence the political agenda so as to transform the public square into a more life-giving space. Here we see the development of Wimberly's succinct call for *prophetic* pastoral care.

In the first essay, Wimberly engages literature in African American and womanist pastoral theology in a discussion of the political dimensions of care. Citing the work of Homer Ashby, Archie Smith, Jr., Emmanuel Lartey, Carroll Watkins Ali, Elaine Crawford, and Carolyn McCrary,†

Wimberly argues that pastoral care and counseling *is* a political process. It is a countercultural movement that orients African American Christians toward a sense of their true worth and value in the eyes of God (164).

The second essay returns to an earlier theme: the importance of the local congregation as the context for pastoral counseling. Here Wimberly generously narrates his own life story of liberation and empowerment, interpreting it through a narrative lens. His upbringing in the black church, especially his experience of observing his father's pastoral ministry, immersed him in "local discourses and communities of wisdom" (170). Wimberly asserts that congregations can empower African Americans to live out of alternative spiritual knowledges and stories, and thus become effective political agents. He continues to explicate this idea using fiction and memoir as case material throughout the book.

These essays illustrate Wimberly's evolving emphasis on the political and prophetic dimensions of the practice of narrative pastoral care. Wimberly's open sharing of his own story exemplifies his transparent and inviting style that enhances the impact of his ideas.

Further Reading

Wimberly, Edward P. "Beyond the Curse of Noah: African American Pastoral Theology as Political." In *African American Religious Life and the Story of Nimrod*, edited by Anthony B. Pinn and Allen Dwight Callahan, 179–89. New York: Palgrave Macmillan, 2008.

• • •

Louis: Chalice Press, 1999); A. Elaine Crawford, *Hope in the Holler: A Womanist Theology* (Louisville: Westminster John Knox, 2002); and Carolyn McCrary, plenary presentation at the Society for Pastoral Theology Annual Meeting, Atlanta, Ga., June 2004.

African American Pastoral Care and Counseling
as Political Processes *

Homer Ashby Jr. sounds the battle cry for contemporary pastoral caregivers in *Our Home Is over Jordan*[1] when he painstakingly outlines the problems that African Americans face. He calls to our attention that the social and economic well-being of African Americans is only becoming worse, and that racial assault fueled by white supremacy is on the rise.[2] Unemployment of African Americans remains twice as high as that of whites. Many blacks seem to have withdrawn from fruitful involvement in politics. Homicide and AIDS, STDs, cancer, infant mortality, hypertension, and other illnesses are disproportionately represented among African Americans. And when it comes to how African Americans are portrayed in the media, Ashby says:

> Two subtle messages are being sent to African Americans: Your insignificance as a participant in the cultural reality of America does not warrant portrayal on the television screen, and (2) your resentment and protest at being ignored is of little concern to us. In both ways African Americans are disregarded and made invisible.[3]

Ashby goes on to talk about other problems African Americans face, including nihilism or the loss of hope that threatens the emotional, spiritual, and physical well-being of African Americans. He discusses the internalized oppression that is at the heart of black-on-black crime and homicide rates, and cautions that a lack of a collective vision for the future among African Americans is leaving us very vulnerable.

Perhaps the most significant thing that Ashby lifts up as a threat to our survival as a people is our loss of a sense of community, our fragmentation as a people. Yes, we have become disconnected and disassociated from each other. We have lost a sense of peoplehood. We can no longer depend on our extended family ties and support systems to sustain us as they once did. Ashby's solution is to encourage us to rediscover the village or communities of care and nurture that will provide all the necessary ingredients for our healthy self-esteem. He says we need an ethic of care that "guides

---

[1] Homer U. Ashby, Jr., *Our Home Is over Jordan: A Black Pastoral Theology* (St. Louis: Chalice Press, 2003).

[2] Ashby, *Our Home*, 1–15.

[3] Ashby, *Our Home*, 6.

* This chapter was previously published in Edward P. Wimberly, *African American Pastoral Care and Counseling: The Politics of Oppression and Empowerment* (Cleveland: Pilgrim Press, 2006), 19–36. Used by permission.

interpersonal relationships, fosters love, builds compassion, constructs systems of support, and denounces violence and abuse in all forms."[4]

As we might expect, he points to the black church as that vehicle for the recovery of the village, for the church embraces the larger plot that undergirds all activities of African American Christians and the wider community. For Ashby, it is in the recovery of our sense as an eschatological people working in partnership with God that we can hope to begin to rebuild our communities and enable African Americans to thrive.

Homer Ashby's program for reestablishing the village functions that once enabled us to thrive in a land of oppression is very important, for indeed without a communal vision we perish. In this book I suggest that we take another step toward healthy personal and communal functioning by acknowledging and drawing on pastoral counseling as an inherently political process that leads African Americans into full participation in the processes that shape their destiny as individuals and as a collective group.

This chapter has two aims. The first is to explore the meaning of pastoral counseling as a political process. The second aim is to examine how African American pastoral counseling has historically attended to the political and social transformation agenda and the link between the personal and public dimensions of life.

This book, then, is about pastoral counseling as a political process. By "political process" I mean the process that enables human beings to become fully involved and engaged in life so that each person can identify, develop, and exercise his or her full human capacities while at the same time enabling others to do likewise for the purpose of contributing to the common good. Participation in all life at all levels, which presupposes living in a democratic society, is what the political process is about. Thus, participating in how one's life and community are governed and administered is essential in the political process. Moreover, enabling people to participate in the political process of self-governing and community building is not a privilege but a God-given right, which God expects us to exercise even when that right is denied and obstacles to exercising it are erected. Pastoral counseling facilitates and enables persons to have the motivation and courage to engage, to get involved, to participate.

Contemporary efforts to limit the participation of African Americans in the political process of this nation take very subtle forms and are not limited by political party. It is not just the tampering with the Voting Rights Act, or making sure that our youth have criminal records, or the use of subtle or effective strategies to get young people to drop out of school that

[4] Ashby, *Our Home*, 12.

obliterate our chances of full participation. Rather, the process of political disenfranchisement subtly entices African Americans to internalize negative conversations, images, and stories about themselves such that there is no need for overt forms of racism. One such subtle mechanism is the negative portrayals of African Americans in the media, as Ashby also noted. Negative media portrayals stimulate internal conversations and lead us to deny our own worth and value, as well as to put down our own institutions and communities.

In this context of internalized racism, the role of pastoral counseling is to enable individuals, married couples, families, and mediating structures that bridge between the individual and the wider society to edit or reauthor the negative internalized stories and identities that African Americans have embraced. The editing needs to facilitate and enable us to participate fully in society.

Such editing is understood as *a practice of the self* that enables individuals and small groups of people to alter the way they have been recruited into identities that are oppressive and self-destructive. Editing is also a *practice of care* exhibited by caregivers who create safe environments and provide help and prompting in understanding the evil of the past and the possibilities for the future that are necessary for persons to revise and reauthor the internalized negative stories frustrating their growth and development.

Practices of the self and practices of care are inherently political processes. Political processes in a democracy by nature are oriented toward facilitating full participation in all of life, including the decision-making dimensions leading to community development and full employment of individual capacities and abilities. The ultimate aim of democratic political processes is to maximize individual and group participation in decision making in ways that benefit the common good. When the practices of self and the practices of care help to facilitate full participation in the democratic political processes of society, then they support full enfranchisement. While racial oppression seeks to limit and control the participation of African Americans in the decision-making processes through recruiting us into negative identities and stories, the practices of self and the practices of care facilitated by pastoral counseling have the power to undo the pejorative recruiting through editing processes.

The terms "practice of self" and "practices of care" are rooted in the practices of conversation and recruiting. These practices are seminal throughout this work. For Michel Foucault, it is discourse or conversation that makes practice intelligible. More specifically, practice provides a group of unifying rules that facilitate the interpretation of reality.[5] The practice of discourse or conversation establishes the order of speaking, the order with which we deal with words, the way we name reality, the way we analyze and classify things, and the way we explain things.

To illustrate how discourse or conversation sets priorities, let us look at the following words uttered in prayer by an elderly assistant pastor following a sermon I preached on September 19, 2004, at National Divine Spiritual Church in Atlanta:

> God, we want you to bless the leaders of this nation, of this community, of this city, and this state. We do not want you to bless only Democrats or Republicans. Rather, we want you to bless all of those in leadership regardless of political party. We ask this petition recognizing that we must ultimately turn to you, God, for all of our expectations. What we can expect from Democrats or Republicans is limited. But our expectations of you include things here on earth as well as things in heaven.

This elderly praying person had lived long enough to understand the limitations of political parties and what they can actually deliver when responding to the needs of people. He recognized that politics focus on scarce resources and that these resources are allocated based on who is in office or in power. Thus, he was helping listeners to understand that the response of political parties to human need is provisional at best. However, what we expect from God goes beyond scarce resources. Indeed, God's grace is unlimited and never scarce.

When this elderly man finished praying, I thought about the goals I was trying to accomplish in this writing project and how we orient our thinking and our lives toward conversations that we have with God and conversations we have in our faith communities. There is a lot to be derived from orienting our conversations toward God, since our identities as human beings come as a result of a gift from God. More precisely, society organizes its conversation based on the honor and shame categories of power, prestige, wealth, position, and privilege, and thus society allocates human worth and value according to those whom it deems worthwhile and honorable. However, God's granting of human worth and value is not limited to human categories of honor or shame, nor are they based on human achievement or merit. Consequently, the prayer of the elderly gentleman sought to orient us properly to God conversation, which is the ultimate source of our identity, worth, and value.

---

[5] Michel Foucault, *The Archaeology of Knowledge and the Discourse on Language* (New York: Pantheon Books, 1972), 46.

Orienting our conversation or discourse toward God is a mark of our belief about what is real, worthwhile, and valuable. Thus, we limit our expectations of what we can expect from Democrats or Republicans, and we participate in the political process knowing that we are strangers and foreigners on earth. Our highest goal is to reach an eternal home (Heb 13–16). This way of thinking about what is real is not only heavenly talk of "pie in the sky by and by." More precisely, this way of defining reality for African American Christians has been the way we have organized our expectations and our priorities.

Real power—political power—lies in the ability to control the practices of discourse and conversation. Moreover, real power enables selected groups of people to not only define reality but then recruit others into realities that may be alien to who they are. For example, the presidential race between incumbent George Bush and Senator John Kerry truly was a battle over who could define reality. Foucault says that the power to define reality is determined socially by who is accorded the right to speak first, the status of the one given the privilege to speak, their competence and knowledge, pedagogic norms, legal conditions, hierarchical attributions, and others; all these contribute to who gets the power to define what is real and not real.[6] The elderly man's prayer, however, helps us to recognize that political processes are conversations based on who can allocate scarce resources. Such political conversations are provisional and do not determine our worth and value as human beings. What we expect from political parties should be related to fair and just distribution of scarce resources, but we should never base our feelings of being worthwhile and valuable on who is in office or on political processes themselves. To do so would be practicing idolatry—that is, making political parties the ultimate grantor of human worth and value.

Thus, we must attend to the practices of discourse and the nature of what gets to be defined as real when we think of the political process. It is clear that skin color is one of the prime definers of who gets the power to speak first and to recruit others into their reality in the United States. Republicans generally do not want to deal publicly with statements about race and prefer to work behind the scenes on behalf of racial justice. Democrats prefer to talk publicly about race as a way to shore up their base within the black community. African Americans trust those politicians more who give open public assent to racial justice, and we distrust those politicians who do not. There are those within the black community, however, who are

---

[6] Foucault, *Archaeology*, 51.

understandably suspicious of the democratic public pronouncements that are disingenuous and hollow.[7]

African American Christians have historically found their self-understanding in God, who is conceived as the ultimate definer of reality. Thus, many Christian African Americans rely more on their theological and faith convictions to orient them to what is real than on what is trumpeted by politicians. Within the African American Christian community, privileging conversation with God is what has given African Americans as individuals and as a group dignity and value that were denied by wider negative cultural images of us.[8]

Given our Christian theological bent, why should we attend to the political processes at all if the ultimate grantor of worth and value is God and not political parties or processes? One answer is that we still must be concerned about how scarce resources are allocated by political processes. We can participate, but we do so recognizing the limitation of such processes. Second, our faith teaches us that we must also express our faith in God and our response to God's gift of worth and value by doing acts of kindness that benefit the common good. Faith and works are united, as the book of James proclaims, and such a belief is rooted in African American convictions that fueled the antislavery movement.[9] So it is the practices of discourse rooted in the faith convictions of many African American Christians that define what is real and important as we participate in political power processes. Thus, we access the decision making that helps to facilitate full participation in all of life as a means of responding to our faith. We do so recognizing that such participation is important and essential, and yet that such participation is not the ultimate grantor of our worth and value as human beings. Political participation enhances God's gift of identity, but it is not the source of it.

Walter Fluker helps us to maintain the distinction between full participation in the political processes and the source of our true and underlying identity. He points out that African Americans sought full inclusion in the United States through the discourses and practices of civility, namely, the practices of recognition, respectability, and loyalty within their religion.[10]

[7] James Perryman, *Unfounded Loyalty: An In-Depth Look into the Love Affair between Blacks and Democrats* (Lanham, Md.: Pneuma Life Publishing, 2003).

[8] Edward P. Wimberly, *Claiming God, Reclaiming Dignity: African American Pastoral Care* (Nashville: Abingdon, 2003).

[9] Margaret Patricia Aymer, "First Pure, Then Peaceable: Frederick Douglass Reads James" (Ph.D. diss., Union Theological Seminary, New York, 2004).

[10] Walter Earl Fluker, "Recognition, Respectability, and Loyalty: Black Churches and the Quest for Civility," in *New Day Begun: African American Churches and Civic Culture in Post-Civil Rights America*, ed. R. Drew Smith (Durham, N.C.: Duke University Press, 2003), 113–41.

The practices of civility use the established rules of wider society to gain access to full participation in society. Yet Fluker shows that the practices of recognition, respectability, and loyalty become problematic if we do not keep in focus that our ultimate worth comes from God and not from practices that seek full acceptance from society. I reiterate: God bestows human worth on the least of these as well as on those whom society values the most. Fluker, however, is right to point out that the practices of civility are not without merit, in that they have the potential to build moral character as well as building up community.

Discourse is a political power process of defining reality. Thus, when African Americans are recruited into negative identities as a means of disenfranchising them, then African American pastoral counseling can step in as a political instrument for editing and undoing internalized oppression.

Therapy has often been thought of as serving the needs of the honor-and-shame culture of society and thus preserving existing racial and gender categories. Any notion that African American pastoral counseling functions to preserve the subordinate status of African Americans is erroneous. Instead, this book draws on Frederick C. Harris' notion that personal efficacy or agency is causally related to political efficacy; reminded through pastoral care and counseling of our personal and communal strength, we try to transform our lives through civic involvement.[11]

Four dimensions of African American pastoral counseling as a political process are our focus here. First, pastoral counseling liberates persons from those internalized conversations and stories into which they have been recruited that limit their full participation in the United States of America and prevent them from developing and exercising their full potential.

Second, pastoral counseling is a political process since it also attends to those mediating structures or institutions that stand between the individual's private sphere and wider cultural public institutions.[12] Mediating structures include those small meaning-making aggregations such as the family, church, voluntary associations, neighborhoods, and support systems that further the process of individuals' internalizing conversations. For Fluker, social networks and mediating structures provide social capital or community networks that enable community engagement that lead to political involvement. Thus, strengthening mediating structures enables African Americans to develop their full potential as well as to enable others to do the same. Pastoral counseling also functions to strengthen support systems that promote full engagement in life.

---

[11] Frederick C. Harris, *Something Within: Religion in African-American Activism* (New York: Oxford University Press, 1999), 81–85.

[12] Harris, *Something Within*.

Third, pastoral counseling is political in the sense that it brings into the public arena insights from the actual counseling process. For example, one role of pastoral counseling in public theology is to bring a critique to modernity. Modernity is characterized by forces that disengage individuals from their communal roots and make them relational refugees.[13] When individuals are relational refugees, cut off from meaningful communal roots, they are more vulnerable to being recruited into negative identities and into conversations that disenfranchise them. Thus, pastoral counseling brings into the public debate over public policy those things that are needed to keep African Americans connected to each other and which build neighborhoods.

Finally, the practices of self are in themselves a political process. In the theory of discourse provided by Michel Foucault, caring for the self is an internal process that is connected with becoming an agent who is active in all of life. He calls this "the political game."[14]

African American Pastoral Counseling and
Social Transformation

In the late 1960s and throughout the 1970s many African American intellectuals bemoaned the fact that the therapeutic movement in the United States had ignored the social agenda of African Americans and of other oppressed people. Black theological intellectuals called this exclusive attention to the personal and psychological aspects of therapy as "navel-gazing." They perceived psychotherapy to be burying its head in the sand, ignoring social ills, a practice completely irrelevant to the historical and social struggles of an oppressed people for liberation. Consequently, the therapeutic movement was relegated to the private dimensions of the lives of African Americans, and the real social and liberation agenda of African Americans belonged to the public domain. Thus, a split between the private and the public dimensions of ministry occurred.

More recently, the international community has leveled the same critique at the therapeutic movement. Emmanuel Y. Lartey has identified the different dimensions of the criticism.[15] As a black African, he recognizes that the therapeutic movement was a middle-class and ethnocentric movement that is slow to react to the socioeconomic position of women, ethnics, and

---

[13] Edward P. Wimberly, *Pastoral Counseling and Spiritual Values: A Black Point of View* (Nashville: Abingdon, 1982); Edward P. Wimberly, *Relational Refugees: Alienation and Reincorporation in African American Churches and Communities* (Nashville: Abingdon, 2000).

[14] Michel Foucault, *The Care of the Self: The History of Sexuality* (New York: Vintage Books, 1988), 81–95.

[15] Lartey, *Living Colour*.

other minorities. In fact, he says that the movement has been characterized by psychological reductionism, sociopolitical apathy, theological weakness, and individualism.[16] Psychological reductionism is the preference for psychological theories of human beings at the expense of social and cultural analysis. Social and political apathy relate to issues of economic and social power, marginalization, access, and social control that impact the lives of people and shape their experiences. The theological feebleness of which he speaks is the tendency of pastoral counseling to replace the faith orientation of Christianity with psychological models and individualism and to neglect the communal and interpersonal dimensions of the therapeutic whole.

As an alternative to the more traditional approach to therapy and pastoral counseling, Lartey has suggested a liberation model.[17] This model takes seriously the concrete experiences and the social location of the poor, the suffering, and the oppressed. Second, a social analysis of the conditions that impact and shape the experiences and lives of the poor, suffering, oppressed, and marginalized are addressed. Third, the theological feebleness of pastoral counseling is addressed by helping the poor and oppressed to interpret and reinterpret their human condition in light of sacred scriptures. Finally, he sees pastoral counseling as the liberation praxis where people in groups encounter each other seeking social transformation of their situation. This latter phase is what he calls symbolic collective action—such as marches, protests, and demonstrations—by the poor that calls attention to the issues that impact their lives.[18]

More recently among African American theological intellectuals, however, there is a fermenting of thought that is gaining a healthy respect for the role of the therapeutic in the lives of African Americans. Echoing much of the similar critique as Lartey, Cornel West has critically examined the social situation that many African Americans are in today. He points out that the cultural structures that once supported black life are collapsing all around.[19] He critiques both liberals and conservatives for ignoring the despair and dread that flood the streets of black America, posing a threat to our very existence. West recognizes that nihilism is more than economic deprivation and political powerlessness. He writes, "It is primarily a question of speaking to the profound sense of psychological depression, personal wholeness, and social despair so widespread in black America."[20] West points out that oppressed people are starving for identity, meaning, and

---

[16] Lartey, *Living Colour*, 79–81.
[17] Lartey, *Living Colour*, 94–102.
[18] Lartey, *Living Colour*.
[19] Cornel West, *Race Matters* (New York: Vintage Books, 1994), 17–31.
[20] West, *Race Matters*, 20.

self-worth. He recognizes that too much attention to the social political realities of black people often means neglecting personal dimensions, and that this contributes to the nihilism or the loss of love, meaning, and purpose. Thus, West calls for the political and the therapeutic to join forces to address not only the sociopolitical agenda of liberation, but also the nihilism that is eclipsing the social and racial progress of African Americans.

Within African American pastoral theology, several voices have emerged that link the ethical/political dimensions with the pastoral. Key in these emerging voices is a view of the self as active rather than passive, a self that has the capacity of transforming itself and others despite the presence of oppression and racism. As early as 1982, Archie Smith explored the relationship of liberation ethics and the practice of psychotherapy.[17] He considered ethics as our response to God's divine liberation activity through action and reflection on God's liberation activity. He built on the concept of the relational self as an agent in the liberation struggle as well as in the authoring of one's own life.[22] Thus, he contended, the self need not be a victim of oppression, but can actively get involved in the transformation of self and others despite racism and oppression. Thus, Smith says:

> Since society and the self are interrelated and interwoven realities, both social ethics and therapy may be seen as part of a praxis that understands social transformation and psychic liberation to be inseparable. Social ethics and therapy employ a reflexive, self-critical methodology which seeks to free human life from fetishism and idolatrous forms of faith and to enable people to reconstitute themselves in light of new self-understanding of a just and liberating social order.[23]

From her particular perspective, Carroll Watkins Ali draws on African American women's experience to focus on the tasks of survival and liberation.[24] For her, survival is the capacity to resist systematic oppression and genocide and to recover the self from abuse and dehumanization. Liberation is total freedom from oppression and the ability to engage in the transformation of oppressive culture through political resistance.

Elaine Crawford, a womanist theologian, also lifts up the concept of the agency of self in the face of oppression.[25] She sees the transformative process of the engagement of the self with God using the creative power

---

[17] Smith, *Relational Self*.

[22] Smith, *Relational Self*, 62–64.

[23] Smith, *Relational Self*, 71–72.

[24] Carroll A. Watkins Ali, *Survival and Liberation: Pastoral Theology in African American Context* (St. Louis: Chalice Press, 1999), 2.

[25] A. Elaine Crawford, *Hope in the Holler: A Womanist Theology* (Louisville: Westminster John Knox, 2002), xvi.

of reinterpretation of scripture as being key to gaining new and liberating perspective on one's self and its relationship to society. Here again the self becomes an agent in the transformation of self and in society.

Carolyn McCrary explores the concept of internalized oppression and how such oppression functions at a depth level in African Americans.[26] She builds on the depth psychological perspective of the British school of psychoanalysis and object relations theory to explicate the power that internalized oppression has on the interior lives of African Americans. For her, internalized oppression results from internalized negative relationships that sabotage personal growth. Therapy then enables internalized oppressive relationships to be replaced by liberating and nurturing ones as the counselee uses the therapist as transitional internalized support to transform existing negative inner relationships.

Homer Ashby is another pastoral theologian who develops the notion of the self as an agent through the concept of home not as a place, but as an attitude that enables African Americans to be at home in the world by engagement with the biblical story and political transformation of space.[27] The process of being at home in a strange land is an interior process involving practices for the recovery of the self and for self-formation, yet the process of interiority is not unrelated to the external process of liberation. Drawing on Watkins Ali's distinction between survival and liberation he says:

> These concrete actions flow from the interior process of self-formation and make themselves manifest in exterior campaigns of liberation. Understood in this way survival is a necessary precursor to liberation. Without a clear sense of identity and destiny it is impossible to act with the necessary internal fortitude to engage in resistance and transformation. A prerequisite to liberation is time and energy devoted to the survival functions. The liberation function rests upon the survival functions in order to bring them to full and satisfactory completion.[28]

For him, then, the survival function, which involves the recovery of identity and of the self, eventuates in political action. Thus, liberation and survival functions are interrelated. In his mind, part of the problem with African Americans in the twenty-first century is the exclusive attention to the liberation function without attending to the survival function.

[26] Carolyn McCrary, plenary presentation at the Society for Pastoral Theology Annual Meeting, Atlanta, Ga., June 2004.

[27] Ashby, *Our Home*, 37–42.

[28] Ashby, *Our Home*, 39.

This chapter has introduced the idea that African American pastoral counseling is inherently a political process that leads African Americans into full participation in shaping their own destiny. Pastoral counseling also operates as a political process in that it attends to the ways in which African Americans have been recruited into negative self-images that destroy human agency and prevent full participation in society. African American pastoral counseling draws on the practices of self and care in the editing process. The practices of the self and care are grounded in the notion of conversation and discourse, which inform what people internalize. African American pastoral counseling has become a countercultural movement because it orients African American Christians toward the ultimate grantor of worth and value: God. As a result, the source of identity and meaning in life shifts away from the honor and shame norms of wider culture.

To a great extent, African American pastoral counseling tries to show the limitations of the political process in the allocation of scarce resources. Though necessary, the importance of political processes for granting worth and dignity must always be tempered by the reality that worth and dignity are gifts from God.

African American pastoral counseling helps us to develop human agency in the direction of contributing to the common good not as a way to earn dignity. Rather, our development of agency and our participation in acts of kindness and justice are attempts to respond to the gift of worth and dignity from God. It is a response to God's love manifested in Jesus Christ.

Finally, African American pastoral counseling has historically attended to the political and social agenda impacting African Americans. What is different today is that the voices of African American pastoral counselors will be heeded more because the restoration of village functions in the African American community and the linking of personal agency with political efficacy pull pastoral counselors into public debate.

• • •

The Parish Context of African American Pastoral Counseling*

We each build the foundation for becoming a self and for developing personal agency through the conversations we internalize in whatever families and networks of relationships we are raised. This chapter looks particularly at the local congregation as an original meaning-making environment, an environment that provides foundational practices for the development of the self. It also explores graduate theological education as a shaping environment for understanding pastoral counseling as a political process.

Pastoral Counseling and the Home

As a boy growing up in a small southern New Jersey home, I used to watch my father accompany people through our living room to his study. My father, a pastor of a small Methodist church, was particularly adept as a pastoral counselor. He had spent many years taking courses and volunteering in hospitals when the pastoral care movement was just attaining credibility in the early 1950s. At the time I witnessed the people tracking through our living room, I had no idea what was going on in the study, though I did surmise that there were some significant and serious conversations taking place between my father and parishioners. Not until much later did I begin to realize that my father was providing pastoral counseling to people, and this realization identified for me the actual source of my initiation into both the profession of pastoral counseling and my understanding of being called to a ministry primarily of pastoral counseling.

But as a child, I was not simply an observer of my father's ministry: I was also privileged to accompany my father on some of his pastoral visitations to parishioners' homes. My father would begin taking Holy Communion to the sick and shut-ins on the first Sunday of each month, and he would continue the rest of that week until he had completed visiting all of those who were not able to come to church. Most of the time, I would be allowed to come inside and watch the activity, but on those occasions that I would be asked to leave I understood that some serious conversation between grown-ups was about to take place at which it would be best if I were not present. Whether hearing the conversations or not, I was being shaped by my father's practice of ministry. For example, my father was always attentive to greetings and finding out about how the parishioners

*   This chapter was previously published in Edward P. Wimberly, *African American Pastoral Care and Counseling: The Politics of Oppression and Empowerment* (Cleveland: Pilgrim Press, 2006), 37–60. Used by permission.

were feeling. He would always engage in conversations with parishioners before he gave them communion. And so I learned the vital importance of attending to people's needs by listening to their stories about life.

Such experiences became the first source of both my knowledge of and skills in pastoral care and counseling. That my primary profession and orientation to work was formed very early in my development prior to most of my formal education is both immensely satisfying and eye-opening.

And there were other such occasions, part of our everyday household activities—occasions for learning pastoral counseling skills by overhearing my parents' dinnertime bantering about the nature of counseling. My mother would say to my father, "You don't know anything about counseling," Quickly adding, "Counseling is not giving advice." My father would respond with just as much assurance and speed: "I don't give advice."

Such brief exchanges between my father and mother reflected the wider academic conversation taking place in the profession of counseling and pastoral counseling. In the 1950s Carl Rogers made popular the notion of nondirective counseling. Rogers cautioned against advice giving and directive approaches to counseling; he urged counselors to employ empathy and trust of the counselees' inner direction in helping the counselee achieve his or her therapeutic goals. To some extent, Rogers was revising his own understanding of what many ministers did in counseling as he saw it; his father was a minister, and he grew up in a parsonage. Rogers' life work was to put in secular language the theological understanding and meaning of self-giving and selfless love. He called such love "unconditional positive regard" and "entering into the internal frame of reference" of the counselee.

My childhood and youth were privileged in that I was a willing witness to this debate about the difference between pastoral counseling as direction and pastoral counseling as nondirective conversation between pastoral counselor and counselee, played out both by my parents and by the field. My mother represented the nondirective, empathic Rogerian perspective, my father the more traditional and directive approach. At the time my maturational age did not permit me to appreciate in any depth what I was learning experientially by listening to my parents' conversation. Nonetheless, a significant foundation was being laid that would propel me naturally into the profession of pastoral counseling.

Part of this natural propulsion was the fact that my mother was a guidance counselor in the Philadelphia public school system, while my father was a pastor and began to attend pastoral counseling classes at what was then known as Temple University School of Theology (later Conwell School of Theology at Temple University). My original formation environment provided the basic foundation for knowledge and skills in counseling that made it easier for me to enter into professional and academic counseling. What I had internalized from my childhood formation surfaced later to be developed into my approach to pastoral care and counseling, which I subsequently called African American pastoral care and counseling.

This formational environment I later mined for nuggets of wisdom. For example, my mother's understanding of counseling came from her training in social work and guidance and counseling. Her understanding of counseling was deeply Rogerian, believing in the capacity of each person to actualize his or her full possibilities given the right supportive emotional environment. On the other hand, my father's understanding of counseling came from experiences in parish ministry as well as from his courses in pastoral counseling in the 1950s and 1960s, when pastoral counseling was becoming part of theological education. He believed in the role of the pastor as a guide who gave wisdom about problems without taking over the decision-making process. He did not mind being active and direct in sharing his wisdom. My father saw the value of counseling psychology for his role as a parish pastor. He understood the role of empathy and attending to the internal frame of the person in creating relationships with parishioners, yet he also knew that he had the freedom to help people to solve problems and to suggest practical solutions. What strikes me now about the conversational environment of my childhood is the fact that my father seemed to be able to capture the essence of counseling, which is empathy, and to use it in his work as a pastor who made strategic intervention with concrete ideas about how to solve problems.

My mother's critique was the fact that my father was not a Rogerian purist. She was correct. He made his parish context central in that he was the leader who offered direction and guidance, yet he did so without making parishioners children. He also took seriously their feelings and their own points of view about their problems. In short, he drew from counseling theory only those ideas and principles he needed to help empower people within his parish.

The context in which one works and lives informs what one does in counseling, I learned. The educational guidance counseling movement and social work contextual world influenced what my mother did with her schoolchildren and youth. What my father did with counseling was also shaped by his work as a pastor in an African American and Methodist context. For example, I recall how my father shared his wisdom with my wife when we lost our first child, who was born two months prematurely—a difficult situation for both of us. My father was very empathic with the loss both of us felt, but it was his sharing of wisdom with my wife that made her have hope. He said at one point that Diana Key, as we named our child, was now with God. He said she came from God and now she was back with God. For my wife, the conversation and my father's words were the funeral and the eulogy that we never had. She felt my dad understood just what she needed emotionally as well as spiritually. His direct words were comforting and offered her a new framework for understanding our loss, one that presented a hopeful perspective.

My mother, on the other hand, besides being empathic, would draw on non-directive-oriented counseling. For example, she would always ask evocative questions that got others to think deeply about their problems without offering much in the way of advice or suggestions. My father, however, employed empathy along with being more direct and sharing his wisdom and also stories.

The practice of counseling is influenced by the knowledge and skills that are implied in the practice of counseling within particular contexts. Michel Foucault is correct because he emphasized that discourse or conversation is an act or event that forms a complete meaning system, and it shapes behavior. Moreover, attention to discourse or conversation also reveals much about the practices that shape professional identity.[1] Indeed, our original conversational environment provides all the knowledge and skills we need to engage in everyday and professional life. What we must do, however, is to mine what is learned from these original contexts in our professional education.

The family of origin or our family of birth is the primary meaning-making environment that provides the original context where our primary needs are met. As infants, we are born into a world that is rich in conversation and discourse as well as in relationships. Originally, we don't have the capacity to participate in conversations, but we have the ability through our relationships with others to catch felt meaning and impressions. As a result, we are then able to form these into words, sentences, and stories as we grow through the life cycle. Our capacity for internalizing relationships and attitudes of others is basic to our existence as persons, and the quality of relationships with others enables us to feel loved, cared for, worthwhile, and valued at a very basic level of our existence as infants. Later in our growth and development the felt impressions formed prior to language make up the foundation, which becomes the source of our identity and personality. At the same time we begin to use words, sentences, and stories to understand ourselves as we develop the cognitive capacities to think, reflect, and tell and retell stories.

[1] Michel Foucault, *The Birth of the Clinic: An Archaeology of Medical Perception* (New York: Vintage Books, 1973), xv–xix.

The family of origin, the family of birth, the family of creation, and the family of rearing are our first memberships in community, and the things learned in these early membership contexts become foundational for us. Thus, the lessons learned in them must be attended to when we begin to think about what influences our basic understanding of reality.

Such reflecting back on our original meaning-making contexts is more than mere reflection; it is a practice of remembering in which we identify and acknowledge those persons who contributed significantly to the stories that shape our identities, our knowledge of ourselves and of the world, and the skills that we employ in eating with others and the world.[2] To recall and to remember stories that shaped our lives in our original meaning-making contexts contributes to our ongoing development and ability to further our identity development as well as continuing to develop the vocation to which we have been called.

For me, a significant example of using the wisdom of the past in the present is the work I am currently doing in spiritual renewal. As a child, my father would tell the congregation his call story at least twice a year. I remember his call story very well. At the time I heard it as a youth, it provided me with the expectation that I would possibly be called to the ministry in a similar way as my father. My own call, however, was different in that my call was not dramatic. I just became aware at sixteen that I wanted to be in ministry. My call was influenced by a group of youth who insisted that I bring the word of God one evening at our youth camp. While I resisted mightily, they insisted just as vigorously.

In the mid-1990s following my heart surgery I revisited my childhood memories of Father's call story. I was flat on my back for at least a week, and I had eight weeks to spend in recovery. I used the time as a spiritual retreat to listen to God, and the result was a reorientation in the way I lived my life. I became a vegetarian, and I knew I had to live my life risking more intimacy with my wife, since I discovered that fear of intimacy is often a major factor in clogging arteries.

My heart problems came during my midlife crises. I realized in resolving my midlife crisis that my father told his call story at times when he needed to be reminded of why he chose ministry as his life's work. As a means of spiritual renewal, I subsequently began to develop workshops based on how my father recalled his call story. My publication of the book *Recalling Our Own Stories: Spiritual Renewal for Religious Caregivers* was the

---

[2] Michael White provides this understanding of remembering practices in *Narratives of Therapists' Lives* (Adelaide, South Australia: Dulwich Centre Publications, 1997), 8.

result.[3] Periodically, I also return to my own call story as a way to renew
my life. More recently, I have begun to recall my miraculous recovery from
bypass surgery as my second call story. My father's pattern of recalling is
call story is something I employ constantly as a means of renewal as well as
a means of sharing with others.

From these original contexts we encounter local discourses and communities of wisdom, which then are often disqualified and relegated by
some contemporary perspectives as invalid folk wisdom that is useless in
negotiating life. We are discovering that our original contexts of meaning
are essential to the way we live today, and to marginalize them and render
them useless severely handicaps our abilities to participate in life at all levels. In other words, recalling practices that lead us to remember the original shaping influences in our lives helps to facilitate our full participation
in life at all levels. In short, our ability to exercise our political agency that
leads to full participation in life involves revisiting those original meaning-
generating contexts associated with our families of origin and birth.

The Parish and Pastoral Counseling

I became the pastor of a local congregation in 1966. I was in my second
year of theological education. In 1968, at the end of my seminary education, I went to another congregation, which I served until 1974. My first
congregation was an all-white congregation in a small town in central Massachusetts near the New Hampshire boarder. My second congregation was
African American in a city environment in central Massachusetts, which I
served until I completed my doctorate in philosophy. In both congregations
I learned a great deal about the political meaning of pastoral counseling.

So I began my pastoral ministry in 1966 in a small town in central
Massachusetts, and shortly after, in the fall of 1967 embarked on my first
Clinical Pastoral Education (CPE) experience at Boston State Hospital.
The Vietnam War was very prominent, and it was the subject matter of
many of our classes. The small town in which I was the pastor had five
churches, and the veterans organizations were strong. The townspeople
took their patriotism very seriously.

My congregation was a joint venture of two different congregations
that had joined together because of declining populations. One congregation was United Methodist, and the other congregation was Episcopal.
Most of the congregants were retired, although there were a few young and
middle-aged couples in the church. To my surprise, many were conservative

---

[3] Edward P. Wimberly, *Recalling Our Own Stories: Spiritual Renewal for Religious Caregivers*
(San Francisco: Jossey-Bass, 1997).

Republicans; prior to coming to this town, I had thought that all people in the world were New Deal Democrats! For the first time I met people who thought that Franklin D. Roosevelt was the worst person on earth because of his economic policies.

Another segment of the congregation was a group of seventy or so young boys who attended a local boarding high school. The Vietnam War was on their minds. While in seminary, we were urged to address the Vietnam War from the pulpit because many felt we should end this war for a variety of reasons. Given the youth and their eventually having to enter the draft, I decided to take a stand from the pulpit against the Vietnam War. I was about to embark on my first real lesson about the nature of politics and its relationship to pastoral care and counseling.

Not long into my sermon on Vietnam, one of the older ladies of the congregation stood up and rushed out of the church. I could not miss the fact that she was very upset and disturbed about what I was saying. I was shocked at her leaving; it rattled me, and I had difficulty completing my sermon without reading it word for word. I did not know what to do or where to turn. My assumption had been that the Vietnam War was unpopular for everybody.

The very next day I went to Boston for my CPE class. In my school reflection group, I brought up what had happened the previous day in church. My clinical supervisor told me to go visit the woman who walked out of the church and to be open to what I would learn. I went, and she gave me an earful about how she felt and why she thought I had committed an unpardonable sin.

This woman had spent all of her adult life as a schoolteacher, and she had had to resign recently due to an incapacitating illness. She indicated that her meaning in life was derived from teaching her young students that "it was my country right or wrong." What I had done was very offensive to her; I had undermined her reason for teaching all those many years.

What surprised me was the fact that I was not able to leave this woman's home for over three hours. In time, I came to find out that she was very lonely, and she appreciated my visits and looked forward to them. Although we differed politically, she thought of herself as a teacher of this young black male in his first pastorate who needed to be educated about how things really are in the world and in that community. My visits helped her to express her deep feelings of loss and also helped her to find meaning in what she could actually do with her life without teaching. In short, I was helping her to find other avenues of meaning making, and she in turn taught me to question my assumptions.

My experience with this woman was a critical lesson in recognizing that pastoral counseling enables people to participate meaningfully in life. Part of the political process is enabling everyone to participate in life as fully as they are able. When obstacles occur, whether they are the result of racial discrimination or incapacitating illness, the practices of care motivate people to keep on "keeping on" despite the circumstances and to find meaningful avenues of participation. This is the true meaning of the political process: the capacity to participate to our fullest ability in life and in decision making.

In this small congregation I learned that the practices of care had empowering possibilities. In 1968 Martin Luther King was assassinated while I was pastor of this congregation. Immediately, the town responded. My wife and I had a steady flow of visitors from my congregation and from the town's people. They were profoundly impacted by the murder of Dr. King. Immediately, I was asked to do a memorial service at my church and to preach a memorial service honoring Dr. King.

These stories that I have told from my family of origin and my first parish show how I began to learn how pastoral counseling is a political process. These original contexts are all communities of close kinship networks, whether blood or fictive ties, and communities of daily support that help us maintain our emotional, interpersonal, and physical integrity as persons. Such networks include not only our families and extended families; they also include voluntary associations like churches, neighborhood associations, and small groupings in which we encounter others on a daily basis.

These communities of original membership provide vital environments and contexts for dynamic and meaningful conversations and discourses that shape our primary orientation to life. Such conversations tell us what is significant and important to life and inform how we live, move, and act in the world. They define for us how we relate to ourselves and to others. They give us clues to what we should internalize from wider culture, and they help us navigate the many conversations that we hear in our lives. These original environments help us shape the overarching meaning system or framework for our convictions and beliefs: who we are as human beings, how we are to relate to others, and how we are to participate in life at all levels. Such a conversational convictional system provides us with messages that inform our worth and value as human beings: they tell us why we are here, what our calling is in life, and how we should negotiate the world outside of our original memberships and formation contexts. In addition, these original contexts model conversational practices, which also help to orient us to what is significant for making meaning in our lives and to have similar conversations ourselves.

In brief, our original membership communities represent social capital or a reservoir of resources on which to draw, enabling full participation in life. Moreover, these original membership communities are mediating structures that stand between the individual and wider society. The role of these mediating structures is to modify the conversational messages of wider society so that they facilitate authentic and meaningful participating in life.

Mining Original Knowledge in Professional Education and the Political Process

In addition to pastoral care in the parish setting, I also learned about pastoral care in graduate professional education. There was a major crisis in my work on the Ph.D. when I was working at the Danielsen Pastoral Counseling Center at Boston University. When I entered the Ph.D. program at Boston University Graduate School in 1971, I had already completed two years of pastoral counseling training at the Worcester Area Council of Churches. I was steeped in Rogerian therapy; I had thoroughly embraced my mother's side of the counseling tradition. The crisis came when I took my performance examination. My professors and supervisors told me that I was not a Rogerian, and that I needed to return to my counseling and try to become more authentic, more fully myself. In other words, they saw a side of me that related to the way my father had integrated counseling into his pastoral identity, and they wanted me to get in touch with this side of me so that my approach to pastoral counseling resonated fully, not only partly, with who I was, how I understood myself, what I had learned from my original family and parish learning contexts. Essentially I was being told to do what Michael White calls re-membership, or returning to our original knowledge and skills learned in early conversational environments.[4] Not only was I given permission to embrace my past, I was also being empowered to actualize who I truly was as a human being and to use it as I participated fully in the academic process. Thanks to their prompting and their insistence, I was learning what political empowerment was all about: discovering the gifts that I had as a human being and using them to make a place for myself and others in society.

To be empowered to the fullest, I had to learn how I presented myself to the world. When I was growing up, I was a very poor student. In fact, I did not learn to read until I was in the eighth grade. My inability to read was hampered by both internal and external processes. The internal processes, I came to learn, were related to the personality character disorder known as

---

[4] White, *Therapists' Lives*, 22.

passive aggressiveness. Passive aggressiveness is a behavioral pattern where anger is neither expressed openly nor directly. Rather, anger goes underground and is expressed through stubbornness and sullen attitudes, and through inefficiency and procrastination. All are strategies used to defeat authority figures.[5] The hallmark strategy used by many passive-aggressive children is the inability to read. For me, having parents who were highly educated and who had high academic expectations was a threat to my own sense of power. Thus, I unconsciously felt that I had to defeat them in order for me to have any autonomy at all.

I mention passive aggressiveness not only because it was an unconscious pattern I used to handle my anger; I lift it up also because it was a convenient cultural pattern that was used by many African American males in pre-civil rights days. One could lose one's life if anger was expressed openly. Anger is a source of personal agency if used properly and constructively, and anger could be channeled in ways that challenged the racial structures and conversations that disempowered African Americans. Thus, any sign of anger, whether constructive or not, would be confronted by whites.

So in fact by being passive aggressive and not learning to read I was disempowering myself. I was not presenting myself authentically to the world, although I would survive and live a long life as a black male. Thus, my first lesson in empowerment came when I realized that I had to claim and demonstrate the intelligence that I actually had and use it proactively.

Pastoral counseling training and my work toward the Ph.D. in pastoral psychology and counseling helped me to claim my intellectual gifts and to mine lessons my parents tried to teach me earlier, which I had been too stubborn to learn then. First, my parents told me that intelligence was not a gift that only a few possessed—as whites insisted. My parents said over and over again that intelligence came as the result of hard work and study. Second, they insisted that I was intelligent, but that I refused to use my intelligence. Pastoral counseling training pointed out that one of my patterns of negotiating the world was to put myself down, falsely presenting myself to the world. My supervisors indicated that I was not playing fair by letting others think that I was not intelligent or less than what I was. They challenged me to present my real self to others, and this was the road to full empowerment. They said I had to risk being myself no matter the consequences; this was the only true way to live.

Not claiming my gifts and intelligence was an unfair game to play. It was my way of consciously determining who was a racist. Racists would automatically buy into the way I initially defined myself without ever trying

---

[5] Norman Cameron, *Personality Development and Psychopathology: A Dynamic Approach* (Boston: Houghton Mifflin, 1963), 650–51.

to find out who I really was. Nonracists would look beyond my initial self-presentation to see who I really was. Nonracists would eventually see who I was and embrace who I was, so I reasoned.

Pastoral counseling taught me to be proactive about how I wanted to be seen by others. I learned not to wait for permission to be myself. Rather, I learned that I was in charge of how I wanted the world to see me. Thus, being an authentic self became a political act of empowerment given the nature of racism in the United States.

The problems that I had in reading also had a legacy in slavery. Learning to read in the cultural climate of slavery was forbidden. Although I was far removed from slavery in that I was born in 1943, the fact that I had a twisted understanding of intelligence despite my parents' conscious attempt to counteract it proves that the cultural legacy of inferiority and superiority surrounding intelligence survived slavery, and I had learned it well.[6] I actually internalized as a child the conviction that real intelligence was a gift that I did not have, and only the gifted had it. I was not one of the gifted people, and neither were my peers. Thus, my own convictional structure disempowered me.

Several learning experiences in the classroom in graduate school helped me to edit my internalized oppression. The first was a course in psychological measurement where I learned about how intelligence was measured. The second was reading Carl Jung's book called *Psychology and Education*; the third relates to understanding the multiple levels of intelligence beyond the emphasis on just intellectual intelligence. The language for talking about multiple levels of intelligence comes from the contemporary movement known as emotional intelligence.

My convictional or belief structure, which was challenged by graduate school, was well established by the time I went to college and graduate school. I grew up in a community context where the dominant cultural conversation driving education was a belief in the inherent inferiority of African Americans. While the message of the innate inferiority of African Americans became explicit at times, the way my peers and I internalized this message was very subtle and hardly conscious. For example, we believed that being smart was an innate gift with which one was born. If one were not gifted from birth, one was predestined to being a mediocre or poor student, and therefore, one person should not try hard to obtain educational things that were out of one's grasp. In my school environment, this belief was never openly challenged, and the really gifted students sat

---

[6] See Catherine Owens Peare, *Mary McLeod Bethune* (New York: Vanguard Press, 1951) for stories of how the prohibition against African Americans reading survived slavery.

in the front of the class, and the mediocre and less gifted students sat in the back of the class.

Of course, I sat in the back of the class believing that I was an average student at best. My father, however, understood how racism worked, and he set out to convince me that I was neither stupid nor average. I remember one incident in the seventh grade, where he called me to his study. He then locked the door and said, "Not one of us will be leaving this study until you realize you are not stupid and that learning is a matter of hard work." Of course, I resisted, but at the end of the day I knew I could learn. He had begun his professional career as a teacher in Florida when segregation was at its highest point in the 1930s, and had long since understood how many students had internalized the dominant conversation of racial inferiority.

The congregation that my father served also tried to counter the racial myth of intellectual inferiority. My Sunday school teacher never believed that my poor reading was due to poor intelligence. She always encouraged me by offering alternative explanations for my poor reading skills.

Because of my father, my Sunday school teacher, and some other teachers along the way, I did internalize an alternative message about learning. Learning was hard work, yet I was capable of doing far more academically than I had earlier understood or believed. It was not until I was working on my doctor of philosophy degree, however, that I began to find theoretical evidence for what my father and church people were saying about intelligence. I took a course in psychological testing and measurement. We had to actually buy the standardized intelligence tests that were administered at that time. We also had to order the explanations about the statistical reliability and validity of each test question. In the process, I learned that each test question was based on concrete but subtle intellectual skills that were not innate, but which could be actually practiced and learned. My high school football coach used to say this, and he urged the African American football players to begin taking the SAT test in the tenth grade like the white students did. Yet most of us did not pay any attention to him. His point was that these tests were not so much aptitude tests measuring innate intelligence but achievement tests focusing on real skills that were taught and reinforced within the educational environment of the school.

It was only when I saw the concrete examples of how intelligence tests are created that I finally accepted that learning was more about hard work and achievement than innate intelligence. Consequently, the mystifying and intimidating belief that whites were innately intellectually superior to black people was finally toppled.

I also learned another significant thing about intelligence while preparing for my German language exam for my Ph.D. I had to read Carl

Jung's book *Psychology of Education* in its original German and be tested on interpreting a passage in it.[7] Chapter 4 is about the gifted child, and this book gave me an understanding of the multiple natures of human intelligence beyond the debate in the United States confining intelligence only to intellectual intelligence. What Jung taught me was that intelligence is more than technical or rational, and it includes what Jung calls the emotional and ethical dimensions.[8] In his essay "The Gifted Child" he says that there are gifts of the mind and gifts of the heart.[9] He summarizes his convictions about intelligence by drawing on his profession as a psychotherapist. He concludes: "Psychotherapy has taught us that in the final reckoning it is not knowledge, not technical skill that has curative effect, but the personality of the doctor. And it is the same with education: it presupposes self-education."[10]

He goes on to say that gifts of intelligence can be used to the extent that the personality grows and develops, and that intelligence is multileveled. Accepting this fact enabled me to embrace my own gifts of intelligence. My formal education at the graduate level opened me to different understandings of intelligence in general and my intelligence in particular that propelled me beyond internalized racist notions of my intellectual inferiority.

My family of origin, my church, and my educational experiences in graduate school helped me to edit wider racist cultural expectations that would have disenfranchised me from full participation in society. Racism by its very nature is political in that it seeks to exclude people from full participation in society by recruiting them into negative stories, plots, and images. Whenever these pejorative images, plots, and stories are challenged and transformed through editing, liberation to be full participants in society at all levels is taking place.

The point of dealing with one's own internalized racism is extremely important, because it helps us to do two things on the structural level. Racism is structural where avenues for full participation in society are systemically cut off. Racism is also symbolic: it exists at the levels of cultural symbols that inform the conversations and ideas we internalize. When structural racism is addressed and eliminated at the policy level, however, racism can still exist at the symbolic level. Thus, symbolic-level racism

---

[7] C. G. Jung, *Psychology and Education*, Bollinger Series (Princeton: Princeton University Press, 1954). This book was the result of translating four of eight essays in vol. 17 of the *Collected Works*. Three of the essays were published in *Psychologie und Erziehung* (1946).

[8] Jung, *Psychology and Education*, 129–30.

[9] Jung, *Psychology and Education*.

[10] Jung, *Psychology and Education*, 130.

keeps us in bondage even if structural racism disappears. It is our challenge to help people continue editing their lives.

Some Final Comments on the Congregational/ Parish Context of Pastoral Counseling

It is clear that my original memberships in local congregations shaped my understanding of racism and how to deal with it at the symbolic and structural levels. The question remains, however: what conclusions can be drawn for the role of pastoral counseling as a political process that grows out of the parish context? Pastoral counseling that takes place within the context of a local African American congregation is influenced by the dominant beliefs and convictions of that congregation, particularly about the nature of human beings and about the way human beings are empowered to participate in society. Two examples can make this case.

First, Alice Wiley, a former doctor of ministry student whose dissertation committee I chaired, helped me to visualize that pastoral counseling practiced within a local congregation takes on the dominant convictions and beliefs of that local congregation. She demonstrated in her dissertation how certain womanist values espoused in a local congregation, of which she and her husband were pastors, shaped the development of a pastoral counseling center within their church. Key in her dissertation were relational values of care and nurture and how important they were in empowering others. She talked about how she prepared her congregation for the counseling center by preaching sermons reflecting the womanist values of relationships and caring and how they were outgrowths of the role of women in extended families and in the life of local churches. She concluded that the convictions and values of that congregation permeated the whole center, particularly because the trained counselors were recruited from the church's membership.[11]

A second example that confirms the fact that pastoral counseling within a parish context takes on the values of the congregation is made by a story that Don Browning includes in one of his publications, *A Fundamental Practical Theology: Descriptive and Strategic Proposals*. It is an example of the congregational care program of a local African American Pentecostal congregation.[12]

---

[11] Christine Y. Wiley, "The Impact of a Parish-Based Pastoral Counseling Center on Counselors and Congregation: A Womanist Perspective" (DMin diss., Garrett-Evangelical Theological Seminary, Evanston, Ill., 1994).

[12] Don S. Browning, *A Fundamental Practical Theology: Descriptive and Strategic Proposals* (Minneapolis: Fortress, 1991), 243–77.

The congregational care is carried out by many groups and departments of that congregation. The pastor delegates responsibilities, but he also supervises the caring activities. His supervision includes creating a shared theology and ethics of care among all who participate in the program. "Many important religious beliefs and values are communicated by the way we care for one another," says the pastor.[13] The caring ministries include lay ministers who visit the sick in hospitals and the elderly in nursing homes, take communion to shut-ins, and staff the prayer phone lines. There were also outreach ministries to prisons and to projects where the poor lived. Browning concludes his observations on the relationship of the caring practices of the congregation with its beliefs and convictions in the following way:

> Given this part of my background, it surprised me to see the extent of psychological language, insights, and attitudes in this African American Pentecostal church. The number of mental health professionals, school counselors, social workers, and teaches trained in psychology far exceeded my expectations. But the moral and theological framework that guided the use of these psychologies was not the framework of most mainline Protestant churches. There was not "triumph of the therapeutic," to use Reiff's felicitous phrase, at the Apostolic Church.
>
> In his preaching, teaching, and example Brazier (the pastor) set the theological and ethical framework for using the modern psychologies. Yet it grew out of the similarities between his experience and the experiences of his people in the inner city and in their congregation with Scripture.[14]

Browning goes on to say that the ethical framework for using modern psychologies was clearly related to married couples, families, and the task of raising children rather than individualism or ethical egoism. The concern was the significance of the black family and its reconstruction. But there was also a strong ministry to singles.[15]

The manner in which convictions and beliefs are espoused within the life of the church impacts the way ministries of care are carried out. Although the church was Pentecostal, there was a great concern for developing persons for outreach to the community. Becoming productive citizens and contributing to the common good were what Christians were supposed to be about. The congregation was also concerned to connect church work with community organizations in order to bring low- and moderate-income housing to the community, to improve local schools, to fight drugs, and to bring businesses and banks to the local community. Although there is a

[13] Browning, *Fundamental*, 253.
[14] Browning, *Fundamental*, 256.
[15] Browning, *Fundamental*.

liberation theology, this theology is subservient to the theology of salvation and redemption, according to Browning.[16] This approach is important to demonstrate that evangelical theology can engage and lead to full participation in society, just as liberation theologies do. Social outreach and political activism cut across theological lines. The family and the local congregation are vital contexts for providing meaningful conversations that can be drawn on for a lifetime. The original shaping contexts provide significant resources to support our full participation in life using all of our gifts.

[16] Browning, *Fundamental*, 253.

6

African American Narrative Pastoral Care (2008)

In this revised edition of his flagship text, Edward Wimberly offers a fuller statement of the relevance of *narrative* approaches to pastoral care in African American contexts.* He offers a model of narrative pastoral care that invites parishioners to analyze the destructive social and political narratives they have absorbed through culture and deconstruct these myths, in order to re-write the scripts and stories they choose to live by, relying on biblical narratives for inspiration. Wimberly also asserts the importance of social support networks to enable parishioners to continue to live out of their preferred, alternative stories.

In the first essay reprinted here, Wimberly explains how black pastors have long understood the value of story-listening and storytelling. He defines narrative pastoral care as a way of helping people find hope through seeing themselves in the faith story. The eschatological hope Wimberly speaks of does not deny experiences of suffering, but rather identifies God's healing presence in the midst of suffering. Wimberly suggests that the narrative practice of the "definitional ceremony" has analogues in the village model of pastoral care in the black church.

In the second essay, Wimberly unpacks the idea of the indigenous storyteller as a model for African American pastors ministering to people in times of grief and catastrophic loss, as in the case of Hurricane Katrina. He recognizes the role of poverty and racism in increasing the suffering of

---

* Edward P. Wimberly, "A Narrative Approach to Pastoral Care," in *African American Pastoral Care*, rev. ed. (Nashville: Abingdon, 2008), 1–15; Wimberly, "Pastoral Care and Support Systems: Illness, Bereavement, and Catastrophic Loss," in *African American Pastoral Care*, 31–45.

African Americans in this disaster. Wimberly stresses the task of drawing people into "God's salvation drama of death and rebirth" (201) and the importance of familial and communal support, as well as public mourning and political accountability in such circumstances.

These essays find contemporary relevance in light of continuing race-related loss of life, including the rising toll of deaths among African Americans due to police violence. How can African American communities process such loss and terror? Wimberly's adaptation of *narrative* care principles together with his emphasis on *prophetic* engagement in public life offer a possible starting place.

Further Reading

Wimberly, Edward P. "Unnoticed and Unloved: The Indigenous Storyteller and Public Theology in a Postcolonial Age." *Verbum Et Ecclesia* 32, no. 2 (2011). doi:10.4102/ve.v32i2.506.

• • •

A Narrative Approach to Pastoral Care [*]

Since the publication of *Pastoral Care in the Black Church* in 1979, I have become firmly convinced that black pastors approach pastoral care through narrative. It is this insight about such an approach to ministry that motivated me to write a supplement to that book.

A truly narrative style of pastoral care in the black church draws upon personal stories from the pastor's life, stories from the practice of ministry, and stories from the Bible. Genuine pastoral care from a narrative perspective involves the use of stories by pastors in ways that help persons and families visualize how and where God is at work in their lives and thereby receive healing and wholeness.

This method of pastoral care involves several dangers. The primary danger is that the pastor's own life experience is so subjective and personal that it might be used imperialistically to lead some pastors to think that "my way is the only way." Second, the narrative approach might lead some to think that a personal indigenous style is all that is needed and that formal training has no place. Third, the narrative style might cause the pastor to be less empathetic and thereby transform counselee/parishioner-centered counseling sessions into pastor-focused counseling sessions.

However, a narrative approach need not be imperialistic, nonempathetic, or pastor-focused. Storytelling can facilitate growth and empathy, be parishioner-centered, and contribute to the essential qualities of any caring relationship. For example, this approach can enable the pastor to enter the parishioner's world of experience and see things through the parishioner's own eyes. It can help the parishioner take full responsibility for making his or her own decisions. It can enable the parishioner to be specific when describing events. This approach can also help the counselor openly discuss things that are occurring between the counselor and the parishioner. Finally, it can help the counselor express his or her feelings about what is taking place in the parishioner's life in ways that lead to growth.

This book is an attempt to demonstrate that an indigenous approach to caring that relies upon storytelling is one style of pastoral care and counseling that takes place in the black church. Not only is this style already used by pastors, it is a basic method used by black people, both lay and clergy, to care for one another. Therefore, this book is written for clergy, seminary

---

[*]   This chapter was previously published as "A Narrative Approach to Pastoral Care," in Edward P. Wimberly, *African American Pastoral Care*, rev. ed. (Nashville: Abingdon, 2008), 1–15 and associated notes. © 2008. Abingdon Press. Used by permission. All rights reserved.

students, and laypeople who are interested in knowing how they have cared for one another and how they can improve that care.

The Nature of Storytelling

Black pastors use many types of stories—long stories, anecdotes, short sayings, metaphors—to respond to the needs of their parishioners. Most specific instances in life situations lend themselves to story formation. For example, stories can be used to address the normal crises people face daily, such as birth, a child's first day at school or at day care; transitions from childhood to adolescence or from adolescence to adulthood; and mid-life, old-age, and death transitions. Likewise, story formation can occur during periods of crisis: losses such as illness, accidents, changes in residence, and a variety of other events that pose threats to someone's emotional or physical well-being. Stories also can be developed during selective phases of counseling to facilitate the counseling process.

In all these ways, stories function in the caring setting to bring healing and wholeness to the lives of persons and families within the black pastoral care context. Henry Mitchell and Nicholas Lewter call such stories *soul theology*, the core belief system that gives shape to the world, that shows how African American people have come to grips with the world in a meaningful way.[1] Narratives and stories embody these core beliefs that permeate the church life of African Americans, and black pastors and congregations draw on this narrative reservoir when caring for their members. These narratives suggest ways to motivate people to action, help them see themselves in a new light, help them recognize new resources, enable them to channel behavior in constructive ways, sustain them in crises, bring healing and reconciliation in relationships, heal the scars of memories, and provide guidance when direction is needed.

Soul theology makes up the faith story that undergirds the stories used by black pastors and parishioners in caring for others. And how that faith story has brought healing and wholeness through storytelling to the lives of African American people is the subject of this book.

The Faith Story

Mitchell and Lewter point out that crisis situations spontaneously express core beliefs.[2] Core beliefs are deep metaphors, images that point to the plots or directions of life. These core beliefs, rooted in stories, manifest

---

[1] Henry Mitchell and Nicholas Lewter, *Soul Theology* (New York: Harper & Row, 1986), 11.

[2] Mitchell and Lewter, *Soul Theology*, 3.

themselves in human behavior as people attempt to live their lives. For the African American Christian, deep metaphors are related to the life, death, and resurrection of Jesus Christ, who liberates the oppressed and cares for the downtrodden. These deep metaphors are especially informed by the Exodus story and God's involvement with God's people. These deep metaphors and core beliefs are anchored in the story of God's relationship with God's people, as recorded in Scripture and as lived out within African American churches.

The plot that gives structure to the deep metaphors of the Christian story is important to the faith story. Plots tell us why we live on earth; they point to the direction life is taking.[3] Plot in the Christian faith story shows us how our lives are connected to God's unfolding story. The faith story, therefore, answers the question of the "ultimate why" of our existence.

The dominant plot that gives life meaning for the African American Christian is what I call an eschatological plot, one that envisions hope in the midst of suffering and oppression, because God is working out God's purposes in life on behalf of persons. The eschatological plot takes suffering and oppression very seriously without minimizing their influence in life. Yet despite the prevalence of suffering and oppression, God's story of hope and liberation is unfolding. Although the final chapter of the story of liberation awaits consummation at the end of time, during many moments along life's journey, there is evidence of God's presence, bringing healing, wholeness, and liberation.

Mitchell and Lewter refer to this eschatological plot that underlies the faith story of black Christians as the providence of God:

> The most essential and inclusive of these affirmations of Black core beliefs is called the Providence of God in Western terms. Many Blacks may not have so precise a word for it, and they may not even know that the idea they cling to so naturally is called a doctrine. But in Africa and Afro-America, the most reassured and trusted word about our life here on earth is that God is in charge. This faith guarantees that everyone's life is worth living. The passage that expresses it best is Paul's famous word to the Romans: "And we know that God works in everything for the good of those who love him and are called according to his plan."[4]

The eschatological plot calls the Christian to faith because each must participate in life and in God's unfolding story, knowing that things will work out in the end. The eschatological plot is important because it does not

---

[3] James Hillman, *Healing Fiction* (Barrytown, N.Y.: Station Hill, 1983), 9–12.
[4] Mitchell and Lewter, *Soul Theology*, 14.

minimize suffering and oppression, nor does it give suffering and oppression the last word.

A goal of the narrative approach to pastoral care in the black church has been to link persons in need to the unfolding of God's story in the midst of life. The African American pastor has narrated, and continues to narrate, stories that help people catch a glimpse of hope in the midst of suffering. It is by identifying with the story that Christians have linked themselves to purposeful directions in life, despite suffering and pain.

The eschatological plot, through which God is working out healing, wholeness, and liberation on behalf of others, has four major functions: *unfolding*, *linking*, *thickening*, and *twisting*.[5] God's plot *unfolds* one scene and one chapter at a time, one cannot know the end of the story until the entire drama is completed. However, by identifying with faith stories, particularly stories in the Bible, one can learn to participate in God's drama, while trusting God's authorship of the drama and God's plan for the final outcome. In counseling within the black church, this often has meant that the pastor must ensure that the counselee who is identifying with a biblical story reads the whole story before coming to any conclusions. For example, it is important that one continues the story of Joseph and the coat of many colors until Joseph is occupying an important government position for the second time. To stop reading this story before its end may leave the reader feeling that life is tragic. Only at the end of the story can we see God's purposes for Joseph revealed. When one reads the entire story, one can envision hope in the midst of tragedy.

When one identifies with stories that have an eschatological plot in Scripture, one is not only pointed toward God's unfolding story in the midst of life, one is *linked* with the dynamic that informs the plot. God's unfolding story is more than a good story with which to identify. It is an ongoing, unfolding story, even today, so when black Christians have identified with that story, they also have linked their lives with the dynamic force behind the events of life. When people are linked to God's unfolding story, their own lives become different. Significant changes take place. People find that life has direction for them, that they have value as human beings. The slaves' identification with Israel's exodus is illustrative of such positive outcomes. By linking their lives with the unfolding plot of Israel's exodus, the slaves focused their attention on God, who was also working on their behalf to liberate them.

The eschatological plot also thickens. *Thickening* refers to those events that intrude into God's unfolding story and seek to change the direction

---

[5] James Hopewell, *Congregations, Stories, and Structures* (Philadelphia: Fortress, 1987), 154.

of that story for the ill of all involved. The plot often can thicken when suffering stakes its claim on us. This thickening could be the intrusion of oppression and victimization that, for a time, hinder our growth and development; and it is at such times that we wonder whether God really cares. However, unfortunate negative interruptions are only temporary, and the story again begins to unfold in ways that help us envision God at work, seeking to *twist* the story back to God's original intention, despite the thickening that hindered the plot.

A pastor who understands the working of God through drama can link people with the unfolding of God's story. Such a pastor seeks to help parishioners develop *story language* and *story discernment* in order to visualize how God's drama is unfolding in their lives. This means that telling and listening to stories become central to the caring process. It also means that people learn to follow the plots of stories, to visualize how God is seeking to engage them in the drama as it affects their lives.

The eschatological plot, with its emphasis on God's healing presence in life despite suffering and pain, has been the driving force behind the narrative approach of the black church. By telling and listening to stories, black preachers and congregants have sought to help people envision God's work in the midst of suffering. They have sought to link people with this activity, so that their lives can have significant meaning, despite the reality of suffering.

In addition to the unfolding, linking, thickening, and twisting of plots, faith stories have four types of therapeutic functions: healing, sustaining, guiding, and reconciling.[6] These are the traditional functions of pastoral care and are very much a part of the narrative approach. However, since a narrative approach to pastoral care cannot determine the impact of a story, one cannot predetermine the impact a story might have on a parishioner or counselee. Nevertheless, stories do influence people's lives in characteristic ways: they can heal or bind up wounds caused by disease, infection, and invasion; they can sustain persons in the face of overwhelming odds and lessen the impact of suffering; they can provide guidance to those affected by the personal and interpersonal obstacles that can hinder people's ability to grow. The goal of pastoral care and counseling, from a narrative perspective, is to use storytelling to strengthen people's personal and interpersonal growth so that they can respond to God's salvation drama as it unfolds and as it has an impact on their lives.

From a narrative perspective, pastoral care can be defined as bringing all the resources of the faith story into the context of caring relationships,

---

[6] These functions are defined in Edward P. Wimberly, *Pastoral Care in the Black Church* (Nashville: Abingdon, 1979), 18–23.

to bear upon the lives of people as they face life struggles that are personal, interpersonal, and emotional. The gospel must respond to the personal needs of individuals and families as they face life struggles. This is best done in the private context of pastoral care, rather than in the public context of preaching or worship. Because the context and intent of preaching, worship, and pastoral care are different, the use of storytelling in each ministry is also different.

Story-Listening

So far, this discussion has been devoted to the storytelling aspect of caring. One might conclude that the telling of stories is the main dimension of a narrative approach to pastoral care. The danger of overemphasizing storytelling, however, is that it may ignore the needs of the person facing life struggles. Story-listening is also an important dimension of African American pastoral care, and the narrative approach is a story-listening as well as a storytelling approach.

Story-listening involves empathically hearing the story of the person involved in life struggles. Being able to communicate that the person in need is cared for and understood is a result of attending to the story of the person as he or she talks. *Empathy* means that we attend to the person with our presence, body posture, and nonverbal responses. It also means using verbal responses to communicate that we have understood and are seeking to understand the person's story as it is unfolding. The caregiver also gives attention to and acknowledges the significant feelings of the person as they are expressed in the telling of the story. It is only when the story has been fully expressed and the caregiver has attended to it with empathy that the foundation is laid for the utilization of storytelling.

The emphasis must be on story-listening to avoid the trap of shifting the focus away from the needs of the person facing life struggles. There are two important ways to prevent this potential abuse of storytelling. First, a growing body of literature on storytelling within the context of counseling and psychotherapy can assist pastors in knowing how to use their own life stories in helpful ways. Second, pastors need to grow in their own personal life so that their life stories and participation in the faith story will be a reservoir of conflict-free and anxiety-free stories. The ways one can use new resources from the counseling literature and can grow so that one's life will be an anxiety-free source of stories will be addressed in later chapters.

Storytelling and Retelling the Story

In an age where the village connections are being continually lost, it is important to utilize communal means of storytelling and story-listening as a vehicle for reconstructing village functions. Michael White put forward one such village reconstructive narrative method, the definitional ceremony. In the year 2000, I attended the Milton H. Erickson Institute in Anaheim, California. Here my narrative understanding expanded by leaps and bounds. Michael White, an Australian family therapist, presented a video of a group of Aborigines whose lives had been disrupted by technological advances. Their traditions for dealing with loss and grief had been disrupted, and he was asked to help them come together in order to grieve the loss of a family member who had been murdered. He called his approach to them the definitional ceremony. The definitional ceremony is a narrative process of storytelling and retelling the story where a person who has an emotional concern or issue tells his or her story. It is then followed by a group of persons retelling the original storyteller's story in light of what struck those hearing the story when the original storyteller told the story.[7] The original storyteller becomes part of the audience, and those who were part of the original audience become storytellers and retell the story they heard, drawing on their own lives. Following the retelling of the story, the original storyteller becomes the storyteller again and begins to retell the story in light of what he or she heard from those who retold the original story. The end result of this phase of retelling the story is that the original storyteller gets an opportunity for catharsis by expressing strong feelings as well as by deriving new perspectives on what he or she had been experiencing. The original storyteller also feels cared for and loved by those who took the time to listen and retell the story. A support system of relational ties is thus created, which sustains the person as he or she goes through the grief process. Thus, the supportive and maintaining function of the village was re-created thro ugh the telling and retelling of stories.

An example of this process of telling and retelling stories will be recreated based on a number of telling and retelling story sessions in which I have participated. This particular story is about the grief and loss resulting from sexual abuse triggered by the death of a parent who was the sexual abuser.

The setting was a class in Inner Healing that I have taught since 1985. In the Inner Healing class, the focus is on the student's own life issues, and the goal is to create an atmosphere where students feel comfortable to tell

---

[7] Michael White, *Narratives of Therapists' Lives* (Adelaide, South Australia: Dulwich Centre Publications, 1997), 93.

stories with which they feel comfortable. One way to create an atmosphere of openness where students feel free to share their own stories is for the professor to begin the process of storytelling himself or herself. Thus, depending on the topic, I would share some concerns out of my own life that I felt comfortable sharing. I do not customarily share stories with which I am currently struggling, however. Rather, I share stories out of my own life with which I have dealt in the past and about which I might feel comfortable sharing more information if asked. The major point of telling my own story is not only to demonstrate transparency but also to make sure that the story is such that it will trigger students to think about their own stories rather than focus on my story. If the stories that I tell are unresolved and recent, they might stimulate interest in my own story rather than enable others to tell their own stories.

Before getting into the actual process of telling and retelling stories, it is important to envisage the classroom as a laboratory for recreating village functions. Every class in seminary is an opportunity for the formation of a village. Here the concept of village refers to the process of becoming a support system of relational ties that fosters an environment for enabling members of the class to maintain their emotional, interpersonal, and spiritual integrity in the face of life's complexities.

Indigo was a member of the Inner Healing class. The topic was domestic violence and how domestic violence serves as a relational means of recruiting family members into negative identities for the purpose of building up the perpetrator of the violence at the expense of the victim. The process of recruiting through the use of domestic violence involves getting the potential victim to internalize a negative identity so that the victim becomes a willing participant in his or her own self-destruction and is always available for abuse by the victimizer. As the topic of domestic violence unfolded late in the semester, Indigo felt comfortable in bringing up her own story of domestic violence that was clearly on her mind due to the death of her biological father.

The background to Indigo's story was that she had been in seminary for one year. The first semester went well, but in the second semester a series of deaths began to take place in her family. It began with the death of her grandmother's boyfriend who had sexually molested her when she was a young girl. She was raised by her grandmother, and her grandmother's boyfriend routinely sexually molested her while her grandmother was at work. He was supposed to be watching her after school. He would tell her not to tell anyone what he was doing, threatening more harm to her. Thus, she kept the experiences of sexual abuse quiet, fearing reprisals. His death brought up memories of her past abuse at his hands that she had not shared with others. She pointed out that his death propelled her into the process of remembering key incidences from the past that she knew she had to tell. She felt all right about recalling the memories of the past abuse, but then a series of tragic events began to take place that she did not understand. These events piled on top of the death of her abusing boyfriend of her grandmother, and these events made her feel that she was under attack for no reason. Her daughter suffered a miscarriage, and she had to take off time from school to take care of her. Her older brother suddenly fell ill and died. She was very close to this brother, so the loss really devastated her. Finally, a favorite grandaunt died, and this almost overwhelmed her. She felt that she had to tell her story for fear that she was going to fall apart.

After hearing her story, I attempted to communicate a few empathic statements, picking up on the fact that she seemed to not understand why all of this was happening to her at this time. She indicated assent to this interpretation. I asked her if she felt all right if I asked others in the class to retell her story and retell it based on the insights that occurred to them as they heard her story. I told her she would get a chance to respond to their retelling of the story after we heard from the others. She agreed to the process.

One person retold the story she heard by focusing on the abuse that she had sustained at the hand of a family member. She indicated that it had come at a very vulnerable time in her life, and she had been threatened with harm if she told. She also said she had carried around the pain in her life until she was an adult, and she finally had to share her story with family members because she found out that her nieces were being sexually molested in similar ways. This reteller of the story told how she exposed the secret of her own molestation when she found out about her nieces' abuse, and she said it caused a negative stir in the family. She pointed out, however, that her telling of the story eventually forced the family to face the deadly secret that was having a negative impact on the lives of others. She said the cycle of abuse was finally disrupted, and the perpetrator was dealt with in the family.

Others came forward and told of their own abuse. One student told of how seminary caused her to face the fact that her father had sexually molested her. She said she went home and confronted her father and her mother as a result of her experiences in seminary. She said her father, to her surprise, confessed to his sexually molesting her, and he indicated he would do whatever she needed to become whole again. He agreed to enter into his own therapy, and he paid for her therapy. She indicated that she was still in the process of healing, and that she felt good about bringing the molestation out in the open.

Several other stories were told. One last story that was told addressed the reason these events took place all at once. This reteller of the story said that she had undergone many losses when she entered seminary. She said she could not figure it out until one day someone mentioned to her that she was under a demonic attack. She pointed out she did not want to accept that answer since it was not part of any theology that she had ever considered. She changed her mind, however, when she realized that the series of negative events began to happen to her when she made a decision to go to seminary. She said when she realized that she was under attack from Satan, she drew closer to God in her prayer life. After a period of time in prayer and after deciding to not give up seminary and to continue toward ordination, she felt better and the attacks stopped.

Following the retelling of Indigo's original story, she got a chance to retell her own story. She told of how supported she felt, and how important it was for her to realize she was not alone and isolated in her story. She said the idea of being under a satanic attack made sense, and she was going to make it a point to address it in her prayer life. She also indicated that she had shared the story of her sexual molestation, and other family members who had been sexually abused by this same step-grandparent came forward and sought her out. She said the retelling of the stories gave her courage to continue on in seminary and to continue to be a healing presence in her family.

Following the telling and retelling of the original story, I had one of the women in the class say a closing prayer. The following week I began to talk about the significance of the definitional ceremony as a means of sustaining and healing persons as well as a means of recapturing the village functions of reinforcing relational ties that sustain people in integrity in the midst of crises and stress.

The Significance of the Narrative Approach

Significance refers to assessing what has been said in light of the role of the narrative approach in re-creating the re-villaging effort in black churches, the effort to evoke and mine the unconscious re-villaging sources lying dormant in the lives of African Americans through eschatological practices, and how the Bible is a vehicle driving this process. The concept of re-villaging rests in a notion that "the village is that small communal network of persons linked together by a common biological, family, cultural heritage living in a particular geographical location where frequent interaction is a reality."[8] Moreover, the village performs certain functions. For example:

> Symbolic functions refer to the ways in which narrative, metaphors and images comprising the worldview and spiritual perspectives of village life work to bring meaning to its members. Ritualistic functions refer to those repetitive patterns of communal life that reinforce the village worldview and values and that assist persons' movement through life transitions. Maintenance functions refer to those support systems practices and values that help people maintain themselves holistically when encountering the problems of life. Reparative functions are those healing endeavors in which the community engages after someone has been hurt or broken. Mediating functions are those mechanisms that transmit the worldview and spiritual values from one generation to the next.[9]

The key is that the definitional ceremony provides a context for carrying out the village functions. According to Michael White, settings for storytelling in a fragmented village are hard to find and they must be created. The definitional ceremony provides such a venue.[10]

The Limitations of the Narrative Approach

In addition to the danger that a narrative approach might focus on the pastor's needs rather than those of the parishioner or counselee, other limitations to the narrative approach must be addressed as well. First, the storytelling approach is not designed to be the only approach to the problems people face. There are times when direct and confrontational approaches are more appropriate. Sometimes pastors in the priestly role must help people face the truth and assess whether the story the person is living out is healthy or unhealthy. The key is that the pastor must help people judge their own stories in light of the faith story. When there is some discrepancy between the person's own story and the unfolding faith story, this truth should be pointed out by the pastor. Moreover, the pastor should help the counselee align his or her own life story with God's unfolding story.

Another limitation of the storytelling method is that it may assume that the people in need have Bible knowledge. But what about those who are

---

[8] Edward P. Wimberly, Anne Streaty Wimberly, and Annie Grace Chingonzo, "Pastoral Counseling, Spirituality and the Recovery of the Village Functions: African and African-American Correlates in the Practice of Pastoral Care and Counseling," in *Spirituality and Culture in Pastoral Care and Counseling: Voices from Different Contexts*, ed. John Foskett and Emmanuel Lartey (Cardiff, Wales: Cardiff Academic Press, 2004), 16–17.

[9] Wimberly, Wimberly, and Chingonzo, "Pastoral Counseling," 16.

[10] White, *Therapists' Lives*, 93.

unchurched or have very few roots in the institutional church? Although the storytelling approach does presuppose some familiarity with biblical stories, many such stories can be used to address the problems people present, if careful thought is given to the reason the stories are being told. One cannot assume that people will find Bible stories objectionable or irrelevant to their needs simply because of their lack of familiarity. Nor can one assume that there is no religious interest on the part of some counselees. However, this does not give the pastoral counselor license to tell religious stories without prior thought or permission from the counselee. It is always appropriate to ask for permission prior to telling the story. And one need not confine oneself to religious stories. There is rich material in African American folklore from which to draw as well.

Summary

Black pastors, to care for persons through storytelling,

1. Draw upon their own experiences in life and ministry, as well as upon Bible stories.

2. Use storytelling in the context of caring relationships, to foster personal, interpersonal, and emotional growth.

3. Use stories as a means of enriching people's awareness of God's drama unfolding in their lives, despite suffering.

4. Link persons with the unfolding of God's drama in ways that bring healing, sustaining, guidance, and reconciliation.

5. Enable parishioners to develop a language that helps them discern God's work in their lives.

6. Use the resources of the church and the narratives that undergird them to attend to the needs of individuals, families, and small groups. This includes worship and ritual.

7. Use stories in the art of counseling to make points, suggest solutions, facilitate cooperation, increase self-awareness, and discover resources for counseling.

8. Use conflict-free and anxiety-free narratives to help people grow emotionally and interpersonally.

• • •

Pastoral Care and Support Systems:
Illness, Bereavement, and Catastrophic Loss[*]

The crisis of loss creates a cessation and interruption of important interacting patterns and sustained relationships that are taken for granted. It is also a rupture in the existing narrative of life, because the experience of loss is the disruption of a narrative. The death of a loved one causes a revising of the story one has been living. For some, a death means fashioning a completely new story for one's life. The crisis is personal and individual, and so is the story about it.

Originally, this chapter illustrated how a pastor from the continent of Africa brought the resources of the church to bear upon a family facing the illness and loss of a loved one. The focus was on how the black church, as a support system, sustained the bereaved family by bringing the unfolding story of God to bear upon the family's needs. This focus on Africa is essential, particularly when we emphasize the loss of the village and the need to recover village functions. Since 1991, however, we have become more aware of catastrophic losses and how devastating they can be. For example, things have changed about how we view the persistence of natural disaster, human frailty, and evil.

The dynamic behind modernity was an optimism and certainty that life was becoming progressively better and that we would overcome many of the human problems of life through science and human effort. Postmodernity, however, has made us aware that the optimism we have felt was a bit naïve. We have become increasingly aware that science has limitations, human progress takes place in small steps, and the hard-fought gains for liberties in civil and human rights have to be refought in each new generation. In the area of race relations, we became aware that catastrophes like Hurricane Katrina have undermined our confidence in the infrastructures designed to protect us. This storm has also made us aware of the reality that racial minorities and the poor are disproportionately affected by natural disaster due to corporate decisions driven by economic interests, racial attitudes, and self-interest politics. Major institutions such as our local, state, and federal governments are ill-prepared for disasters, and our insurance industry, designed to help us recover from losses, is a dismal failure. While Hurricanes Katrina and Rita had an impact on everyone, the consensus is that ethnic and racial minorities and the poor were not only

[*]   This chapter was previously published in Edward P. Wimberly, *African American Pastoral Care*, rev. ed. (Nashville: Abingdon, 2008), 31–45 and associated notes. © 2008. Abingdon Press. Used by permission. All rights reserved.

more vulnerable but more affected as well. For example, the levees were stronger and held up better in more affluent areas of New Orleans than in the poorer areas. While this is not a new awareness to the African American community, it is still a hard pill to swallow, and it is disheartening to know that while things have changed racially, they seem to have remained the same. The end result is that we have had to revise our optimistic orientation toward life, and we have had to adopt a more realistic appraisal of human possibility.

From a pastoral care viewpoint, we have had to understand and more fully address the reality of human catastrophe and the role of human lament in recovery from disaster. We have not only had to deal with the individual nature of loss and bereavement, we have had to deal with the public nature of grieving resulting from natural disasters and human evil.

We will return to the subject of public grieving later in this chapter when we explore catastrophic loss.

The Nature of Bereavement

Bereavement results from the sudden cessation of a close and abiding relationship.[1] Bereavement often elicits negative emotions such as grief or mourning, which come after the death of a person who has had a particular place in one's life. What follows is generally characteristic pattern as the bereaved tries to fill the void made in his or her life by this loss.

The basic tasks for the bereaved person are to achieve emancipation from bondage to the deceased, readjust to a world in which the deceased is missing, and form new relationships.[2] Another task is to revise and edit one's life story without the deceased. These tasks are difficult because the impact of the death of a loved one is apt to stun bereaved persons to the point of immobilization and disorganization.

Those who suffer grief sometimes want to avoid the pain associated with the experience. After many attempts on the part of the bereaved to avoid that pain, the grieving process itself must be accepted if adequate mourning is to take place. According to Erich Lindemann, once the grief process is accepted, the bereaved begin to deal with the memory of the deceased person, and this, in turn, is followed by relief in tension. Moreover, Lindemann discovered that if others care for the bereaved for four

---

[1] This definition is contained in Erich Lindemann, "Symptomatology and Management of Acute Grief," *Crisis Intervention*, ed. Howard J. Parad (New York: Family Service Association, 1976), 7.

[2] See Lindemann, "Acute Grief," 7–21, for his reference to basic tasks for the bereaved.

to six weeks, that is an appropriate length of time to help them reach an uncomplicated and undistorted grief reaction.[3]

Certain characteristic symptoms appear in persons suffering bereavement. Lindemann enumerates the following four components of the grief syndrome: body distress, guilt, hostile reactions, and loss of patterns of conduct.[4] As a result of the impact of loss, the bereaved might suffer tightness in the throat, shortness of breath, the need to sigh, empty feelings in the stomach, or a lack of muscular power. The senses are altered to the degree that there may be a sense of unreality and a feeling of increased emotional distance from others.

Often, guilt and hostile anger are evident when the bereaved accuse themselves of negligence and look for evidence to corroborate this allegation. Moreover, they may exhibit anger toward relatives and friends of the deceased through a loss of warmth in relationships and a feeling of abandonment on the part of the bereaved.

Death of a loved one disrupts usual patterns of interaction, resulting in a restlessness, an inability to remain in one place, an aimless moving, or a continued search for something to do. There is also a general lack of capacity to initiate and maintain patterns of activity, for the grief sufferer discovers that many of the activities that were done with the deceased or in relationship to the deceased have lost their meaning.

There may be preoccupation with the image and memory of the deceased, often an attempt to deny the death and recover the presence of the lost loved one.[5] There is a yearning or seeking for the loved one, an attempt to achieve reunion with the deceased.[6]

Normal grieving is characterized by three phases. First, the grief sufferers yearn for the lost loved ones and experience anger toward the loved ones for abandoning them. The second phase begins when the bereaved accept the fact that neither yearning nor anger will bring the loved ones back. This leads to despair and disorganization in the lives of the bereaved. Following this phase is a period of reorganization, in which the bereaved turn toward the world and begin to find new relationships and meaning in life. During this period, the grief sufferers either begin the task of revising and editing the old story or begin to develop a new story without the deceased.

---

[3] Lindemann, "Acute Grief," 7–21.

[4] Lindemann, "Acute Grief," 7–21.

[5] John Bowlby, "Pathological Mourning and Childhood Mourning," *Journal of the American Psychoanalytic Association* 11 (July 1963): 501.

[6] C. Murray Parkes, "Seeking and Finding a Lost Object: Evidence from Recent Studies of the Reaction to Bereavement," *Social Science and Medicine* 4 (1970): 187–201.

During the process of grief work, it is important for the bereaved to experience and express their yearning for and anger toward the deceased. In this way they can give up the deceased and accept the fact that the deceased is gone forever. Only then can they accept the reality that loved ones are separate from themselves and can be lost. Failure to consciously experience and express the yearning for and anger toward the deceased leads to an arresting of the grief process, which eventuates in inappropriate attempts to carry out a reunion with the deceased and, ultimately, to pathological mourning.[7]

Bereavement Ministry: Case Example from a Black African Pastor in a Black Church

This is a report of an African pastor who ministered to a dying parishioner and the parishioner's family before and after his death. The focus of the pastor's concern was a black male in his late fifties who was dying from cancer. Prior to the discovery of the malignancy, the parishioner had sustained injuries in a serious car accident, and initially, the illness was linked to complications associated with that accident. However, during the period of convalescence it was discovered that he was terminally ill with cancer of the liver. When told of his disease, the parishioner did not accept the prognosis, refusing to admit he was dying. Rather, he insisted that a good job was waiting for him and that he would return to work.

The parishioner's immediate family consisted of a second wife and a son from his first marriage. The second wife did not live with the husband at the time of his illness; the father and son were estranged and had not seen each other for many years.

The parishioner's extended family consisted of two younger sisters who lived in the area and an older sister living in the Deep South. The two younger sisters had a good relationship with their brother, were upset about his illness, and were concerned about his inability to accept the fact that he was dying. The older sister, however, had a much closer relationship with her brother, probably because she had taken care of him during his childhood.

The man's relationship with the pastor was a comfortable one. The pastor had visited the parishioner periodically in the hospital since the accident. The pastor was concerned about the dying man's inability to accept his impending death, and he expressed this concern to the two younger sisters. While talking with the sisters, the pastor discovered that the dying man probably would be much more willing to talk about his problems with

---

[7] Bowlby, "Pathological Mourning," 505.

his older sister. Therefore, the pastor sent for this sister, and she came as a result of the pastor's initiative. The pastor found that the dying parishioner was able to express his fears to his older sister and finally was able to accept the fact that he was dying. The pastor also contacted the man's son and informed him of his father's condition. As a result of this effort, the son and father were able to establish some form of reconciliation before the father died.

Following the death of the parishioner, the pastor turned his concern to the bereaved family. He discovered that the second wife, the three sisters, and the son had become a fellowship group for one another. The pastor helped strengthen this support system by using the wake and the preparation of the funeral service to facilitate the grief process among the members of the fellowship group. He found that their participation in preparing the funeral service stimulated them to express their feelings concerning the beloved brother, husband, and father.

This African pastor had trained many laypeople in his congregation for times of bereavement. After discovering that many of the parishioners were from the South and the West Indies, and seeming to automatically know what to do in terms of the crisis of loss, he exploited many of those natural leanings and involved these persons in discussion groups surrounding such crises. When there was a need for these persons' services within the congregation, he would call on them to assist others.

The pastor trained these laypeople to share stories from their own lives to encourage the bereaved to share their stories of hurt and pain. He informed them that a brief story from the lives of the caregivers could assist the bereaved to review their own relationships with the deceased and enable feelings of bereavement to be expressed. The pastor warned them, however, to tell their stories in ways that kept the bereaved person's needs for grieving central.

According to the African pastor, much of his knowledge concerning bereavement ministry was a result of his African heritage. Death was accepted as a fact of life in his community in Africa, and many extended family obligations were associated with the death of a loved one and the bereavement process.[8] As "eldest son," the pastor's obligation to the family during the bereavement period had consisted of assisting with funeral

---

[8] For readings in African pastoral care and counseling, see Abraham Adu Berinyuu, *Towards Theory and Practice of Pastoral Counseling in Africa* (Frankfurt: Peter Lang, 1989), 82–98; Abraham Adu Berinyuu, *Pastoral Care to the Sick in Africa* (Frankfurt: Peter Lang, 1988); Masamba ma Mpolo, "African Pastoral Care Movement," and "African Traditional Religion, Personal Care In," in *Dictionary of Pastoral Care and Counseling*, ed. Rodney J. Hunter (Nashville: Abingdon, 1990), 11–12, 12–13.

arrangements and carrying out the father's wishes concerning the remaining family.

His participation in a consultation group and a seminar on death, dying, and bereavement were also very helpful in shaping his bereavement ministry.

A Narrative Reflection on the Case

The Black Pastor as Diagnostician

In the case just described, the pastor became aware that the parishioner refused to accept the fact that he was dying of cancer. This refusal to accept a given reality is called denial. Following the diagnosis, the pastor actively sought to ascertain what sources existed within the family to assist the dying patient through his difficulty and to help him face the reality of death.

The pastor became cognizant of several family resources. The patient's second wife revealed a concern about him and attempted to lend support. In addition, the pastor discovered three sisters, who emerged as the most significant sources of support for the dying patient. An adult son, whose communication with his father had been nonexistent for a period of time, also was considered a potential avenue of support.

Aside from family resources, the pastor assessed resources within the church for support of the dying parishioner. Some members had been trained to be of assistance, and religious ceremonials would provide support. The pastor also became aware that traditions among the members, particularly those from the South and West Indies, provided a set of customs that defined the responsibility of church members and friends to persons in crisis. Thus, a framework existed with which to support the parishioner and ease him in his dying moments. Through the support of the family, the social network, the church and its heritage, and the values of the black subculture that defined the behavior of persons toward others in crises, the pastor recognized the existence of a variety of resources available before and during death, as well as throughout the subsequent bereavement of the family.

Of great help to the black African pastor were the influential cultural patterns in Africa that informed his sensitivity to the role of extended families in ministering to the dying. He used knowledge from his past, and the sensitivities toward the role of support systems acquired from his background in his bereavement ministry to the congregation.

The key to the use of the cultural patterns of the extended family, the support system, and the funeral was the fact that these patterns were embodied in the central narrative of the faith tradition. Those in the

extended family were part of God's unfolding story; those in the caring support system of the church were part of God's unfolding story. When these
people shared stories of bereavement from their own lives, they included
testimonies of God's presence in the midst of death. Moreover, the support
system shared a common faith story, which, when shared, held out hope in
the midst of tragedy.

The wake and funeral were vehicles for assisting the family through
the grieving process. As part of caring, the pastor purposely employed the
funeral and the wake to help the bereaved discern God's presence in the
midst of their grief. Through the funeral and wake, they could encounter
the spacious resources of God's story of grace and hope.

The funeral also laid the groundwork for enabling the bereaved to
revise and edit their stories. Images of God's presence in the lives of those
who were bereaved in Scripture held out hope for developing new life scenarios. The liturgy of the funeral gave the message that God will assist you
in fashioning a new story without the presence of the deceased.

The parishioner in this case had been largely uncommunicative about
his condition, with the pastor as well as with two of his sisters. However,
after learning of another sister, with whom the brother would be willing to
talk, the pastor facilitated the arrival of the third sister, which resulted in
the dying patient's discussion of his fears and his acceptance of the fact that
he was dying. Moreover, after the pastor brought the dying man and his
sister together, they began to share stories of their lives together when they
were young. These memories and stories helped to shore up his courage so
that he could face the task of dying; they secured the bonds between the
dying man and his sister. He was sustained and nurtured by sweet memories and died knowing that his life was worthwhile and that he was loved.

Essential to the narrative understanding of caring ministry to the
bereaved is the envisioning of the funeral and the caring as being linked to
God's unfolding drama in our lives. God's unfolding story is a drama made
up of episodes, scenes, chapters, and a plot. The funeral and the ministry
of caring in God's name are miniplots in the midst of God's unfolding macroplot. The macroplot of God involves death and rebirth made possible by
Jesus Christ. The salvation drama is made up of dying with Christ and rising with Christ. Therefore, in ministry to the dying and the bereaved, the
task is to draw the people into God's salvation drama of death and rebirth.

Reunion of the loved ones with a dying patient is one illustration of
how renewal and rebirth are possible despite the imminence of death.
In the described case, the resources of God's ongoing story of salvation
undergirded and enabled the rebirth of new relationships. The act of being

drawn into God's salvation drama offered new possibilities and hope in spite of pain and suffering.

As the bereft are drawn into the salvation drama, the foundation is also being laid for them to begin to revise and edit a different narrative, one that is without the loved one. By being linked with God's unfolding drama of death and rebirth, the bereft find courage to begin a new life and a new narrative without the deceased. A new narrative is begun with hope and expectation, knowing that God is in the revising process.

The Pastor as Mobilizer of Support Systems

The African heritage of the caring pastor in this case made him sensitive to the role of support systems in life transitions. His cultural heritage has built into it traditions of community support and ceremonial practices to aid those in life transitions. These supports and practices gave him a special sensitivity toward knowing how to utilize support systems in bereavement situations with families outside his cultural background.

The major role of the African pastor in the crises of dying and bereavement was to bring the resources of the support system to bear upon the emotional and interpersonal needs of the dying patient and the grieving relatives. By accomplishing this, the pastor:

1. provided opportunities for relatives and friends to identify and empathize with one another

2. provided opportunities to share in a common story of the faith tradition

3. provided a ritual and worship context for linking and connecting with a meaningful religious plot that brought renewal and rebirth in the midst of suffering

4. provided a loving and caring group of laypersons and family who facilitated the expression of feelings of grief and mourning

5. encouraged the lay caregivers to help the grief sufferers use stories from their own lives as a means of facilitating the grief process

In order to assist the support system in the case of bereavement and dying, the pastor helped the bereaved and the dying parishioner to maintain significant ties with others, which helped them sustain their emotional and spiritual well-being in the face of death. The support system helped the dying man and his family satisfy their needs for love, affection, and continued participation in meaningful relationships in the midst of suffering.

The use of a support system enabled the pastoral care to be the best within the African and African American church context. The support system helped sustain the dying man during his last days on earth. It brought healing through the renewal of relationships, helped guide the grief sufferers through the grief process, and enabled the bereaved and the dying man to be linked with the ongoing drama of God's salvation.

Re-Villaging Analysis

This revision lifts up the need to reestablish village functions within the African American church as a legitimate twenty-first century function. This case draws on a study of an African minister pastoring an African American church and relating it to support systems originally took place in the late 1970s. It was an illustration of the function of support systems. The goal of the illustration was to be more intentional about making sure these support systems were not lost given the demise of such networks due to cultural trends. My original thinking was that these supportive traditions would not really collapse, believing that the loss of the traditional village would never happen. It has happened, and it is necessary to attend to some of the village functions that were evident in the case as a means to set the theoretical stage for re-creating village functioning today. The main assumption of this section is that a village can never be re-created; however, village functions can be reestablished.

I begin with the emphasis on the indigenous storytelling whose role in the creation of village functions is to assist in communal healing. The communal healing function is to help restore the family relational ties; to use the Bible to evoke the eschatological plot and its practice of drawing persons into the unfolding story of God; to transform people's lives by connecting them with hidden and unconscious resources that lead to resilient strategies in the face of difficulties; and to help people edit the negative beliefs and convictions that might hinder their ability to be resilient. In the case presented above we see illustrated the restoration of relational ties, and we get a glimpse of the use of biblical resources to connect people with the unfolding plot of God. We need to say more about how resilient resources and practices were evoked when stories were elicited, however.

Resilient practices emerge out of the storytelling process itself. In fact, resilient practices are part of the healing function of re-villaging, where the indigenous storyteller facilitates the storytelling process, and from the storytelling process new insights are stimulated for bouncing back from loss. In our publication *The Winds of Promise: Building and Sustaining Clergy Families* my wife and I define resilient practices as engaging in the storytelling process from which people are able to gain access to hidden and unused opportunities for managing life's twists and turns.[9] Spiritual lifelines often emerge from our storytelling that provide opportunities to see the next steps in moving through difficulties that we face in life. This was evident when the family members became aware of God's plot of reconciliation and healing unfolding in their lives so that old relationships could be reestablished. While no actual biblical story was named in the case, they nonetheless became aware of an active and connecting dynamic at work that enabled them to transcend past hurts and problems. This dynamic force was already at work, but it was outside their awareness, and the storytelling enabled them to become aware and connect with it. It was this previously hidden dynamic that enabled them to reconnect with each other and to find support for each other in the dying process and in the grief that they were experiencing.

Catastrophic Loss

In addition to the private grief of human beings, events like the Columbine shootings in Colorado in 1999, the 9/11 attacks, and the Katrina catastrophe of 2005 have made us aware that grief has a public side. The public nature of grief has not been satisfactorily addressed by pastoral care and counseling as a discipline. In an article by Larry Graham entitled "Pastoral Theology and Catastrophic Disaster" delivered at the Society for Pastoral Theology in June 2006, Graham points out that such events as the Columbine shootings, 9/11, and Katrina forced us to struggle with how caregivers can help themselves and others come to terms with the corporate and public dimensions of grief and loss, which had been ignored in pastoral theology. Pastoral care normally confined its thinking about grief and loss to the personal and private realm. Thus, Larry Graham raises the concern of how pastors and pastoral theologians can rethink the public and corporate nature of loss and grief. Toward this end, Graham lifts up several practices, and one such practice is the role of lament as a resilient practice.

In Graham's exposition of lament, he credits a phone conversation with me for introducing the meaning of lament. In my books, *Claiming God, Reclaiming Dignity: African American Pastoral Care and Counseling* and *The Winds of Promise: Building and Sustaining Clergy Families*, I define lament as crying out and complaining to God about our current predicament, being honest about God's role in the cause of such predicaments, and expecting

---

[9] Anne E. Streaty Wimberly and Edward Powell Wimberly, *The Winds of Promise: Building and Maintaining Strong Clergy Families* (Nashville: Discipleship Resources, 2007), 35–50.

God to respond. Lament as an ancient biblical practice was designed to draw people into conversation with God so that the resilient resources that God has for bouncing back from catastrophic circumstances can be activated. Lament actively questions God's role in causing the catastrophe, but such complaints are not considered blasphemy. Rather, it is considered an appropriate response to helplessness and a genuine invitation for God to be present in the lives of those who suffer. In blasphemy, there is no genuine acknowledgment of God's existence or desire to be engaged with God.

Of significance is the reality that public and corporate lament is a resilient practice. First, lament provides connection with God, who is the ultimate source of new opportunities and hidden resources for bouncing back from loss, devastation, and catastrophe. Second, in addition, public and corporate grieving are re-villaging practices as well. They assist in the symbolic function of re-villaging by bringing to life certain narratives, metaphors, and images that embody the spiritual resources of the faith traditions. See, for example, the many psalms of lament and the laments found in the book of Job. There is also the re-villaging public aspect of the ritualistic recitation of the psalms of lament provided in biblical tradition. Third, public and corporate lament perform the maintenance function of securing relational ties needed to overcome devastation. Fourth, corporate public lament assists in the reparative function, so that healing the hurt and brokenness of those affected by catastrophe can take place. Finally, lament enables the spiritual and relational values of the faith tradition to be mediated to those who have faced catastrophe. This is the mediation function.

Indeed, the role of the pastor as indigenous storyteller is critical in times of catastrophe. The symbolic role of the black preacher as village leader is essential during catastrophe as well as during the recovery phase after catastrophe. One thinks of the role that the Reverend Lance Eden, pastor of First Street United Methodist Church in New Orleans, played during Katrina as well as into the recovery phase. During Sunday morning worship he led his congregation and the many volunteers who came from all around the United States in public and corporate lament during public worship. Not only this, he also led his congregation and volunteer in restoring the homes that were salvageable and helped reestablish communal networks that Katrina disrupted. *Ebony Magazine* and *Colors Magazine* acknowledged his leadership efforts during the Katrina recovery. In fact, the November 2005 issue of *Colors Magazine* featured an article on Eden's work entitled "After the Storm: Special Report from the Gulf Coast."[10]

---

[10] *ColorsNW Magazine*, "Special Report from the Gulf Coast," November 3, 2005, http://www.colorsnw.com/cover_story.html, no longer available.

The article in *Colors Magazine* lifts up, in effect, Eden's role as indigenous storyteller in the re-villaging and recovery effort in New Orleans. It says:

> In the part of town known as Indian Village, Lance Eden offers a history lesson about the area his family calls home. Serious and thoughtful, all who speak of Eden see a great leader in the making. Someone who is wise enough to be able to say he doesn't know and confident enough to take the lead when the need arises. Eden sees the preservation of his family history as part of his responsibility not just to his kin but to the history of Slidell. The history of his family stretches back centuries, and as a history buff, he has taken to compiling and keeping stories for future generations.[11]

The life of the Reverend Lance Eden as minister and indigenous storytelling is an illustration of how the African American tradition re-creates itself over and over again. While the tangible evidence of a family's life such as mementos and pictures were lost in many cases, the storytelling traditions and re-villaging functions continue as the stories are still retold. The symbolic role of African American preachers is alive and well as the work of Lance Eden reveals. We who taught Lance at Interdenominational Theological Center and helped form him spiritually and professionally are very proud of his work. At the age of 27, he has the wisdom and maturity of a much older, seasoned minister. We are happy that the tradition of the indigenous storyteller continues in our graduates.

---

[11] *ColorsNW Magazine*, "Special Report."

7

Narrative Care in the Contexts of Trauma (2011)

E dward Wimberly's scholarship continually addresses situations directly related to his practice of pastoral care. In this article from the *Journal of Health Care for the Poor and Underserved*,* Wimberly describes a collective narrative approach used to care for traumatized persons, clergy, and their families in the aftermath of hurricanes Katrina and Rita. Wimberly emphasizes the importance of storytelling in community, not only during periods of catastrophic loss, but also later, as people begin to experience recovery and solidify a sense of healing and resilience.

Wimberly draws upon research that he and Anne Streaty Wimberly conducted together as they worked with clergy families under the auspices of the Louisiana Conference of the United Methodist Church, the Office of Faith and Health.† The couple offered a retreat for religious and spiritual leaders and their spouses, who began to tell the stories of their own survival of the hurricanes in New Orleans and on the Gulf Coast. Here Edward Wimberly reflects on their work with these couples, who had also experienced vicarious trauma and compassion fatigue. He emphasizes the efficacy of storytelling in safe and supportive environments, where survivors of trauma can find support and understanding from each other. Wimberly also highlights the value of religious and spiritual traditions in the development of life-giving story lines.

---

* Edward P. Wimberly, "Story Telling and Managing Trauma: Health and Spirituality at Work," *Journal of Health Care for the Poor and Underserved* 22, no. 3 (2011): 48–57.

† Anne E. Streaty Wimberly and Edward P. Wimberly, *The Winds of Promise: Building and Maintaining Strong Clergy Families* (Nashville: Discipleship Resources, 2007).

As climate change escalates, bringing more and more weather-related disasters, Edward Wimberly's work on this issue remains apt. It is part of a growing body of literature on pastoral responses to collective traumatic events.* Wimberly's salient point is that caregivers must establish strategies and practices of self-care when caring for those experiencing trauma and catastrophic loss as well as later, after the crisis is over. They need to tell their stories in ways that help them make meaning and identify their ongoing purpose.

Further Reading

Wimberly, Anne E. Streaty and Edward Powell Wimberly. *The Winds of Promise: Building and Maintaining Strong Clergy Families*. Nashville: Discipleship Resources, 2007.

• • •

---

*   See, for example, Storm Swain, *Trauma and Transformation at Ground Zero: A Pastoral Theology* (Minneapolis: Fortress, 2011); and Michelle Walsh, *Violent Trauma, Culture, and Power: An Interdisciplinary Exploration in Lived Religion* (New York: Palgrave Macmillan, 2017).

Story Telling and Managing Trauma: Health and Spirituality at Work[*]

Religious and spiritual caregivers are often first responders to catastrophic events including natural disasters (such as earthquakes and hurricanes) or man-made acts of war or terrorism. Religious caregivers and spiritual leaders must learn to take care of themselves in the presence of trauma while managing the trauma in the lives of others. This is no easy task. In fact, religious caregivers, spiritual leaders, and their families are affected greatly by catastrophic events in their own lives and in the lives of those for whom they care. This was particularly the case for religious and spiritual leaders and their families of those affected by Hurricanes Katrina and Rita. In a previous publication, the author of the present article wrote:

> When we began writing this book, Hurricanes Katrina and Rita had not occurred. However, during the completion stage, these two catastrophic events struck New Orleans and the Gulf Coast. Clergy families were among the many whose lives were turned upside down in the wake of the devastation. As the stories of clergy families who survived the hurricanes began to unfold, we were reminded that, as clergy families, we are not immune to the ravages and trauma of unforeseen events and the difficult task of managing our lives in their aftermath. We are not beyond the need for care and succor.[1]

Given the vulnerability of religious caregivers and spiritual leaders to catastrophic events as first responders, it is incumbent upon them to learn to take care of themselves in the midst of trauma. This essay seeks to address that need.

First, this essay will introduce several meanings of trauma and explore a narrative or story-telling model of managing catastrophic losses in the lives of people as well as to help caregivers care for themselves as they care for others. Then, the focus shifts to managing trauma through the use of story-telling and story-sharing.

Definitions. In the area of preventive and mental spiritual health there are key terms that must be defined. These definitions include core terms in crisis theory, stress management, and trauma. In crisis theory, a *normal*

---

[1] Anne E. Streaty Wimberly and Edward P. Wimberly, *The Winds of Promise: Building and Maintaining Strong Clergy Families* (Nashville: Discipleship Resources, 2007), 135.

[*] This chapter was previously published in *Journal of Health Care for the Poor and Underserved* 22, no. 3 (2011): 48–57. © 2011 Meharry Medical College. Reprinted with permission of Johns Hopkins University Press.

life crisis is where people face obstacles which they cannot handle by their accustomed problem-solving means, and they must call upon emergency problem-solving resources, including appeals to others (family, friends, other caregivers) for help.[2] Such normal problems include transitions such as the birth of a child, the movement of a child to adolescence, the transition into young adulthood, marriage, middle age, older adulthood, and death. There are also situations of loss including illnesses, accidents, and unexpected deaths. Moreover, there are crises such as retirement, relocation, and divorce. The point is that these transitions call for preventive intervention, whether in the form of education or brief support from caring networks of people or some other mode.[3]

Stress calls for more expertise from those who intervene than milder crisis intervention does. Stress often manifests itself when people or families face two or more life transitions at the same time. For example, people may be facing the mid-life crisis while at the same time an elderly parent gets sick or children leave home for good.[4]

Trauma differs from both crisis and stress; it completely overwhelms people's problem- solving capacities and often prevents them from integrating the traumatic occurrences into their lives.[5] It causes complete helplessness in the face of real threats to the self, to loved ones, to one's body, as well as to one's sanity. It produces extreme confusion and insecurity, and it challenges a person's sense of fitting in the world and his or her reliance on institutions that normally buffer people from disaster.

Trauma can be caused by psychological catastrophes such as sexual abuse, violence, witnessing abuse and violence, experiencing earthquakes, volcanic disruptions, war, mass violence, and displacements due to floods and other events. Even long-term exposure to violence and milder verbal abuse can eventually constitute trauma.

Psychologically, trauma overwhelms an individual's psychological, emotional, and spiritual inner resources. People responding to trauma can easily become detached from their emotions and numb to what is going on. There are feelings of loss of meaning, despair, loss of self-esteem, and depression.

[2] Edward P. Wimberly, *African American Pastoral Care*, rev. ed. (Nashville: Abingdon, 2008), 47–70.

[3] Edward P. Wimberly, Reuben Warren, and Anne Streaty Wimberly, "Exploring the Meaning and Possibility of Black Fatherhood Today," in *Multidimensional Ministry for Today's Black Family*, ed. Johnny B. Hill (Valley Forge, Pa.: Judson Press, 2007), 41–56.

[4] Edward P. Wimberly, *Counseling African American Marriages and Families* (Louisville: Westminster John Knox, 1997), 70–74.

[5] C. M. Parkes, "Disaster, public," in *Dictionary of Pastoral Care and Counseling*, ed. Rodney J. Hunter (Nashville: Abingdon, 1990), 285–87.

Evidence-Based Support for Religious Narrative
Approaches to Trauma

As of the winter of 2007, there was no evidenced consensus or "a clear set of recommendations for intervention during immediate and mid-midterm post mass trauma phases."[6] As a result, a group of experts from different but related fields of trauma were assembled to provide such a consensus. e result included the establishment of five empirically supported intervention principles, designed to guide trauma intervention efforts.

These essential functions include:

1. promoting a sense of safety

2. promoting calming

3. promoting a sense of self- and collective efficacy

4. promoting connectedness

5. promoting hope.

In the most comprehensive review of trauma intervention to date, these interventions including prevention, support, and therapeutic modalities are found in a variety of therapy professions and religious communities. These five essential principles will be used to assess the validity of a narrative approach to trauma intervention used by the author and an intervention team in response to Hurricanes Katrina and Rita.

The approach used in this presentation developed out of this author's training in community mental health while a Ph.D. student at Boston University and while training at the Solomon Carter Fuller Community Mental Health Center in Boston, Massachusetts in 1973–1975. The author was hired as a Pastoral Consultant Assistant whose role was to learn to work with ministers and their churches in providing community mental health primary prevention through early case-finding, consultation and education. At that time, the idea of religion as an actor in community mental health had already been around a long time, its public role having been recognized since the signing of the Community Mental Health legislation in 1963 by President John Kennedy.[7] One of the first efforts to link the community mental health movement to the Black Church was completed by this author, who used a primary prevention approach to community mental health that was supported and developed by the Dr. Solomon Carter

---

[6] Stevan E. Hobfall et al., "Five Essential Elements of Immediate and Mid–Term Mass Trauma Intervention: Empirical Evidence," *Psychiatry* 70, no. 4 (2007): 283–315.

[7] Gerald Caplan, *The Theory and Practice of Mental Health Consultation* (New York: Basic Books, 1970), 330.

Fuller Community Mental Health Center in Boston.[8] The point is that the religious organizations and community mental health practitioners are and have been closely connected in their joint efforts to foster improvement in the quality of mental health in communities. Recent evidence-based research speaks poignantly to the role of religious institutions and religious practices in improving mental health in communities.[9]

With regard to the role of religion in the aftermath of the Hurricanes Katrina and Rita in the New Orleans area and on the Gulf Coast, efforts to work with clergy including Africans, African Americans, and Whites and their families (all of whom were first responders as well as victims) took place approximately three months after the disastrous event. This event was organized by the Louisiana Conference of the United Methodist Church, the Office of Faith and Health, an organization intended to provide ongoing support for clergy members and their families as they continued to struggle with disaster as well as to help them employ self-care as they responded to trauma.

While the effort was to help clergy and their families to care for themselves as well as others, a major focus also was to test out the research method which is called *narrative inquiry*. Narrative inquiry is all about how those being researched are able to use the telling and retelling of their stories to bring meaning to their lives when going through everyday life as well as when facing trauma and disasters.[10] The emphasis in this method of doing research is to observe how those facing trauma and disaster tell and retell stories within community with others in such a way that they find plot-lines that help them see purpose in their lives. Within the context of the particular experience with New Orleans pastors and their families, the emphasis was on how they drew on their faith traditions to develop resilience in the face of trauma.

While the method of research was qualitative, the results of this intervention effort are recorded in a book co-authored by the author of the present essay and his wife.[11] The narrative inquiry project found:

1. story-telling and retelling are very useful to help connect people with plotlines present in their faith orientation

---

[8]   Edward P. Wimberly, *Pastoral Care in the Black Church* (Nashville: Abingdon, 1979).

[9]   Stephen B. Roberts and Willard W. C. Ashley, Sr., eds., *Disaster Spiritual Care: Practical Clergy Responses to Community, Regional and National Tragedy* (Woodstock, Vt.: SkyLight Paths Publisher, 2008).

[10]   D. Jean Clandinin and F. Michael Connelly, *Narrative Inquiry: Experience and Story in Qualitative Research* (San Francisco: Jossey-Bass, 2000).

[11]   Wimberly and Wimberly, *Winds of Promise*, 135–56.

2. the participants (numbering over 50) were able to participate fully in telling and retelling stories which took place in small groups

3. several people who had been disconnected from family and friends were able to grieve these losses

4. many moved to new locations when either their homes or churches or both were lost and were able to make new friends

5. the several rituals designed through movement and interaction with others proved to be the most meaningful to people

6. recalling stories three months after the hurricanes was very useful in helping people envisage purposeful movement along a hopeful plot-line

Of particular significance is the validity of the five empirically supported principles of intervention for evaluation of a narrative approach to trauma intervention used by the author at the retreat for clergy and their families three months after Hurricanes Katrina and Rita. For example, in terms of promotion of safety, all respondents found it very important to be with others who shared their sense of calling to vocation. In several cases there were stories told by spouses of clergy whose church members had lashed out against them in anger. Clergy families could empathize with each other. They had come to realize that parishioner anger was a normal reaction to their losses. Group story-telling and story-listening established a safe space to talk.

The second essential element of intervention is the promotion of calming. Promotion of calming was not so evident, however. Three months after the disaster most of the clergy and their families were beyond the initial shock of the event, and they were at the stage where they were putting their lives back together. What they needed was to discern the meaning in the midst of tragedy.

The promotion of sense of self-efficacy and collective-efficacy is the next essential intervention method. It was clear that most of the participants three months into the aftermath of Katrina and Rita had come to grips with their emotions, had done effective problem-solving, had begun to reestablish relationships, had found new places to live, and had begun to establish their ministries. It was helpful, however, for them to have a space to review what they had accomplished as well as to bring meaning to their lives. For them, the retreat helped them envisage the positive movement forward after three months.

Of real significance is the concept of social or communal efficacy. Narrative storytelling and listening with other clergy and their families increase their ability to be resilient in the rebuilding of their lives and ministries. It also gave them courage to return to their ministries with renewed faith and vigor. Moreover, they were able to affirm that self-care in community was preferable than to remain alone as families.

The fourth essential part of intervention was the promotion of connectedness. Narrative fosters community and community-building. Coming together for story-telling and story-listening and performing group rituals supported this intervention strategy. For example, each morning and at the end of each day, the group would march around the room taking two steps forward and two steps backwards before finally taking progressive steps forward. The goal was to remind the group that life's pilgrimage was exactly in starts, stops, regressions, and progressions. Yet, the end would be reached.

The final essential intervention is instilling hope. Indeed, the use of narrative intervention strategies helps in achieving positive outcomes. Most importantly, narrative helps people bring meaning to their lives, meaning based on seeing some positive progress in their lives and using stories of faith to visualize hopeful ends. Some very encouraging stories of finding hope in the midst of tragedy were told in ways that encouraged everyone present.

In addition to functions with regard to clergy, there is also qualitative evidence that lay people also drew on religious values and practices and spirituality while surviving the storms of Katrina. The conclusions of a qualitative study of older Black Katrina survivors revealed that regular communication with a supernatural power, faith as a source of guidance and protection, daily Bible reading, the use of devotional materials, and helping others because of devotion to a supreme being, all contributed to emotional and spiritual resilience.[12]

Closely related to the use of a religious retreat for clergy was the use of what was called a The Hurricane Choir, which was a community-based intervention in the post-Katrina period.[13] The reality is that this research was designed to monitor the response of victims of Katrina to stress and disruption in their emotional and coping lives while they participated in

---

[12] Erma J. Lawson and Cecelia Thomas, "Wading in the Waters: Spirituality and Older Black Katrina Survivors," *Journal of Health Care for the Poor and Underserved* 18, no. 2 (2007): 341–54.

[13] Robin Harvey et al., "The Hurricane Choir: Remote Mental Health Monitoring of Participants in a Community-based Intervention in the post-Katrina Period," in *Journal of Health Care for the Poor and Underserved* 18, no. 2 (2007): 356–61.

the Hurricane Choir. The concept was brilliant, and it was based on natural religious and spiritual support that would come from participating in a spiritual practice, which not only involved music, but also faith symbols and stories on which those participating in the choir could draw. Moreover, the collection of data took place as the participants went online to record their responses to questions that would reveal how social networks and religious practices helped with their coping. Unfortunately, results had not been tabulated at the time the article needed to be published. Therefore, only preliminary outcomes were reported. Nonetheless, this model of doing innovative research drawing on religious and spiritual practices, lends support for replicating this study in the future.

In the next section additional literature research will be presented with regard to the need for first responders to practice self-care in the face of responding to others confronting trauma.

Impact of Trauma on Caregivers

Trauma not only overwhelms those who experience it directly; it also affects seriously those who care for those who experience trauma, especially first responders. First responders as caregivers, whether religious or not, must practice self-care if they are going to be effective working with those facing trauma. There are two dangers that caregivers face. The first is *compassion fatigue*, and the second is *vicarious traumatization*.

Working with survivors of disasters has a tremendous impact on caregivers. This is especially the case for clergy, professional counselors, social workers, health care workers and others. Compassion fatigue is exposure to both primary and secondary traumatic stress, and its cumulative impact can be powerful.[14] Burnout occurs when the caregiver loses the capacity to function physically, mentally, emotionally, and spiritually. They have become exhausted.

Symptoms of compassion fatigue include difficulty separating work from personal life; lower toleration of frustration; increased outburst of anger and sometimes rage; dread of working with certain people; over-identification with others, and projection of one's own feelings onto those who have been traumatized.

Closely related is what is called *vicarious traumatization*, the harmful effects of trauma arising from working with people who have been traumatized. Like compassion fatigue it comes as a result of deep empathic engagement with those who have been traumatized. It affects the inner

---

[14] Dorothy S. Becvar, "The impact on the family therapist of a focus on death, dying, and bereavement," *Journal of Marital and Family Therapy* (2003): 469–77.

emotional and spiritual life of the caregiver, and it takes its toll on the caregiver. Burnout is often the result, and the caregiver loses the ability to function physically, mentally, and emotionally.

Symptoms of vicarious traumatization include changes in one's worldview and spiritual orientation to life; challenges to one's meaning and purpose for life; raising questions about the ultimate meaning in life; and despair and loss of hope.

Thankfully, there are means of self-care for the first responder, especially if he or she is a religious caregiver. There are also resources for those caregivers who confront compassion fatigue and vicarious traumatization.

Self-Care in the Face of Trauma

Religious caregivers in the Judeo-Christian and Muslim religious traditions in North America often become entranced by a vision of ideal caregiving. In fact, such an ideal dominates many professions, whether religious or not. The vision is one of flawless delivery of empathy or attunement, and the expectation it generates is that we will sacrifice ourselves completely to achieve it. It is, however, unrealistic and beyond human capacity to provide perfect empathy. The best we can do is to provide something we can call *good-enough empathy*, which is within our human capacity. Even good-enough empathy, however, requires that we periodically care for ourselves emotionally, physically, and relationally so that we are replenished. In other words, there must be rest periods after the times the caregiver provides caring for others.

The vision of ideal caregiving disrupts our ability to take care of ourselves and to get rest and relaxation. Below is a quotation that speaks clearly to the problem of self-care when caregivers believe that they can provide perfect empathy:

> The emphasis on perfection has led people to describe the effort to achieve empathy as having "sucked the life out of the caregiver," and as having "the potential to contaminate" us as caregivers if we have no place to turn to for emotional and spiritual renewal. How to renew and sustain our vital spiritual and emotional life as religious and professional caregivers, and thus replenish our energy, remains a crucial need in the face of the demand for perfect empathy.[15]

Self-care in the face of trauma is essential. Historically, every age provides means and methods of self-care. These methods can be religious or

---

[15] Edward P. Wimberly, *Recalling Our Own Stories: Spiritual Renewal for Religious Caregivers* (San Francisco: Jossey-Bass, 1997), 7.

non-religious. They can be spiritual and appeal to universal audiences. Perhaps the best illustration of self-care in the twenty-first century is the *Oprah Winfrey Show*, where significant practices of self-care take place. Marcia Z. Nelson outlines ten significant practices that Oprah teaches on her daily television program.[16]

While the practices of Oprah appeal to a very wide audience, there are self-care practices in the Judeo-Christian and Muslim traditions as well. There is the concept of Sabbath rest in both the Old and New Testaments. For example, the book of Hebrews in the New Testament builds on the Hebrew practice of rest while on the journey. In this tradition, people rest periodically while on life's journey so that they can be replenished for the future pilgrimages. Key parts of the journey are periods of time out for rest and worship. In this tradition it is believed that the transcendent being significantly participates in the renewal taking place in Sabbath rest. The entire concept in education of sabbatical leave is built on this religious tradition. Muslims also have traditions of pilgrimage, which function similarly to the Judeo-Christian Sabbath.

In the Judeo-Christian religious tradition the concept of *lament* refers to conversation with the transcendent being and complaining about how difficult the journey in life is.[17] Complaining to the deity is permitted and encouraged because it is believed that such openness facilitates replenishment for the journey, which comes as a result of conversation with the divine.

Sabbath rest is also a period for internalizing conversations that help caregivers to edit their notions about providing perfect empathy. It is only when we are at Sabbath rest that caregivers recognize their limitations, and this periodic rest reminds them that they are human and vulnerable. We are not super-human. In short, Sabbath rest is essential for self-care and for recovering from compassion fatigue, vicarious traumatization, as well as from burnout and exhaustion.

Practices for Dealing with Trauma

Religious and spiritual caregivers have access to the best resources in the social, behavioral, and counseling psychologies as well as to healing and self-help resources of religious and spiritual traditions. Among behavioral and social science management strategies is the story-telling tradition,

---

[16] Marcia Z. Nelson, *The Gospel According to Oprah* (Louisville: Westminster John Knox, 2005).

[17] Edward P. Wimberly, *Claiming God, Reclaiming Dignity: African American Pastoral Care* (Nashville: Abingdon, 2003), 113–15.

which involves enabling people to tell their stories about their experiences of facing trauma. Telling stories about the trauma people face requires an audience of caring and sympathetic and empathic people. One of the major drawbacks of living in modern life is that the forums or places where people can have an audience to tell and listen to stories are in limited supply. Thus, one of the major functions of managing trauma is to ensure that there are forums and audiences where people can tell their stories.[18]

Key in providing audiences for story-telling and story-listening for people facing trauma is how story-telling in forums or caring communities fosters resilience in the face of trauma. Resilience relates to the capacity to muster one's inner and outer resources for meeting the challenges that people face when confronting trauma.

Resiliency practices are strategic activities that should be performed if people are to face trauma in their lives head on. Resiliency practices include the following story-telling practices: the practice of unmasking; the practice of inviting catharsis, the practice of relating empathetically, the practice of unpacking the story, and the practice of discerning and deciding how to move further on the journey beyond trauma.[19]

The practice of unmasking is letting what has happened to us take story-telling form. It is a process of story-sharing. "Unmasking refers to our allowing internal and unspoken happenings and circumstances of our lives—challenges and promise—to come to life in narrative form."[20] It helps us bring the hidden and inner dimensions of our experience of trauma to manifest itself so there can be healing.

The leaders in organized story-telling process for caregivers must be transparent with their own stories of dealing with trauma. When the leader tells a true story from personal experience, s/he provides a model for telling stories as well as for handling trauma. In doing so, the leader builds a foundation of empathy for the stories that caregivers will hear from others and helps them bring insight to those stories.

There are other benefits to helping caregivers to unmask their stories. Unmasking stories where others are present helps the caregivers to feel that their need for connecting with others gets satisfied. It also leads eventually to the caregivers seeing meaning and purpose in their problems. It gives them a sense that they are not alone, and it also helps them to get in touch with feelings and to give these feelings a name. The underlying premise to story-sharing during the unmasking phase is that there will be cathartic moments where there is release of negative emotions and honest feelings of

---

[18] Wimberly, *Claiming God*, 102.
[19] Wimberly and Wimberly, *Winds of Promise*, 36–49.
[20] Wimberly and Wimberly, *Winds of Promise*, 38.

the heart. Such catharsis cleanses the soul and opens up room for new and better feelings.[21]

The next practice of story-telling is *inviting catharsis*. Catharsis may occur at any point of the story-telling experience. Catharsis or expressing feelings is always good, especially if it cleanses the body of negative feelings. Yet, those who lead the story-telling practices must create a safe space for the caregivers to tell it like it is. ". . . Catharsis is the 'unburdening' of the heaviness that has accompanied holding onto a troubling or challenging experience or circumstance." People comment on how wonderful it feels to being given uninterrupted space to tell their stories.[22]

The practice of relating empathically is always important when people are in the midst of catharsis. Connecting to the feelings when there is an opportunity for the leader is comforting to the story-sharer. Those surviving trauma especially feel good when they know they can trust others with their stories. Connecting empathetically is all about helping people to recognize that others share the same experiences and strong feelings that they feel and experience and that they are not alone.

Catharsis is not enough, however. As caregivers tell their own stories, strong feelings are released; the experiences and feelings must be understood, and some meaningful frame or perspective needs to be employed as the leaders help the caregiver to reflect on these feelings and experiences. This phase of the story-telling is called *unpacking stories*. The significance of story-telling is that what happened during the trauma often reappears time after time until it eventually becomes a small memory without force in the trauma sufferer's life. There is need to update and make meaning out of what happens so that it is possible to live triumphantly without feeling overwhelmed and always vulnerable. The experience of trauma will never be forgotten, but its power to perpetuate trauma and pain lessens over time, and practices such as spiritual renewal exercises, reauthoring or editing, and interpreting and putting the experience in plot language helps to tame the influence of the trauma.[23]

The point to unpacking or putting the meaning of the experience in plot language is essential to tame the trauma. Plots are ends toward which our lives are going. There are several ends to stories, and the most important thing for caregivers to discover is that traumatic stories are not the end of the story. Not all traumatic stories have to have tragic endings. The significance of story-telling with an audience is to discover the truth that trauma, though powerful, is episodic rather than permanent. Most religious

---

[21] Wimberly and Wimberly, *Winds of Promise*, 12.
[22] Wimberly and Wimberly, *Winds of Promise*, 43.
[23] Wimberly and Wimberly, *Winds of Promise*, 45.

and spiritual caregivers will eventually help those suffering from trauma to connect their trauma experiences with the hopeful plot that under girds their religious and spiritual traditions, and in so doing they are able to help the trauma victim to discern that trauma is not the end to the story.[24]

The final practice in story-telling is moving forward. This step is an outgrowth of unpacking practice where persons recognize the episodic nature of the trauma and link their lives with the plot associated with their faith, religious, or spiritual tradition. Religious plots in the Judeo-Christian tradition as well as in the Muslim traditions are hopeful. That is, they are moving toward ends that give life ultimate meaning.[25] In fact, spiritual traditions are all about connecting with the positive plots at work in the world that provide people meaning.

Spirituality and health are all about connecting with the universal healing dimensions in all of life. Religious traditions of the first responders have resilient resources including epic stories from which they can draw for spirituality and health. ese resources can be drawn on for story-telling and story-listening. Moreover, those who practice spirituality, such as Oprah Winfrey's television show, also help people suffering from trauma to tap into resilient spiritual practices. Indeed, health and spirituality in the face of trauma are at work all around us through narrative and healing resources of resiliency.

---

[24] Wimberly, *African American Pastoral Care*, xiii.
[25] Wimberly and Wimberly, *Winds of Promise*, 48–49.

8

Pastoral Theology in a Wesleyan Spirit (2011)

Edward Wimberly, a lifelong Methodist, plumbs John Wesley's theology
and its resources for the church in *No Shame in Wesley's Gospel.** Wimberly highlights Wesley's evangelical goals as well as the therapeutic dimensions of Wesleyan class meetings. Wimberly also stresses Wesley's refusal
to divorce personal salvation from the work of social transformation. In
so doing, Wimberly shores up the theological mandate for his own move
toward more public and *prophetic pastoral care.*

In the first essay, Wimberly examines a number of Wesley's writings
on slavery, noting in particular his "rhetoric of the heart," by which Wesley sought to convince his audiences of the evil of the African slave trade
(229). For Wesley, slavery was an affront to the gospel: it hindered slaves'
freedom to respond to the gospel; and it damaged the souls of those who did
the enslaving as well. Wimberly notes Wesley's theological claim: it is not
possible to gain spiritual happiness from an unjust economic system that
rests "on the backs of other human beings" (224). Wimberly sees in Wesley
a model for how to hold evangelism and public political witness together in
the twenty-first century.

The second essay expands upon the thesis that personal and social
transformation are linked, not only in Wesley's theology, but also in that

---

* Edward P. Wimberly, "Shame, Slavery, and Economics of Hope: Wesley's Public Theology," *No Shame in Wesley's Gospel: A Twenty-first Century Pastoral Theology* (Eugene, Ore.:
Wipf & Stock, 2011), 78–93; Wimberly, "Practical Public Theology: Civil Rights and
the Wesleyan Spirit," *Wesley's Gospel*, 94–109.

of Martin Luther King, Jr. and Cecil Wayne Cone.* Wimberly highlights the centrality of African Americans' personal relationship with God as the key to deconstructing and overcoming the shame inherent in the legacy of slavery.

This is the heart and soul of Wimberly's pastoral theology. Here we see how his theology undergirds and enlivens his commitment to prophetically inflected pastoral care, wherein individual, spiritual, and communal needs are recognized as interwoven aspects of the human experience. Wimberly teaches that a relationship to God is the source of agency and power to resist evil and oppression in this world (249).

Further Reading

Wimberly, Edward P. "No Shame in Wesley's Gospel." In *The Shame Factor: How Shame Shapes Society*, edited by Robert Jewett, 103–16. Eugene, Ore.: Cascade Books, 2011.

• • •

---

* Martin Luther King, Jr., *Strength to Love* (New York: Harper & Row, 1963); Cecil Wayne Cone, *Identity Crisis in Black Theology*, rev. ed. (Nashville: AMEC, 2003).

Shame, Slavery, and Economics of Hope: Wesley's Public Theology*

I see not how you can go through your glorious enterprise in opposing that execrable villainy which is the scandal of religion, of England, and of human nature. Unless God has raised you up for this very thing, you will be worn out by the opposition of men and devils. But if God be for you, who can be against you? Are all of them together stronger than God? O be not weary of well doing! Go on, in the name of God and in the power of his might, till even American Slavery (the vilest that ever saw the sun) shall vanish away before it.

Reading this morning a tract wrote by a poor African, I was particularly struck by the circumstance that a man who has a black skin, being wronged or outraged by a white man, can have no redress; it being a "law" in our colonies that the oath of a black against a white goes for nothing?[1]

This quote from John Wesley was taken from a letter to William Wilberforce, who was a member of the British Parliament. In the letter, Wesley encouraged him to take action for change against the vile system of slavery.[2] England outlawed participation in slave trading in 1807. In this chapter, I aim to show that Wesley saw a connection between human bondage and its impact on the souls of those who did the enslaving as well as on those who were enslaved. He saw that earning one's living and wellbeing at the expense of others was the major source of sin. Thus, the primary basis of his rhetorical practices dealing with slavery was his awareness that one's wellbeing in life ultimately did not depend on one's economic wellbeing, but was based on the One who created the economy in the first place.

The significance of this chapter for our contemporary society is that we can learn—from past traditions of faith and what they have to teach us—about the limitations of investing our happiness totally in "this world's"

---

[1] John Wesley, *Journals and Diaries*, in *The Works of John Wesley: The Bicentennial Edition*, ed. W. Reginald Ward and Richard P. Heitzenrater (Nashville: Abingdon, 1976), 7:242.

[2] David N. Hempton, "Wesley in Context," in *The Cambridge Companion to John Wesley*, ed. Randy L. Maddox and Jason E. Vickers (New York: Cambridge University Press, 2010), 72; Ted A. Campbell, "John Wesley as Diarist," in Maddox and Vickers, *Cambridge Companion*, 130; Rebekah L. Miles, "Happiness, Holiness, and the Moral in John Wesley," in Maddox and Vickers, *Cambridge Companion*, 217.

* This selection was previously published in Edward P. Wimberly, *No Shame in Wesley's Gospel: A Twenty-first Century Pastoral Theology* (Eugene, Ore.: Wipf & Stock, 2011), 78–93. ISBN 978-1-61097-193-5. www.wipfandstock.com.

economic systems. Moreover, they teach us that our happiness as human beings cannot rest on the backs of other human beings. More precisely, it is not possible to gain identity by forcing others into human shame and humiliation in order to bolster human privilege and economic superiority at the expense of others. Rather, our happiness rests in responding to God's love for us through love and service to others. Therefore, after this chapter introduces Wesley's rhetorical devices to address the evils of slavery, I will introduce the implications of Wesley's thoughts on slavery for the twenty-first century. The first implication will address how injustice challenges those being oppressed to confine their worth and identity as human beings to earthly, cultural, derogatory, shaming, and damaging images of their humanity and worth. Secondly, the chapter will address the implications of Wesley's practical theology for addressing unjust economic systems of exploitation.

It is key that we not only can visualize Wesley's therapeutic and healing dimension of this salvation theology at work, but also can see his justice-oriented theology in which people are held accountable for their sin. Wesley sought to help heal the damages inflicted on black people as a result of slavery as well as to heal the identities of white slave owners who sought their worth and identity at the expense of others. He also wanted slave owners to realize that their efforts to achieve identity, power, authority, and economic security on a faulty economic system was also sinful, for which they would suffer judgment.

Wesley's Evangelical Rhetorical Goal

Wesley's rhetorical and practical theological goal was not to make Christian public theologians who were politically aware citizens. In fact, becoming public theologians was a latent effect of his effort to save souls. His goal was evangelical, and he wanted all human beings to have a personal relationship with God as well as to respond to God's grace at work in their lives through loving God, self, and neighbor. Indeed, this chapter takes very seriously Robin Lovin's conclusion that Wesley's primary agenda was fostering a relationship with God.[3] In fact, Lovin states:

> Wesley strongly opposed slavery, not because he believed that "all men are created equal;" but because he believed that the slave, like everyone else, has a soul that can be addressed, claimed, and redeemed by God. Thus the slave, like everyone else, needs the freedom to respond to

[3] Robin Lovin, "Human Rights, Vocation, and Human Dignity," in *Our Calling to Fulfill: Wesley's Views on the Church in Mission*, ed. M. Douglas Meeks (Nashville: Kingwood, 2009), 109–23.

the word of grace proclaimed. The equality that Wesley understood was evangelical, not political, and he probably would have understood claims to human dignity on behalf of sinners in need of conversion as a positive hindrance to the reception of the gospel.[4]

Wesley believed slavery hindered and blocked human beings relationship with God. It made it difficult for those who enslaved others to trust in God who was the source of the enslaver's true identity, worth, and dignity. It also made it difficult for those who were enslaved to feel close to God due to being enslaved by other human beings.

Wesley understood that slavery as a system and slave trading as an ideology were grounded in a *this-world*-oriented narrative that sought human happiness, identity, worth, and dignity at the expense of other human beings. To base one's identity and worth at the expense of others was sin and idolatry for Wesley. Moreover, this sin and idolatry had horrific consequences for others. Thus, slavery and slave trading put the salvation of the slave owner and the slave trader at peril just as it did those who were enslaved. As a result, Wesley felt he had to convince the slave owner and trader that their economic practices put their souls in jeopardy just as it did the souls of those enslaved. Therefore, Wesley's rhetoric of persuasion not only dealt with the soul and sin, but also with the economic system. His fundamental concern was to get the slave owner and trader to adopt a new form of economics that did not lay one's hope for happiness and worth on this world's exploitive and oppressive economic system.

Wesley was all about developing an economics of hope that freed black people in slavery as well as liberated whites who enslaved others. At the foundation of his theology for combating slavery was his therapeutic and healing model of salvation. His healing and therapeutic salvation theology speaks volumes to the twenty-first-century understanding of shame as well as the humiliation caused by colonialism and the economic efforts of whites who enslaved blacks to gain worth and identity by exploiting others.

For the economic system of slavery to work, slave owners and traders felt they had to stigmatize black people in slavery by labeling them as less than human and no better than animals. Wesley saw how this system of stigmatization was a major obstacle for the black person in slavery's relationship with God through Jesus Christ. Moreover, slavery was also was a form of idolatry blocking the enslavers' relationship with God as well. In short, slavery functioned as a method of reinforcing the humiliation and shame that destroyed not only the worth of those in slavery, but also the worth and value of those who owned slaves and practiced slave trading.

[4] Lovin, "Human Rights," 109–23.

It was only in a relationship with God in Jesus Christ that true worth and value was bestowed. Because slavery destroyed the souls and happiness of two races of people, Wesley was convinced that this economic system had to be abolished.[5]

Wesley and Public Rhetoric

Wesley had a simple motivational rhetoric. It was addressed directly to those in his reading and hearing audiences. George Lawton examines Wesley's literary roles as a publicist. A publicist is one who addresses public events through preaching, letter-writing, and producing educational tracts, as a diarist, pamphleteer, critic, and editor.[6] Lawton concludes that Wesley's homiletic and writing styles used a very simple rhetorical framework. Wesley told the audience what he intended to do, then he executed his intention, and finally, he told the reader and listener that he had completed his task.[7] He says Wesley's rhetoric in sermons had a therapeutic diagnostic precision, possessing clinical insight and accuracy. He used this therapeutic rhetoric to connect with his audience.[8] His use of prose was ordinary, and his language was always crystal clear, appropriate, penetrating, reasoned, and yet persuasive.[9] He was careful to adopt the people's common language, assuring that he would bond and communicate with them.[10]

Moreover, his sermons, as well as his vast publications, found their way into the homes of people and were part of many informal and formal conversations. In other words, his rhetoric was not just therapeutic. It was also a nurturing rhetoric, which nurtured the growth of persons as they were led by God's spirit into perfect love. His writings and thoughts were very much part of the public arena, both inside and outside the church. He could have been what social ethicist Robert Franklin calls a public theologian, particularly since he brought his faith unapologetically into the public arena.[11]

---

[5] Manfred Marquardt, "Social Ethics in Methodist Tradition," in *T&T Clark Companion to Methodism*, ed. Charles Yrigoyen Jr. (New York: T&T Clark International, 2010), 294–96.

[6] George Lawton, *John Wesley's English: A Study of His Literary Style* (London: Allen & Unwin, 1962), 240–65.

[7] Lawton, *Wesley's English*, 240.

[8] Lawton, *Wesley's English*, 242.

[9] Lawton, *Wesley's English*, 244.

[10] Lawton, *Wesley's English*, 245.

[11] Robert M. Franklin, "Travelin Shoes: Resources for Our Journey," *Journal of the Interdenominational Theological Center* 25, no. 1 (1997): 3 and Robert M. Franklin, *Another Day's Journey: Black Churches Confronting the American Crisis* (Minneapolis: Fortress, 1997). See also Edward P. Wimberly, *African American Pastoral Care and Counseling: The Politics of Oppression and Empowerment* (Cleveland: Pilgrim, 2006), 126–27.

Lawton points out that Wesley's thoughts and writings were public news in the eighteenth century. In fact, he says:

> Methodism was news. Largely by what Wesley called "singularity," i.e. full-blooded Christianity which contrasted noticeably with formal churchmanship—Methodism made an impact upon almost every community. As news, it stirred many a pen up and down the country.[12]

Wesley wrote excellent tracts or treatises where he appealed to public religious common sense and reason. He would make his persuasive conclusions, drawing on the religious understanding common at that time.

Wesley's characteristic therapeutic and nurturing rhetorical style was to grab the attention of his audience immediately. This was the case in this treatise. He declared immediately in the first paragraph his transparent intent to give a plain account of his religious principles and actions, trusting his innate writing wisdom that this would be the most appropriate way to connect with his reading audience.[13] In the second paragraph, he indicated the problem he would address in the treatise. He drew the audience's focus to "numerous follies" and miseries of human beings who had no religion or whose religion was lifeless and formal. He, then, pointed out that it would be great if it were possible to convince those people that God gifted humanity with religion. Not only was religion a gift, it was the source that gave humankind the love of God, the source of all good and love in life. God loved us first, and God was the fountain of all good we hope to enjoy.[14]

To summarize, Wesley's practices of persuasion were therapeutic in the sense that they sought to heal the sin of those seeking to establish human identity and happiness at the expense of others. This sin was evident in the oppressive slave-based economic system and in slave trading.

Wesley's Public Rhetoric and Protest Against Injustice

About two-thirds of the way through his *Thoughts Upon Slavery*, it is clear that Wesley's rhetorical techniques changed to a diatribe, which marked his shift away from the rhetoric of nurturing and therapy to a combative argumentative strategy to refute slavery.[15] It is clear that Wesley was making an impassioned argument, heightening an emotional rhetoric. He emphasized that there was a clear difference between justice and injustice and between

---

[12] Lawton, *Wesley's English*, 260.
[13] Wesley, *Works*, 3.
[14] Wesley, *Works*, 3.
[15] Robert Jewett, *Romans: A Commentary* (Minneapolis: Fortress, 2007), 25. Here, Jewett describes diatribe as a combative strategy.

cruelty and mercy. He talked about the injustice of taking Africans from their native land removing the rights guaranteed to all Englishmen.

His major premise was that all slave holding was inconsistent with natural justice. It was inconsistent with mercy. He attacked the profit motive and stressed that it was the heart of slavery. The most significant argumentative challenge, however, was his point that slavery was idolatrous economic system where those who engaged in it laid up for themselves treasures on earth and sought happiness through riches. He relied heavily on his ultimate premise, which was all happiness and virtue began with God and certainly did not rest in the slave-based economic system.

In this shift to diatribe, Wesley changed to what Carey calls the emotional rhetoric of sentimentality. This radical shift separated Wesley's approach from the rhetoric of Benezet. In part 4 of his treatise on slavery, he began with this shift of rhetoric, and it continued to the very end of the tract. In addition, Wesley continued his rhetorical diatribe by confronting vigorously the slave traders' slaving activities. He indicated that he would address his main writing audience, the captains of the slave ships, the merchants who dealt in slave trading, and the planters who extracted free labor from those enslaved. He made sure that those in his audiences in England and in the American colonies knew that he was addressing them.

Wesley clearly stated his first and second premise theologically in the form of a question and then an answer. He said:

> Is there a God? You know there is. Is he a just God? Then there must be a state of retribution; a state wherein the just God will reward every man according to his works. Then what reward will he render to you? O think betimes! Before you drop into eternity! Think now, "He shall have judgment without mercy that showed no mercy."[16]

In his last direct comment to them after indicating that liberty was a human natural right, he wrote the following words:

> If, therefore, you have any regard to justice, (to say nothing of mercy, nor the revealed law of God), render unto all their due. Give liberty to whom liberty is due, that is, to every child of man, to every partaker of human nature. Let none serve you but by his own act and deed, by his own voluntary choice. Away with *all* whips, all chains, all compulsion! Be gentle toward all men; and see that you invariably do unto every one as you would he should do unto you.[17]

---

[16] John Wesley, *Thoughts Upon Slavery* (London: R. Hawes, 1774), http://gbgm-umc
.org/umw/wesley/thoughtsuponslavery.stm, no longer available.

[17] Wesley, *Thoughts Upon Slavery*.

After the above statement, he prayed a prayer of petition, not on behalf of the ship captains, merchants, or planters; rather, he addressed those blacks who had been enslaved.

> O thou God of love, thou who are loving to every man, and whose mercy is over all thy works; thou who are the Father of the spirits of all flesh, and who are rich in mercy unto all; thou who has mingled of one blood all the nations upon earth; have compassion upon these outcasts of men, who are trodden down as dung upon the earth! Arise, and help these that have no helper, whose blood is spilt upon the ground like water! Are not these also the work of thine own hands, the purchase of thy Son's blood? Stir them up to cry unto thee in the land of their captivity; and let their complaint come up before thee; let it enter into thy ears! Make even those that lead them away captive to pity them, and turn their captivity as the rivers in the south. O burst thou all their chains in sunder; more especially the chains of their sins! Thou Savior of all, make them free, that they may be free indeed![18]

The most significant dimension of this prayer was Wesley's theological connection between the need for justice and evangelism. Wesley comprehended that slavery and slave trading hindered God's work in the lives of all persons, and slavery blocked and hindered the enslaved black people's relationship with God as well as the slaveholder or slave trader's own relationship with God by engaging in the slave-based economic system. Theologically, Wesley did not separate the souls of human beings from their economic, political, social, and cultural situation. Persons were whole human beings, and their souls and spirits interacted with their social and cultural context. Thus, Wesley expected those who based their entire system of survival on the backs of others to be judged harshly by God, and they needed to renounce their evil ways or face retribution.

From my own rhetorical analysis above, it is clear that my conclusions about Wesley's authorship of *Thoughts Upon Slavery* are very similar to Carey's conclusions. Indeed, Wesley followed the work of Benezet, and the rhetoric employed by Benezet was very logical and rational. This was the case in the first three sections, but the rhetoric shifted dramatically in the fourth and fifth sections of the treatise. I used the rhetorical term diatribe to describe Wesley's shift, but I like Carey's use of the term *sentimental rhetoric* to describe the shift in rhetoric. This dramatic change separated the writing of Wesley in the tract from the writing style of Benezet.

Carey concludes that Wesley's work departed from the geographical and legal (rational) argument, and utilized rhetoric of the heart to match

---

[18] Wesley, *Thoughts Upon Slavery.*

Wesley's emphasis on feeling religion.[19] I agree with Carey that his rhetoric not only shifted toward the literary use of emotion and sentimentality, but it shifted away from a political tract to an enthusiastic political sermon characteristic of Wesley's ecclesiastical context and ethos.

Of critical significance is Carey's statement that Wesley brought his private "feelings into the public sphere."[20] This made Wesley a "sentimental hero" or "a man of feeling:" Carey says that this was an "ironic strategy, and the true implied reader" in Wesley's audience was a feeling person, or one who was "shocked by the slave owner's brute insensibility because he has the sensibility required to be capable of being shocked in that way."[21] In short, Carey is suggesting that Wesley's intended reading audience were those persons who would be moved by Wesley's compassion. I must say that there must have been women reading this tract in the general public as well as in the society meetings.

Carey also indicates that eighteenth-century rhetorical sentimentality rested on the capacity of the writer and speaker to generate empathy, or the ability to imagine the feelings of another.[22] This relates to what I have identified in earlier places as therapeutic rhetoric, known as the motivational sequence. This was a major characteristic in all of Wesley's sermons. The motivational sequence was the effort to identify the concern or problem with which the audience was struggling and then address it in the sermon. Thus, Wesley's use of the language of the heart is consistent with his rhetorical style in other sermons.

Wesley and the Twenty-First Century Black Community

Wesley was concerned that slavery had an impact on the souls of the black people who were enslaved. I was struck considerably by Wesley's ending of *Thoughts Upon Slavery*. Suddenly, the tract ended with a prayer, which focused on the captivity of those enslaved without addressing the slave owners who were the subject of the tract. I not only noticed this sudden shift, but I also noticed the ending poem, which, frankly, upset me. He used what I thought were anger triggering and inciting words that would be totally unacceptable to twentieth-century and twenty-first-century African Americans. The poem was written as follows:

[19] Brycchan Carey, "John Wesley's *Thoughts Upon Slavery* and the Language of the Heart," *Bulletin of the John Rylands University Library of Manchester* 85, nos. 2–3 (2003): 283.
[20] Carey, "John Wesley's *Thoughts*," 283.
[21] Carey, "John Wesley's *Thoughts*," 284.
[22] Carey, "John Wesley's *Thoughts*," 284.

The servile progeny of Ham
Seize as the purchase of the blood!
Let all the Heathens know thy name:
From idols to the living God
The dark Americans convert,
And shine in every pagan heart![23]

I was suspicious of his identifying of enslaved Africans with Ham to justify slavery in the American colonies, but I was also disturbed by the word *pagan*. I was ready to dismiss Wesley as a modern-day typical racist who believed in the inferiority of black people. I was so disturbed that I looked up the term pagan, and discovered it was not a derogatory term, but a descriptive word for non-Christians. He was not using it in the sense of the word *heathen*, which in racist language was derogatory, implying or meaning uncivilized. The word heathen was used to justify the ill treatment of black people in slavery. It is clear that Wesley was not using the term pagan to justify slavery. Wesley even used the word heathen earlier in the tract, but it was in the sense of non-Christian and not uncivilized.

Yet, I remained mystified by his relating black folk with the cursed children of Ham, however, until I read J. Gordon Melton's account of Wesley's impact on slavery in the American colonies, and Warren Thomas Smith's assessment of Wesley on slavery, as well as Carey's account of Wesley's rhetoric.[24] As a result, my spirit became more forgiving, and I could embrace Wesley's genuine concern for the black enslaved as well as for their freedom from captivity.

The shift to this poem at the end of the treatise on slavery was unexpected, and it seemed out of place. Rhetorically, however, it made sense. Wesley's rhetoric always took into account those who would be reading his treatises. Therefore, he was addressing not the slave owners or slave traders, exclusively. Rather, he was addressing those in the societies and those in the public who might be persuaded by his anti-slavery and anti-slave-trade sentiments. Therefore, he wanted to be sure that they saw the connection between slavery and its slave trade and the negative impact both had on those enslaved. I am sure his rhetoric was to incite in his audience moral outrage against slavery.

When I look at the implications of Wesley's rhetoric for the twenty-first century, I also think of persons who might be interested in Wesley's thoughts on slavery in congregations. How would we translate Wesley's

---

[23] Wesley, *Thoughts Upon Slavery.*

[24] Warren Thomas Smith indicated that *Thoughts Upon Slavery* was Wesley's genuine work in *John Wesley and Slavery* (Nashville: Abingdon, 1986), 91; J. Gordon Melton, *A Will to Choose: The Origins of African American Methodism* (New York: Rowman & Littlefield, 2007), 25; Carey, "John Wesley's *Thoughts*," 284.

rhetoric so that we in this century can visualize the significance of Wesley's thoughts for today? First, it is important to envisage modern-day segregation, prejudice, and beliefs in the inferiority of people of color as a political process. As a political process these negative activities and convictions seek to restrict the access of people of color to the limited economic resources offered by society. I understand racial politics as "limiting access to the vast range yet finite supply of resources needed for human fulfillment."[25]

Wesley dealt with overt racism and forceful and oppressive enslavement of Africans in the colonies and in England. One subtle and less overt strategy used today among the white majority is to recruit African Americans, Hispanic Americans, Asian Americans, and immigrant Americans of color into negative stereotypes so that they internalize these negative images. When these negative stereotypes are internalized by these groups, the devalued people become less of a threat economically.

To say this in Wesleyan language, negative images of people of color today help people of color to define themselves as inferior and "less than" others. The end result is settling for jobs and roles in society that majority people do not want. In the Wesleyan spirit, this internalization of the negative images of themselves causes devalued people to limit their identity and worth to these negative and stereotypical images. When this happens, the danger is that this internalizing blocks people of color from seeing themselves as children of God. Thus, the same end result takes place, whether it was overt slavery or subtle recruitment into negative images.

From the standpoint of practical theology in the Wesleyan spirit, Wesley's rhetoric is still applicable for those who are the white majority. His evangelical language would include being concerned about one's neighbor. It would also include the awareness that restricting others to limited economic resources is developing one's group identity and worth at the expense of other, less valued groups. This is indeed sin, but it also damages the soul of those who employ these negative images as well as being detrimental to those who are victims of such negative images.

Wesley and Twenty-First Century Capitalism

Another twentieth-century and twenty-first-century concern is whether Wesley's thoughts really addressed the structural issues related to the capitalistic economic system that was emerging as a result of the burgeoning Industrial Revolution. One assessment of how Wesley addressed the structural issue was given by Manfred Marquardt. His goal was to assess John Wesley's thinking about individual and collective economic ethics.

---

[25] Wimberly, *Politics of Oppression*, 12.

Marquardt believes that all of Wesley's economic thinking rested on Wesley's three simple rules of "gain all you can; save all you can; and give all you can." He stated: "In fact, these rules appropriately sum up Wesley's own practices and his congregational teachings concerning handling money and other economic goods."[26]

The third rule, which focused on giving all you could, was key in Wesley's thinking. Indeed, this rule was focused on making sure that human beings did not lay up their treasures on earth and that they kept their eyes focused on God's present but not yet rule and reign.[27] Placing one's hope for identity, meaning, and happiness in this world's treasures was clearly a tragic choice, and it would eventuate in disastrous consequences in a person or community's life.

Marquardt sought to explore to what extent Wesley's thinking eventually led people to embrace the capitalistic spirit. His concern was to assess whether or not those who followed Wesley embraced the first two of the economic rules, which were to earn all you could, and save all you could. Marquardt clearly believed, as Wesley did, that the third rule—giving all you could—would prevent people laying up for themselves treasures on earth.

Marquardt, however, came to the conclusion that Wesley did contribute to the spread of capitalism. However, while there were some aspects of Wesley's thinking that contributed to the spirit of capitalism, Marquardt believes that Wesley's theology countered this effort to embrace capitalism. He concluded:

> At the same time it must be observed that some fundamental expressions of Wesley's economic ethics thoroughly contradicted the "spirit of capitalism" and, historically considered, worked against that spirit. Alongside the radial social obligation connected with property ownership, these elements specifically included demands that the state intervene in the economic process (to be considered in the next section), and rejection of coupling economic success to favorable standing with God. Indeed, Wesley gave no sign of proving the certainty of faith by good works or earthly prosperity, in the sense of practical syllogism.[28]

I agree with Marquardt's assessment of Wesley's thoughts on economics. Yet, in Marquardt's assessment of Wesley's thoughts on capitalism, he

---

[26] Manfred Marquardt, *John Wesley's Social Ethics: Praxis and Principles*, trans. John E. Steely and W. Stephen Gunter (Nashville: Abingdon, 1992), 35.

[27] John Wesley, "The Danger of Riches," in *The Works of John Wesley* (Grand Rapids: Baker, 1998), 7:1–15.

[28] Marquardt, *Social Ethics*, 41–42.

demonstrates that Wesley's ethical thinking clearly addressed some of the structural dimensions of capitalism. It was clearly important to participate in the economic system so that the basic needs of human beings could be met. Yet, placing one's hope for happiness and identity in the economic system was shortsighted and self-deceptive.

Overall, however Marquardt did not believe Wesley really addressed social structural issues. There is some thinking that Wesley did not try to change social structure, and that he was only interested in the souls of the poor. This was Marquardt's conclusion. He says that Wesley rejected structural changes in society.[29] However, Wesley's concern for the souls of the oppressed, his tract *Thoughts Upon Slavery*, and his passionate rhetorical diatribe against slavery had the impact of leading the Methodist movement to attack the evils of slavery. The impetus helped to bring slave trading to an end in England.

I am convinced that Wesley's addressing structural dimensions of ethical living is clear in Wesley's practical theology dealing with the injustice of slavery and slave trading. Slavery was a vital reality for Wesley and for his time period, both in England and in the American colonies. It is important to address how Wesley's evangelical theology, grounded in justification and sanctification, had an impact on social structural issues related to slavery. For African Americans living in the twenty-first century, this is the most important issue for testing whether Wesley's theology and thinking are relevant for our contemporary faith and practice.

Scholars' assessments concerning the transforming aspect of his thoughts on slavery are mixed. Some say his thoughts have had a transforming impact on social structure. Others say there was no real impact at all.[30] I take the stand that Wesley's pre-Enlightenment rhetoric was an engaged and relationally reasoned rhetoric, which did not artificially separate reason and experience. Wesley always kept reason and revelation connected and did not join reason only with sense data as did John Locke, whose thinking Wesley understood and challenged. Pre-modern thinking trusted the relationship between the knower and the One who provided the knowledge, and this thinking also envisioned the link between knowledge and virtue. In fact, Wesley's view of revelation and reason as coming from

[29] Marquardt, *Social Ethics*, 134.

[30] M. Douglas Meeks, "A Home for the Homeless: Vocation, Mission, and Church in Wesleyan Perspective," in *Our Calling to Fulfill: Wesleyan Views of the Church in Mission*, ed. M. Douglas Meeks (Nashville: Kingswood, 2009), 1–10; Lovin, "Human Rights;" Theodore W. Jennings, Jr., *Good News to the Poor: John Wesley's Evangelical Economics* (Nashville: Abingdon, 1990), 181–98; Marquardt, *Social Ethics*, 133–138; and Richard P. Heitzenrater, "The Poor and the People Called Methodists, 1729–1999," in *The Poor and the People Called Methodists*, ed. Richard P. Heitzenrater (Nashville: Kingswood, 2002), 15–38.

God and leading to virtue in life was his basic point in "Earnest Appeal to Men of Reason and Religion." The point is that Wesley's thoughts did not artificially separate evangelically relating to God through Jesus Christ and a person's responsibility to demonstrate that relationship by living responsibly. Moreover, this spread of Wesley's emphasis on the relationship between the personal processes of justification and sanctification on the societies meant that people within those societies would implement his ideas in their daily lives, depending on their stations in life. The effort of the societies was to help people to internalize the virtues that came from their relationship with God and to live them out in the world.

Further support for connecting evangelical emphasis and social transformation come from some African American political scientists. Contemporary, African American, political science thinking addresses the connection of social transformation and personal transformation. For example, there is a connection, tie, bond, and correlation between personal agency and facilitating the agency of others in the evangelical thinking of African American Christians. Frederick C. Harris points out this causal relationship between the two. The discovery of personal efficacy or agency occurs when an individual realizes that he or she has power to influence his or her condition in life. Then he or she becomes civically involved on behalf of others, illustrating the facilitation of agency. This was particularly the case with African Americans.[31]

Realizing, from my experience as an African American Christian, that there is a holistic connection between personal transformation and engagement in social and political transformation, I was led to look for these same connections in Wesley. Wesley's emphasis on neighborly love, which was a response to God's justifying love, was enacted communally. In the societies, his sermons and tracts were systematically studied. Readers were expected not only to internalize the value and virtues in their lives, but also to live them out in their daily lives and their work. Therefore, Wesley's thinking was not just for the personal edification of believers. They were expected to make a social witness against slavery. In fact, this was the conclusion of some Wesley historians, as we shall see later in this essay.

Summary and Conclusions

This chapter began with the statement that Wesley's primary goal was not to make public theologians. On the contrary his practical theological goal was to enable all persons to have a meaningful relationship with God.

---

[31] Frederick C. Harris, *Something Within: Religion in African-American Activism* (New York: Oxford University Press, 1999), 81–85. See also Wimberly, *Politics of Oppression*, 28–36.

Wesley was concerned, however, with the reality that slavery hindered those enslaved from having a meaningful relationship with God. I indicated that Wesley's publicly addressing slavery from his evangelical perspective would have latent consequences and eventually would change the slave system. My analysis not only confirms this, but also confirms, validates, and reinforces Wesley's conscious effort to possibly change social structure by moving what Cary called the implied reader to consider addressing the slave trade as an economic system.

My contention in this chapter is that Wesley's pre-Enlightenment theology, focusing on happiness and virtue, permitted him to do public theology in a way that held evangelism and political action together. The use of relational, nurturing, emotional, rhetorical, and diatribe theory, applied to Wesley's sermons and tracts, helps to illustrate his holistic approach. His concern for the relationship of persons to God, as well as his speaking to the need for virtuous love in addressing public issues of vital concern for all, were consistent. For me, his commitment to the abolitionist movement to end slavery needs to be the center of all of our efforts to understand Wesley as a public theologian.

A final point needs to be mentioned about Wesley and those enslaved in the American colonies. According to Love Henry Whelchel, Wesley's ministry in the Americas from 1735 to 1737 was significant for Wesley and subsequently influenced his work to abolish the slave system. He endeared himself to those Africans in slavery in the Americas because of his concern for their welfare, physical and spiritual. In fact, Whelchel points out that the popularity of Methodism for the enslaved Africans was because of Wesley's ministry among them.[32] The point is that Wesley had firsthand experience with the slave system from his experiences in the Americas and in England, and his passion for the slaves' physical and spiritual plight was real. Indeed, Wesley's theology was orthodox in the sense that relational privileging of a relationship with God was not only right belief but was connected to right behavior and practice or orthopraxis with regard to slavery. Wesley's theology and his evangelical thinking had practical and socio-structural consequences.

Clearly, John Wesley's relevance for the twenty-first century is his conclusion that there is an economics of hope. The hope is in an economy of practical theology that rests human hope clearly in God's present but coming and unfolding rule and reign. Limiting our hope to earning all we can and saving all we can without giving all we can causes us to place our hope

<hr/>

[32] Henry L. Whelchel, Jr., "'My Chains Fell Off': Heart Religion in the African American Methodist Tradition," in *"Heart Religion" in the Methodist Tradition and Related Movements*, ed. Richard B. Steele (Lanham, Md.: Scarecrow, 2001), 103.

in this world rather than in God's unfolding realm. Moreover, to place our hope in this world's economic systems will also cause us to seek our own identity and worth at the expense of others. Thus, a practical theology of the economics of hope in the Wesleyan spirit connects to God's life and God's future.

• • •

Practical Public Theology: Civil Rights
and the Wesleyan Spirit *

One of the major characteristics of black Wesleyan practical theology is the refusal to divorce personal salvation from the work of social transformation.[1] Martin Luther King Jr. maintained this tradition of not separating personal and social transformation. This is obvious in his sermon entitled "Transformed Nonconformist."[2] Cecil Wayne Cone also believes liberation theology should not separate personal and social transformation. Moreover, this unity is found in the conversion tradition of African American Christians.[3] This chapter argues that the artificial separation of personal and social transformation undermines the liberational struggle of African Americans. *There is a strong legacy of uniting the personal and social transformation dimensions in African American church history, and it must be recovered if African American practical theology is going to be effective in the twenty-first century. For too long, liberation theology kept these two dimensions separate, but there is evidence that this alienation is over and that there is a healthy integration of these two dimensions.*

Historically, this unity can be seen in the conversion tradition of black Christians in slavery and freedom as well as in the Civil Rights tradition, particularly in the sermons of Dr. Martin Luther King Jr. This chapter explores the Wesleyan and evangelical roots of the Civil Rights Movement, particularly in the slave conversion tradition and in selected sermons of Martin Luther King Jr., and gives attention to their presence in black theology. Attention will be given to the rhetorical, practical theological strategies of both Wesley and King. Both remind us that we are citizens of two worlds. There is the world of the "here and now," but there is also the world that is "present and not yet" of God's rule and reign.

The basic theme of this chapter is that the similarity between Wesley and King lay in their rhetoric about living in two worlds. King sought to convince those in the Civil Rights struggle to be "transformed nonconformists."[4] He also asked white Christians to "be not conformed to this

---

[1]   Henry L. Whelchel, Jr., "'My Chains Fell Off': Heart Religion in the African American Methodist Tradition," in *"Heart Religion" in the Methodist Tradition and Related Movements*, ed. Richard B. Steele (Lanham, Md.: Scarecrow, 2001), 116–17.

[2]   Martin Luther King, Jr., *Strength to Love* (New York: Harper & Row, 1963), 10.

[3]   Cecil Wayne Cone, *Identity Crisis in Black Theology*, rev. ed. (Nashville: AMEC, 2003).

[4]   King, *Strength to Love*, 10.

*   This selection was previously in Edward P. Wimberly, *No Shame in Wesley's Gospel: A Twenty-first Century Pastoral Theology* (Eugene, Ore.: Wipf & Stock, 2011), 94–109. ISBN 978-1-61097-193-5. www.wipfandstock.com.

world."[5] John Wesley's eighteenth-century rhetoric also addressed the drawback of basing human happiness on this world's riches and, especially, on this world's economic system of slavery and slave trading. His sermons "The Danger of Riches" and "The More Excellent Way" and his treatise *Thoughts Upon Slavery* all addressed the sin of human beings laying up for themselves treasures on earth rather than in the world that was coming but is not yet.[6]

This chapter also explores Anglican and Wesleyan emphasis on evangelism of black people in slavery and its connection to the African American conversion tradition. There was a strong evangelical conversion tradition among black Christians in slavery, which carried over into the early twentieth century and up to the time of the Civil Rights Movement. This presentation links this conversion tradition with King's connection of personal and social transformation.

With regard to the issue of shame, it is clear that the Christian conversion tradition, beginning in slavery and continuing up to the present time, was the source of black people's capacity to deal creatively with the shame and degradation caused by racial oppression and injustice. In fact, it was in the Negro spirituals that it is possible to envisage the connection between social protest, civil rights, justice, and the overcoming of shame. Anne Streaty Wimberly writes:

> The struggle of persons to deal with the trauma of stigmatization and shame is not easy. In truth, it cannot be assumed that black people in slavery did not succumb to their experiences of personal, social, and physical brutalization. In fact, Ronald Salzberger and Mary Turck contend that, for some, the brutalities of slavery resulted in what historian Nell Irvin Painter called "soul murder," insofar as persons experienced an irreversible deadening feeling of self. However, in the very real situation of unspeakable harm faced by black people in slavery, the spirituals were born; and the music attested to the ability of many to overcome shaming attitudes and continue on amidst brutalizing circumstances.[7]

---

[5] King, *Strength to Love*, 157.

[6] John Wesley, "The Danger of Riches," in *The Works of John Wesley*, ed. Thomas Jackson (Grand Rapids: Baker, 1998), 7:1–15; John Wesley, "The More Excellent Way," in *Sermons I*, ed. Albert C. Outler, *The Works of John Wesley: The Bicentennial Edition* (Nashville: Abingdon, 1976), 1:26–37; John Wesley, *Thoughts Upon Slavery* (London: R. Hawes, 1774), http://gbgm-umc.org/umw/wesley/thoughtsuponslavery.stm, no longer available.

[7] Anne Streaty Wimberly, "Overcoming Shame in Slave Songs and the Epistle to the Hebrews," in *The Shame Factor: How Shame Shapes Society*, ed. Robert Jewett (Eugene, Ore.: Cascade, 2011), 80.

Rhetoric in the Storytelling of African Americans
in Slavery and Freedom

Anglicanism, which was the faith tradition of John Wesley, provided instruction in the Christian faith to enslaved African Americans as early as the mid seventeenth century, but a peculiar thing took place. Early on, black Africans in slavery exercised control over what they learned from the Anglican missionaries. Albert J. Raboteau points out:

> For slaves brought their cultural past to the task of translating and inter-preting the doctrinal words and ritual gestures of Christianity. Therefore the meaning which the missionary wished the slaves to receive and the meaning which the slaves actually found (or, better, made) were not the same. The "inaccuracy" of the slaves' translation of Christianity would be a cause of concern to missionaries for a long time to come.[8]

Raboteau continues his emphasis on the freedom slaves enjoyed to inter-pret and reinterpret Christianity in light of their own African cultural and religious experiences. He also goes on to say that "powerful emotionalism, ecstatic behavior, African dance, and congregational verbal responses were all part of the conversion and evangelical dimension of Protestantism."[9] In short, Raboteau's analysis lays the groundwork for the basic argument of this presentation. That is to say, the similarity between Wesley's use of rhet-oric and King's rhetoric in selective sermons and writings lay in American Protestant evangelical revivalism.

It is important to lift up the holistic conversion tradition of black people in slavery and its aftermath. The black conversion tradition represents a vast reservoir of orally narrated conversion stories, which were originally told as enslaved people experienced God and received salvation. These conversion experiences of formerly enslaved people were collected in the 1920s and 1930s as researchers interviewed black people who were once enslaved. These orally narrated conversion stories became a rhetorical style of witness taking place within the African American church. It was this tradition that influenced the theology of Martin Luther King Jr. and Cecil Cone.

The conversion tradition was not only an important influence on the thinking of King and on his effort to keep personal and social transforma-tion in dynamic tension: Cecil Wayne Cone sees the conversion tradition of black people in slavery as an important source of black and liberation the-ology. In contrast to his brother, James Cone, he visualizes the conversion

---

[8] Albert J. Raboteau, *Slave Religion: The "Invisible Institution" in the Antebellum South* (New York: Oxford University Press, 1978), 126–27.

[9] Raboteau, *Slave Religion*, 149.

tradition as the source of the essence of black religion and liberation. In short, his work testifies to the holism of the personal and social in addressing oppression.

Cecil Cone's argument in *Identity Crisis in Black Theology* is that it is black peoples' experience of God in the midst of suffering, oppression, slavery, and betrayal that is the source of liberation theology, not Black Power or the Civil Rights Movement.[10] James Cone took the Enlightenment tack of distrusting completely the conversion experience tradition and rooted his theology in the correlation of black theology and liberation theology with Black Power. Cecil Cone argues that black theology should reach back to the history and culture of black people in Africa.[11] For him, it was the conversion tradition growing out of slavery that enabled this African connection.

Cecil Cone says that black religion is "an experience expressed in a confessional story of Black people's relationship with God," and this is the major source of doing black theology.[12] This experiential understanding of black theology is also the source of the rhetorical thesis of this presentation. I agree with Raboteau's assessment of the convergence of how African Americans in slavery developed their own hermeneutical lenses for interpreting their encounters with God. African tradition gave this conversion tradition its distinctiveness.

Wesley and King

The conversion tradition of black people in slavery and its aftermath is the source of the holism of personal and social transformation. It is the conversion tradition that provides the link between Wesley and King's emphasis on rhetoric. There is correspondence between the rhetoric of King's "two-world" emphasis and Wesley's "two-world" emphasis. Could Wesley's anti-slavery rhetoric and Kings civil rights rhetoric—in his sermon "Paul's Letter to American Christians"—represent a novel way to transcend political divisions between black Christians and white Christians? Moreover, is it worth pursuing?

Dr. King, in "Paul's Letter to American Christians" in *Strength to Love*, focused on Romans 12:2, and he reminded Christians that we are citizens of two worlds, "the world of time and the world of eternity. Our loyalty, he

---

[10] Edward P. Wimberly, "The Significance of the Work of Cecil Wayne Cone," in *The Identity Crisis in Black Theology*, by Cecil Wayne Cone (Nashville: AMEC, 2003), 11.

[11] James H. Cone, *My Soul Looks Back*, Journeys in Faith (Nashville: Abingdon, 1982), 60.

[12] Cone, *My Soul*, 15.

says, needs to be grounded and rooted in eternity and not in earthly customs and institutions that have fostered slavery, racism, and segregation."[13]

In like manner, Wesley recognizes the danger and limitations of grounding one's identity, worth, happiness, and meaning in this world's promises of riches. Wesley denounced vehemently slave owning and slave trading. His rhetoric not only drew on the notion of choosing the more excellent way, but reached angry emotional levels in trying to convince the slave owner and slave trader that their wellness as human beings was in jeopardy. He also believed slavery blocked God's effort to bring African Americans happiness on earth and in eternity.

Wesley's Rhetoric Context

Thoughts Upon Slavery, published in the year 1774, shows John Wesley's rhetoric or effort to convince those who forced black people into slave labor and who forcefully removed them from their homes in Africa that bondage and slave trading were contrary the gospel and natural law.[14] This economic system also put the soul of slave traders and owners as well as the souls of those enslaved into mortal danger. His rhetoric was addressed not only to those who were enslaved. It was also directed at the general public as well as the Wesleyan societies or small religious formation groups.

Wesley's rhetoric was clearly grounded in a theology of happiness. His theology of happiness was based on the belief that true happiness is only in relationship with God and not in the slave system. He tried to convince slave owners and traders that wealth coming out of the system of slavery did not produce glory. He said:

> For first, wealth is not necessary to the glory of any nation; but wisdom, virtue, justice, mercy, generosity, public spirit, love of our country. These are necessary to the real glory of a nation; but abundance of wealth is not.[15]

Wesley also warned the slave owner and trader about the retribution that comes from stealing humans and trading slaves. He said:

> Is there a God? You know there is. Is he a just God? Then there must be a state of retribution; a state wherein the just God will reward every man according to his works. Then what reward will he render to you? O

---

[13] See Edward P. Wimberly, *African American History Month Daily Devotions 2009* (Nashville: Abingdon, 2008), 5.

[14] Wesley, *Thoughts Upon Slavery*.

[15] Wesley, *Thoughts Upon Slavery*.

think betimes! Before you drop into eternity! Think now, "He shall have judgment without mercy that showed no mercy."[16]

The point is that according to Wesley's theology laying up for yourselves treasures on earth rather than in the present but coming reign of God led away from true happiness in God and would end in being judged negatively by God.

Wesley's Rhetorical Strategies

What were the familiar rhetorical strategies that John Wesley used to convince people to choose a relationship with God and the world that was unfolding related to God's rule and reign? I have found that many of Wesley's sermons use what is called in modern rhetoric the motivational sequence. The first strategy is to get the attention of those in the audience. The attention-getter is usually a provocative statement such as the following: In Wesley's sermon "The Circumcision of the Heart," which is based on Romans 2:29, Wesley began immediately with the problem he wanted to address in the sermon. He said, "If Christ be risen, ye ought then to die unto the world, and to live wholly unto God."[17] His rhetoric went straight to where he expected the readers and hearers to focus their minds and hearts. He wanted them to focus on what it meant to be alive to the world but to be dead to God. Being alive to God involves being renewed by the Spirit of God daily.

After getting the audience's attention, he introduced the problem that he wanted the readers and hearers of the sermon to consider. This was the need to have a circumcised heart, or the testimony, in their hearts, that they were "children of God." As a result, they must give themselves totally to God and not to the desires of this world.[18] His goal was to convince those in the audience that real joy, hope, and happiness began first with a relationship with God. Wesley wrote:

> Let every affection, and thought, and word, and work, be subordinate to this. Whatever ye desire or fear, whatever ye seek or shun, whatever ye think, speak, or do, be it in order to your happiness in God, the sole end as well as source of your being.

---

[16] Wesley, *Thoughts Upon Slavery*.

[17] John Wesley, *John Wesley's Sermons: An Anthology*, eds. Albert C. Outler and Richard P. Heitzenrater (Nashville: Abingdon, 1991), 25.

[18] Wesley, *Sermons*, 26–27.

He continues:

> Have no end, no ultimate end, but God. Thus our Lord, "One thing is needful." And if thine eye be singly fixed on this one thing, "thy whole body shall be full of light." Thus St. Paul, "This one thing I do; I press toward the mark, after the prize of the high calling in Christ Jesus." Thus St. James, "Cleanse your hands, ye sinners, and purify your hearts, ye double minded." Thus St. John, "Love not the world, neither the things that are in the world. For all that is in the world, the lust of the flesh, the lust of the eye, and the pride of life is not of the Father, but is of the world." The seeking happiness in what gratifies either the desire of the flesh, by agreeably striking upon the outward senses; the desire of the eye, of the imagination, by its novelty, greatness, or beauty; or the pride of life, whether by pomp, grandeur, power, or the usual consequence of them, applause and admiration; "is not of the Father," cometh not from, neither is approved by the Father of spirits "but of the world;" it is the distinguishing mark of those who will not have him reign over them.[19]

The key point in all of this is what is called rhetorical invention. That is to say that all of Wesley's insight and logic is grounded in the authority of Scripture. Yet, Wesley takes his theology to another level by linking the circumcision of the heart on what he calls "inbred pollution." If people are to be perfect, they must add love to their lives, which is the perfection of happiness.[20] Thus, Wesley's rhetoric served the ends of justice, mercy, and love of neighbor. He links personal and social transformation, and it was this linking that eventually led Wesley to condemn slavery and slave trading.

King's Rhetorical Context

King's rhetorical context and strategies have some major themes in common with John Wesley's. While I am not making a causal link between Wesley and King, I have earlier referred to King's theological understanding of the two-world orientation to time, which grew out of what is called the slave conversion tradition, which was greatly influenced by Anglicanism. Moreover, what King and Wesley had in common was a context that was completely shaped by slavery. Thus, I will say something about the rhetorical context of King as well as his rhetorical strategies.

Dr. Martin Luther King Jr's rhetorical context was the Civil Rights Movement period of the 1950s and 1960s. He came to public notoriety because of the Montgomery Bus Boycott of 1955, initiated when Mrs. Rosa Parks violated the official white segregationist bus seating policies, which

---

[19] Wesley, *Sermons*, 28–29.
[20] Wesley, *Sermons*, 28–29.

made it unlawful for a black person to refuse to give up his or her seat for a white person. In fact, by segregationist convention and law, she should have taken a seat in the back of the bus. Her refusal to give up her seat set off a firestorm of reaction s among whites and propelled the African American community into one of the most spiritual and human agency actions of protests in United States history.

Dr. Martin Luther King Jr. was pastor of Dexter Avenue Baptist Church and, by his own testimony, indicated that his concern was not about moving off into the prophetic ministry in the pursuit for social justice. His concern was to pastor his church, develop his congregation, and build up the community surrounding his church. Dr. King's intention for this congregation became very clear to me when Dr. Murray Branch—who replaced Dr. King at Dexter Avenue Church and was an Old Testament Professor at the Interdenominational Theological Center—invited me to the now historic Dexter Avenue King Memorial Church to lead that congregation in relational renewal in the late 1970s. It was at that time that I saw Dr. King's strategic plan for the church, and it was clear that he did not intend to address the problems of racial inequality. But it was in the context of segregation, human lynching, and injustice for black people that the Civil Rights Movement was born when Dr. King and Mrs. Rosa Parks answered God's call to action.

King's Rhetorical Strategies

King always had several audiences that he addressed when he preached or wrote his letters. His rhetorical style, like Wesley's, was first to get the audience's attention and then to introduce the problem he would address. After introducing the problem, he would then introduce what he thought would be the solutions, and finally he would help them take actions to solve the problem. I want to briefly examine the rhetorical methods used in two of King's sermons.

The first is "Paul's Letter to American Christians." It was published on November 4, 1956, approximately eleven months after the Montgomery Bus Boycott. His attention-getting method was to draw on a biblical letter-writing genre in the New Testament and to use the rhetorical method of speech-in-character. Speech-in-character is the creative style used to get the attention of others. It either drew on the writer's own biography or on someone else's to cleverly get the message across to the audience.[21] King used the biblical character of the Apostle Paul, knowing that both white and black Christians' attention would be riveted to what would follow.

[21] Robert Jewett, *Romans: A Commentary* (Minneapolis: Fortress, 2007), 1019.

After completing the customary biblical pattern of an epistolary greeting, King contemporized his letter and made it speak to the modern situation. He did this by referring to the advances in science and the marvels of technology. Yet, he suddenly turned to focus on the lack of human progress in the moral and spiritual area. After giving specifics of the inability to foster brother and sisterhood and progress in war, he went to the heart of the problem he wanted to address. This problem is what he called giving "ultimate allegiance to man-made systems and customs."[22] He went on to say:

> American Christians, I must say to you what I wrote to the Roman Christians years ago: "Be not conformed to this world, but be ye transformed by the renewing of your mind." You have a dual citizenry. You live both in time and eternity. Your highest loyalty is to God, and not to the mores or the folkways, the state or the nation, or any man-made institution. If any earthly institution or custom conflicts with God's will, it is your Christian duty to oppose it. You must never allow the transitory, evanescent demands of man-made institutions to take precedence over the eternal demands of the Almighty God.[23]

King also returns to this theme of belonging to two worlds in the sermon "Transformed Nonconformist." Here, he also talked about the same theme that Wesley trumpeted often, and this theme was happiness. Wesley and King's rhetoric had the same source: the gospel of Jesus Christ. King wrote: "When an affluent society would coax us to believe that happiness consists in the size of our automobiles, the impressiveness of our houses, and the expensiveness of our cloths, Jesus reminds us, 'A man's life consisteth not in the abundance of the things which he possesseth.'"[24]

The similarity of Wesley and King's theology rested in their common understanding of the time dualism that was Pauline to the core. We live in two worlds. We live in the world of now and the world that is present but not yet; it is coming, and it is where God will reign and rule. Jesus inaugurated the coming of the new age, and God will complete it at the end of time.

It was indicated earlier that the common source of this time orientation to the two worlds came from Anglican missionary emphases. Wesley spent several years in the American colonies during slavery, and he befriended many persons who were in slavery. This experience as well as his knowledge of slave trading in Britain eventually led to his anti-slavery effort.

Those persons in slavery took what the missionaries preached and taught and transformed it into a message and strategy that would eventually

---

[22] King, *Strength to Love*, 157.
[23] King, *Strength to Love*, 157–58.
[24] King, *Strength to Love*, 11.

lead them out of slavery. King built on this tradition, and added non-violent protest to it, to fashion the Civil Rights Movement. His loyalty was always to the vision that he saw growing out of Paul's theology, that we must be committed to the world that is coming rather than to this world's riches and human-made customs.

The Civil Rights Movement and Black Power: A Bridge to Personal and Social Transformation

I was never convinced that the wedge driven between personal and social transformation was as wide as some in the Black Power Movement indicated. My theological mentor was James Deotis Roberts, and his theology became the theological underpinning of my doctoral dissertation, which I defended in November of 1975, while in my first year of teaching at ITC. I was very happy when Cecil Cone's book appeared in 1975 as well, because it also confirmed that the wedge between personal and social transformation was artificial in black theology.

Cecil asked me to write a brief statement endorsing the revised edition of his book *The Identity Crisis in Black Theology*, which appeared in 2003.[25] I was more than delighted to write something, since his work had given me courage to say what I had to say about social and personal transformation and about conversion. In my statement, I said the following about Cecil's book:

> In summary, *The Identity Crisis in Black Theology* is a forerunner to post-Enlightenment theology. It trusts our experience as African American Christians with God in the midst of suffering. From the experience, we draw hope and courage from God to resist enslavement, to overcome racism, sexism, classism, homophobia, and ageism, as well as strength to resist being recruited into negative identities. Moreover, our experience with God enables us to become co-workers in liberating others from oppression.[26]

What struck me as significant also was James Cone's embrace of the personal dimension of transformation in his book *Risks of Faith*. In it he becomes transparent about his upbringing in Macedonia AME Church in Bearden, Arkansas.[27] He said:

---

[25] Cone, *Identity Crisis*, 11–12.

[26] Cone, *Identity Crisis*, 12.

[27] James H. Cone, *Risks of Faith: The Emergence of a Black Theology of Liberation, 1968–1998* (Boston: Beacon, 1999), ix.

Every Sunday and sometimes on weeknights I encountered Jesus through rousing sermons, fervent prayers, spirited gospel songs, and the passionate testimonies of the people. Jesus was the dominant reality at Macedonia and in black life in Bearden. The people walked with him and told him about their troubles as if he were a trusted friend who understood their trials and tribulations in this unfriendly world.

He continued:

Like the people of Macedonia, Jesus became a significant presence in my life, too. I do not remember the exact date or time I "turned to Jesus," as the conversion experience was called. At home, church, and school, at play and at work, Jesus was always there, as the anchor of life, giving it meaning and purpose and bestowing hope and faith in the ultimate justice to things. Jesus was that reality who empowered black people to know that they were not worthless human beings that white people said they were.[28]

In 1999, there was no longer a division between James and Cecil. Personal transformation and social transformation were linked as they were for Wesley and King. What is of more significance as well was that the Anglican and Wesleyan missionary influence enabled black people in slavery to fashion their own understanding of Jesus and God and their presence in their lives to inform their theology. With this convergence between King and Wesley and the Cone brothers, the next section will explore the implications of this rhetorical and theological correspondence for practical theology.

Implications: Practical Theology in Civil Rights and Wesleyan Spirit

The rhetorical strategies of Wesley and King have implications for practical theology in the Civil Rights and Wesleyan spirit, which will be developed. The thrust of the implications will be a model of narrative and strategic theology that holds in tension evangelism, narrative therapy, nurturance, and public theology.

Practical theology from a narrative frame is all about helping people with whom we are ministering to identify the major metanarratives at work within their immediate meaning-making context. Metanarratives are those dominant story plots existing within people's meaning-making context that compete for people's allegiance and influence their choices. We have established that Wesley and King adopted a biblical and theological frame that envisages the world as being made up of two distinct levels,

---

[28] Cone, *Risks of Faith*, x.

which are a this-world-oriented metanarrative and one oriented with the present-but-not-yet, coming rule and reign of God.

Understanding reality in light of these two competing worldviews has all kinds of limitations. I will name two. The first limitation is that all metanarratives are social constructions by those who are in power and have the ability to persuade people, through coercive or non-coercive means, to choose their conception of reality. This is the deconstructive postmodern critique. That is to say that we need to be suspicious of all metanarratives, because they are formed as the result of the powerful people in culture.

A second limitation is the argument that posing two separate metanarratives is a dualistic conception of reality, which is out of step with modern holistic conceptions of reality. One is spiritual and the other is material.

My response is that all conceptions of reality are social constructions of reality, but it is impossible for human beings, no matter how intelligent we are, to live without metanarratives. Given this understanding of human finiteness, I opt for a Pauline view of reality, which Wesley and King embraced. A Pauline dualism is an eschatological time dualism, and it is related to past, present, and future time dimensions. All human metanarratives are social constructions using time-oriented analogies and emphases. Moreover, no thinker has found ways to transcend time categories in conceptualizing reality.

Power is very much a factor in the development of metanarratives. This was no less the case in the slave conversion tradition or in the theology of Martin Luther King Jr. There is, however, one major difference between the metanarratives developed by oppressors and those that came from black people in slavery and its aftermath. The metanarratives of the powerful come from alliance to an idolatry of this world's values, and these values indicate that it is possible to gain identity, happiness, economic prosperity, and wellbeing at the expense of others. Black people in slavery and its aftermath—especially in the conversion experiences of black people in slavery and its aftermath—did not find their source of power in the world or in themselves. Rather, they found their power in God and in God's present but coming rule and reign in this world. This metanarrative was not an expression built on the backs of others through oppression and exploitation. No, it was rather a metanarrative that came from their relationship with God and God's present but not yet rule and reign. This relationship with God was the source of their agency and power to speak to the forces of evil and oppression in this world.

Practical theology from a narrative frame is all about the ecclesiology and the task to persuade people to choose the present-but-not-yet eschatological plot, which in the eyes of Wesley, King, and the Cone brothers includes all facets of ministry in degrees of emphasis. My own critical emphasis, however, focuses on the need to recover the village functions of the small group, primarily because of what Cornel West calls cultural nihilism. Cultural nihilism is based on the reality that the mediating structures that stand between human beings and the wider structures of society have collapsed, such as the family, extended family, voluntary associations, small groups, networks, and fellowships. The result has been the loss of love, the loss of meaning, and the loss of purpose.[29] This means that practical theological strategies, including public theological strategies, need to target the use of mediating structures as the venues and arenas for helping people make decisions about the choice between two plot narratives.

Deconstructing Metanarratives

The basic premise of the narrative approach to practical theology is that all metanarratives must be deconstructed so that they focus on God's present and coming world of reality rather than on the this-world orientation. The deconstructive rhetoric must focus on those who promote oppression as well as those who are the victims of oppression. In narrative practical theology, the strategies for deconstruction are externalization and internalization. Externalization is the process of helping people, whether victims or perpetrators of oppression, to examine their beliefs and convictions about themselves, their relationships with others, and their relationship with God.[30] Internalization is helping people examine the convictions and beliefs that they have internalized or into which they have been recruited by those who are oppressors.[31]

Externalization is a rhetorical process wherein people are asked a series of questions designed to help them reflect on their deeply held convictions. For example, for oppressors these questions would begin with how they as human beings first established their identities in life. These questions would include issues such as those related to when they learned that status, position, power, wealth, and social standing were important, and how essential these dimensions are for their happiness, identity, and wellbeing. A second focus for the oppressor is whether or not it is acceptable to use others as means to the ends of achieving happiness, identity, wellbeing, and worth in life.

---

[29] Cornel West, *Race Matters* (New York: Vintage, 1993).

[30] Edward P. Wimberly, *Recalling Our Own Stories: Spiritual Renewal for Religious Caregivers* (San Francisco: Jossey-Bass, 1997).

[31] Edward P. Wimberly, *African American Pastoral Care and Counseling: The Politics of Oppression and Empowerment* (Cleveland: Pilgrim, 2006).

After these questions are answered, the next series of questions would involve whether or not strategies of gaining identity have actually been effective in achieving happiness, identity, worth, and dignity. Here, the focus is on trying to help those who have established their identities at the expense of others to assess whether they are really happy and fulfilled. The criteria for doing this kind of evaluation is whether or not those involved feel that there is something missing in their lives.

For victims of oppression, the questions are different. The questions have to do with those convictions and beliefs about themselves that resulted from being coerced and recruited into negative identities. These convictions and beliefs are explored by exploring themes and feelings related to social status, self-esteem, value, worth, honor versus shame, and self-regard. The key is to help people speak out loud or externalize these convictions and beliefs about themselves and others and to access whether or not they are happy or satisfied with them. Following this, then, the focus is on what to do with these beliefs and convictions.

Whether one is an oppressor or a victim of oppression, the key is to reauthor or re-edit the metanarratives or beliefs and convictions that one holds about oneself. Key in this process is the discernment of what God is doing in one's life to update one's metanarrative. Indeed, the focus is on the fact that God cares about whether the metanarrative is oriented toward this-world values and how those values lead to self and other destruction. Indeed, God desires our wellbeing and happiness and knows that the source of our ultimate happiness is the metanarrative oriented toward the world that is present but still coming. Our happiness is in being grounded in God and God's future.

Conclusion

The basic argument of this concluding chapter is that personal and social transformation, of human beings and of society, are key emphases that we must recover in the twenty-first-century practical theology. Keeping these two dimensions apart distorts reality and makes it difficult to make an impact on human behavior and on social structures. The rhetorical ideas of John Wesley and Martin Luther King Jr. were drawn on as examples of how rhetoric can be used to foster personal and social transformation and to hold them in creative tension. Moreover, both the conversion tradition of black people, in slavery and freedom, and the reconciliation between James and Cecil Cone, in their thinking about personal and social transformation, also speak to the clear necessity of holding these two dimensions in tension. The conclusion is that human happiness requires human beings to attend to their personal relationships with God as well as their relationships to others and to social institutions and structures. One without the other prevents true personal and social transformation. Moreover, overcoming shame begins first in our relationship with God, and from that starting point, we begin to construct relational and ethical responses concerned with our neighbor and our neighbor's wellbeing. Through our relationship with God and with others shame can be overcome.

9

African American Pastoral Theology in Practice: The Gathering of the Village (2017)

In *The Gathering of the Village for Justice and Participatory Democracy: The Concerned Black Clergy of Atlanta*,* Edward Wimberly offers a history of Concerned Black Clergy of Metropolitan Atlanta, Inc. (CBC), an organization that Wimberly has been a part of for over thirty years.† Wimberly compares the model for this meeting of pastors and community leaders to the concept of the African village, in that it provides a safe environment for listening to each member of the community and honors each person's perspective. Wimberly attributes the CBC's longevity and record of accomplishment to the village model and its traditions and practices of telling stories to a public audience. This practice is also consistent with collective narrative therapy.‡ The three broad themes in Edward Wimberly's corpus of work—the focus on the *context* of the black church, the use of *narrative* models of care, and the theological mandate to work for *prophetic* and political change—are all exemplified in this account. As in much of Wimberly's work, the finely woven interconnections between personal, communal, and public care become evident.

---

* Edward P. Wimberly, *The Gathering of the Village for Justice and Participatory Democracy: The Concerned Black Clergy of Atlanta* (Atlanta: ITC Press, 2017). Here we reprint chapter 3, "The Gift of Audience, Pastoral Imagination, and Public Theology," 39–52.

† See the CBC website at https://www.concernedblackclergy.com/.

‡ David Denborough, "A Storyline of Collective Narrative Practice: A History of Ideas, Social Projects and Partnerships," *International Journal of Narrative Therapy & Community Work* 1 (2012): 40–65. For another pastoral adaptation of collective narrative practice, see Tapiwa N. Mucherera, *Meet Me at the Palaver: Narrative Pastoral Counseling in Postcolonial Contexts* (Eugene, Ore.: Wipf & Stock, 2013).

CBC is a remarkable organization that was founded in 1983 in the wake of the "Murdered and Missing Children" crisis. Between the years of 1979 and 1981, at least twenty-nine children and young adults were murdered in Atlanta, in a case that has recently been re-opened.* Black pastors in Atlanta came together in part to provide a forum where the mothers of the murdered children could tell their stories, process their grief, and secure funds to help bury their children (256). The black pastors who founded CBC saw the vulnerability of the poor and minoritized black community and decided to work together with community leaders to address holistically the issues of violence, poverty, homelessness and struggle in the community.

In this essay, Edward Wimberly reviews the history of CBC, emphasizing the link between the pastoral wisdom that comes from caring for parishioners and the need to address the larger social and political issues that have an impact on the community (256). Wimberly traces the legacy of this wisdom and pastoral imagination to the work of the Reverend Dr. Martin Luther King, Jr. Wimberly also notes how CBC has evolved to be an interracial and interfaith organization that effectively responds to the needs of the community. This kind of village-based community forum that addresses injustice in ways both political and spiritual offers a much-needed model for our time.

Further Reading

Wimberly, Edward P. "Forum-ing: Signature Practice for Public Theological Discourse." *HTS Teologiese Studies / Theological Studies* 70, no. 1 (2014). doi:10.4102/hts.v70i1.2079.

• • •

---

* Joshua Sharpe, "Continuing Coverage: Atlanta Child Murders," *Atlanta-Journal Constitution*, March 30, 2019, https://www.ajc.com/news/crime--law/says-escaped-the-atlanta-child-murders-suspect-now-talking/IHE056DNiE9FJZMgrFRpdM/.

The Gift of Audience, Pastoral Imagination, and Public Theology[*]

Pastoral imagination helps us to move away from past ways of thinking in order to embrace new, creative, and strategic practical thinking based on new information and circumstances. Therefore, imagination gives us the freedom to revise traditions of care that are taking place between individuals, couples, families, small groups, and during ministry in the public arena to embrace justice. Justice fosters opportunities for all human beings to participate in a democratic society to the fullest extent possible. In short, pastoral imagination facilitates the care of persons and is an inherently political process.

Four major themes and related legacy practices have dominated the more than thirty-year history of the Concerned Black Clergy of Atlanta group (CBC). The first is the spark that ignited its beginning. The mothers of the "Missing and Murdered Children" sought an audience with a group of black clergy who met regularly at the old Paschal's Restaurant on Martin Luther King Jr. Drive, and from this the group was born, along with its focus on helping the oppressed and needy. The second is the lasting impact of the Civil Rights Movement on the Concerned Black Clergy of Atlanta (CBC). The third is the practice of electing successful black pastors to be the president of CBC and function as public theologians in residence. The fourth practice is what I called forum-ing or providing a safe public forum in which people can practice public theological democracy.[1] These four signature activities and related practices distinguish the CBC's work from any other organization.

It is important to understand CBC's history in light of these themes and practices. Such practices develop out of human conversations, discourses, and discussions which are repeated over time, and they shape the ways in which organizations define themselves.[2] In a similar fashion, the language practices of narrative therapy bring healing to individuals, to families, to communities, and to public problems related to the poor and underserved.

---

[1] Edward P. Wimberly, "Forum-ing: Signature Practice for Public Theological Discourse," in *HTS Teologiese Studies / Theological Studies* 70, no. 1 (2014), https://doi.org/10 .4102/hts.v70i1.2079.

[2] Wimberly, "Forum-ing." See also Michael White, *Narratives of Therapists' Lives* (Adelaide, South Australia: Dulwich Centre Publications, 1997) and Michel Foucault, *The Archaeology of Knowledge and the Discourse on Language* (New York: Pantheon Books, 1972).

[*] This chapter was previously published in Edward P. Wimberly, *The Gathering of the Village for Justice and Participatory Democracy: The Concerned Black Clergy of Atlanta* (Atlanta: ITC Press, 2017), 39–52. Used by permission.

I track and describe these four ways of telling the story of CBC, a story prompted by divine intervention. But I begin with a brief statement about the social and historical context in which public ministry exists.

The Crisis of the Missing and Murdered Atlanta Children

Rev. Albert Love, Pastor of Boatrock Baptist Church in Atlanta, and an employee of the Christian Council of Atlanta at the time of the formation and charter of CBC in 1983, pointed out that the initial impetus for the formation of CBC came as the result of the mothers of the "Missing and Murdered Children of Atlanta." These mothers came to the black clergy meeting held at Paschal Restaurant in order to find care and sympathy for their grieving and to secure money to bury their sons who were murdered.[3] At that time the gathered black clergy responded to the mothers by giving them an audience and providing them with a forum and a safe space for them to tell their stories. The clergy present heard the mothers' grief and pain at the loss of their children. The clergy understood the fact that these murders were attacks on the poor, black and vulnerable children. These ministers drew on their self-understanding as pastors and ministers of the Gospel, and they reached out to these mothers. More than this, they were able to recognize that there was a public dimension related to the murders. This public dimension was the ongoing and consistent vulnerability of the poor, underserved, minorities, and black communities that needed to be addressed by the entire Atlanta community.

More recently, the nation was similarly horrified by the massacre of 26 people in Newtown, Connecticut on December 14, 2012, twenty of whom were children. In an article entitled "Massacres, Mental Health and Black Kids" in an online magazine called *The Root*, there was a discussion of the role of mental health as one of the reasons for the shooting.[4] The article noted that there was some skepticism about the role of mental illness of the shooter, and whether this was the motive and cause for the murders. Could mental illness be the key factor in these murders? When reviewing the commonalities between the December shootings, the murders of the "Missing and Murdered Children of Atlanta," the shooting and murders at Columbine High School in Littleton, Colorado, and those murders of children in Newtown, Connecticut, mental illness is a common factor in these

---

[3] Albert Love, Interview, June 12, 2012. In a follow-up to the interview with Rev. Albert Love on June 12, he mentioned that he felt the initial impetus for the formation of CBC was the mothers of the "Missing and Murdered Children" seeking an audience with black clergy at Paschal's Restaurant.

[4] Ivory A. Toldson, "Massacres, Mental Health and Black Kids," *The Root*, December 27, 2012, https://www.theroot.com/massacres-mental-health-and-black-kids-1790894675.

three shootings. Gilbert Caldwell in the foreword to my book *Relational Refugees: Alienation and Reincorporation in African American Churches and Communities* makes the connection between mental health and the violence of April 20, 1999 at Columbine High School in Littleton, Colorado. He suggested that "the young man who shot Jews, African Americans, and Koreans in Illinois" fit into the category of being what I call a "relational refugee."[5] Relational refugees are people who do not feel at home in the world; "and feel cut off from significant communities and relationships, who live as refugees outside the boundaries of the church."[6] The common factor in the mental instability of the shooters at Columbine High School and at Sandy Hook Elementary School is that they were relational refugees who used violence as a response to feeling disconnected and being relational and cultural misfits in society.

If such relational disconnection is at the heart of our cultural experiences today, it is possible to visualize how CBC's emergence is a late twentieth-century phenomenon. It has also become a twenty-first century response to the cultural reality affecting all of society that Cornel West describes as nihilism. For him, nihilism is a cultural reality for all people in the United States. Nihilism is the loss meaning, loss of purpose, and the loss of love. It is the social malaise which is the major characteristic facing all persons in our society.[7]

Fortunately, throughout its history CBC has viewed ministry holistically, and it has included the personal, social, cultural, and public theological dimensions of ministry. It has connected violence, mental health, scarcity of material resources, spiritual and mental health resources, the loss of village connections, becoming relational refugees, and public policy. Three dimensions make CBC's history and response to such fragmentation are described. These are:

1. the "gift of audience," or what is now called "forum-ing"

2. the role of the pastoral leadership in the succession of CBC presidents based on the leadership model of Dr. Martin Luther King and the Civil Rights Movement

3. public theology as a result of pastoral imagination and public conversations.

---

[5] Gilbert H. Caldwell, foreword to *Relational Refugees: Alienation and Reincorporation in African American Churches and Communities* by Edward P. Wimberly (Nashville: Abingdon, 2000), 12.

[6] Caldwell, foreword to *Relational Refugees*, 12.

[7] Cornel West, *Race Matters* (New York: Vintage Books, 1994), 17–31.

The Gift of Audience and Forum-ing

To tell their stories, people need a safe space, and they need an audience. The forum is such a space and audience. Presently, it uses the practice of narrative therapy. Narrative therapy emphasizes the role and necessity of having an audience to whom persons can tell their stories of being overwhelmed by the process of living. Having safe places to tell, to revise, and to retell their own stories is viewed as fundamental and foundational to growing and developing our self-identity and self-esteem. Safe-space audiences can be formed in a variety of places, but the best environments for early childhood and youth development storytelling are in multi-generational, cohort-peer relationships with teens. In other words, safe-spaces for telling stories can be in a variety of spaces. Forums for telling stories for youth and young adults can happen within small groups or in larger intergenerational village and community life. Narrative therapy has basically emerged out of a group of people observing how others confronting trauma "make contributions to the lives of others who are going through similar difficulties."[8]

African American churches have also provided this kind of audience experience. Audiences make significant contributions to the lives of others who are undergoing trauma. Intentional efforts to provide such audiences need to continue. The audience practice of CBC is something that CBC has consistently exercised since its inception.

There are several regular and inclusive activities that are carried out at the beginning and at the end of each Monday morning meeting. At the beginning of the meeting the role of the president is to help assure that there is the right atmosphere, that those who attend have opportunities to be heard. The first opportunity comes at the very beginning of the Monday morning meeting right after the chaplain gives the opening prayer. Following the prayer, the president announces that each attendee can introduce herself or himself giving their name, the name of their church or organization, and their role in CBC, if any. The president makes sure that there is eye contact with each person.

At the end of the CBC Monday morning meeting, the president announces that those still present are invited to form a circle and join hands for a final prayer by the chaplain or someone designated by the president. Before the chaplain gives the final prayer, the president of CBC moves to each person in the circle and asks him or her to make any announcements about an upcoming event during the current week. The president moves around the circle clock-wise to give each person an opportunity to provide the date, time, and place for the activity and the nature of the activity. It

[8] West, *Race Matters*, 17–31.

could be a committee meeting, a community meeting, a church meeting, a political meeting, or something else. The role of the president is to assure that people give only date, time, and place. The purpose of the opening activities and the closing activities is to assure that people attending know that they are welcomed and encouraged to join and to return.

There are also practices that are encouraged when the presentations are the order of the day. Once the speakers have given their presentations, the audience is given opportunities to raise questions. However, statements are discouraged. Moreover, confrontation, being discourteous and disrespectful, is not tolerated. The key is to make sure the forum is a safe space for all.

CBC and the Legacy of Pastoral Leadership

Dr. Martin Luther King and his pastoral ministry, which connected the role of pastor of the flock with public ministry, became the living legacy for CBC. When the Montgomery Bus Boycott commenced in Montgomery in the 1950s, Dr. King was pastor of Dexter Avenue Baptist Church. A teaching colleague of mine at Interdenominational Theological Center (ITC) who is now deceased, Dr. G. Murray Branch, was the pastor of Dexter Avenue Baptist Church after the death of Dr. King. During a one-week visit conducting a workshop, Dr. Branch showed me Dr. King's church administrative notes at Dexter Avenue, and it was clear that Dr. King's primary allegiance was to his pastoral and preaching duties. In fact, he was reluctant to lead the Montgomery Boycott Movement because of his sense of responsibility to his pastoral ministry. He maintained his role of pastor at Dexter and later at Ebenezer Baptist Church for a long time while heading up the Southern Christian Leadership Conference (SCLC).

The fact that every elected president of CBC of Atlanta has been a successful local pastor is no accident. As an adopted practice from the Civil Rights Movement, electing pastors to the presidency of CBC has become a signature of CBC. In short, it is the pastor as public theologian that represents CBC's enduring leadership model for transforming pastoral and public leadership.

After conducting this study of CBC, an enduring insight from my research is that it is important to describe in more detail this pastoral, prophetic, and public leadership role that captured the minds of the CBC's leadership. Earlier, I mentioned what Dr. King wrote about the preaching ministry when he was attending Crozer Theological Seminary. When he later pastored Dexter Avenue Baptist Church in Montgomery, Alabama, he expanded this theme many times.

Dr. Branch concluded that King's genius for ministry lay in his linking his pastoral ministry with public theology and care for the community. Yet Dr. Branch pointed out that it was the community that discerned Dr. King's aptitude for public leadership before he recognized it in himself. Consequently, Dr. King had to be persuaded by the community to combine his concern for his pastoral ministry with his concern for the community. What he theorized in seminary about learning social justice through caring for the lives of people within the church and in the community only became real when he became a fulltime minister. Therefore, King brought to the Civil Rights movement a pastor's heart and compassion for the needs of the poor.

Using today's language of pastoral practice, King brought to the Civil Rights Movement and to public theology a practice of pastoral imagination. Pastoral imagination is a form of practical theological reflection that is critical, reflective, integrative, and novel. It allows the pastor to draw on academic theory, research, and practice, tailoring and translating them in order to use them to assess particular problems in precise situations in which the pastor finds himself/herself.[9] King began to demonstrate a keen sense of pastoral imagination while at seminary, and it served him throughout his pastoral and public ministries. This pastoral imagination is illustrated in the seminary paper that I mentioned earlier. Before he concluded it by observing that he was a "profound advocate of the social gospel," he noted, "I must be concerned about unemployment, slums, and economic insecurity."[10]

While the term pastoral imagination is used originally in *Educating Clergy* to talk about teaching practices that stimulate the pastor's imagination through use of the seminary curriculum, here I use it to describe an accomplished reality in Dr. King's ministry. Pastoral imagination takes the wisdom learned from caring for parishioners outside the church and demonstrates the connections between the parishioners' problems and the social and cultural problems impacting their lives as well as those who lived in the community. In short, Dr. King made the connection between the individual lives of human beings and the problems facing them and the social and cultural factors that compounded these problems. Being a pastor provided him with empathic power to feel what his parishioners felt, but he

---

[9] Charles R. Foster et al., *Educating Clergy: Teaching Practices and Pastoral Imagination* (San Francisco: Jossey-Bass, 2006).

[10] Martin Luther King, Jr., *The Papers of Martin Luther King, Jr.: Advocate of the Social Gospel, September 1948–March 1963*, ed. Clayborne Carson, vol. 6 (Berkeley: University of California Press, 2007).

also took it to the next level, which is called advanced public empathy and the care for others.

In the context of this history of CBC, advanced public empathy. means identifying with the feelings of persons facing poverty, hunger, discrimination, and oppression, while at the same time recognizing that these problems have a social and cultural component beyond the particular person. In short, most problems have a systems component.

Finally, King's legacy also set the stage for the CBC to become a practical context for fostering participatory democracy. Participatory democracy is all about our developing our personal agency which eventually will propel us into the public arena where we practice political agency. That is to say, through the practices outlined above, particularly the gift of audience and forum-ing, participants' lives are transformed, and they become involved politically and civically, for example, by determining politically how public resources are to be allocated.[11]

The King Legacy and CBC

The presidents of CBC all possessed the skills of advanced pastoral imagination and empathy. All had college and seminary training, and they had made the transition from the academy to the church and to the public arena. They were selected because they empathized with the problems of their parishioners, the poor, the unemployed, and the homeless, and they had developed pastoral imaginations. Consequently, they were able to find effective ways to address with imagination public social and theological concerns.

The following persons have been the pastoral leaders of CBC over the years:

> Bishop Cornelius Henderson was the first president elected and he served from 1984 to 1987. He was pastor of Ben Hill United Methodist at that time. His gifts to CBC were his vast connections within both the African American and White communities. He was well respected and liked in both these communities. He had an exceptional gift of empathy for people and their needs, and he possessed exceptional organizational skills.

Early in the development of CBC it had to address issues related to the building of the Georgia Dome, where the Atlanta Falcons Football Team was the home team. In the building of the Dome, many churches were impacted and had to be moved. CBC advocated for the churches, the

---

[11] Edward P. Wimberly, *African American Pastoral Care and Counseling: The Politics of Oppression and Empowerment* (Cleveland: Pilgrim Press, 2006), 28.

churches were more equitably compensated as a result, and the Vine City Community Development Association was formed.[12]

Bishop McKinley Young was the second president, and he served CBC as president from 1988–1991. He was also the pastor of Big Bethel AME Church during that time. He was well schooled in grassroots political actions and protest activities. He helped to lead the efforts to make sure the churches were compensated for the property that the Georgia Dome was displacing.

The Rev. Dr. James Allen Milner was the third president and served as president of CBC from 1992 to 1993, but he left CBC early to avoid a conflict of interest related to his own funding for his homeless programs and the need to raise money for CBC's outreach to the homeless. His contribution to CBC was his expertise and knowledge of working with homeless persons and their families. He also had the respect of the funding community. He is pastor of Chapel of Christian Love. Moreover, as a teen in high school he marched with Dr. King in Atlanta, and he spent time with Rev. Joseph Lowery and Rev. David Abernathy. More recently, he was the chair of Mayor Shirley Franklin's monthly luncheons for clergy.

Insights into Dr. Milner's leadership and pastoral imagination are found in his book *God's Special Provisions for the Poor.*[13] Aside from his work as a pastor, he has directed ministry to homeless persons and their families over the years. He brought to CBC this concern, and he has helped to brand CBC as a religious institution that cares for the needs of the homeless.

CBC has long addressed the needs of the homeless. In fact, it was one of the first public issues that CBC addressed. CBC helped churches to form clusters to provide food and shelter for the homeless. Several feeding and sheltering organizations were founded, and some are still in existence today.

Rev. Dr. Gerald Durley was the fourth president of CBC, and he is the recently retired pastor of Provident Missionary Baptist Church. He served CBC from 1994–1997. He brought to CBC expertise in community mental health, public health, and community service and outreach through the church. He was also the president of the Atlanta Christian Council. He possessed the excellent gift of making connections with people who had influence in the business community and with churches.

Key to Dr. Durley's presidency of CBC was the mentoring that he in turn had received at Ebenezer Baptist Church. Persons who worked under

[12] The references to the presidents of CBC and their activities related to public theology are found at www.concernedblackclergy.org/3501/3522.html, no longer available. Some of this material is taken *verbatim* from this site.

[13] J. Allen Milner, *God's Special Provisions for the Poor* (Atlanta: Chapel of Christian Love Books, 2010).

the mentorship of Dr. Joseph Roberts at Ebenezer Baptist Church learned to be sure to do their public theological homework.

Rev. Timothy McDonald was the fifth president of CBC, and served from 1997–2004. He was on the staff at Ebenezer Baptist Church and likewise under the mentorship of Dr. Joseph Roberts. He is very astute in systemic analysis of social problems, and can speak the truth to power very effectively. Moreover, he was a community organizer long before he got involved in CBC. In his role as community organizer, he used his understanding to assess community problems related to poor and underserved communities and how the powers in charge could be influenced to address those problems with equity. He is pastor of First Iconium Baptist Church.

Rev. Darrell D. Elligan, was the sixth president of CBC from 2006–2009, and is the pastor of True Light Baptist Church. He understands corporate America and how effective institutions work. He brought to the CBC presidency a concern for established and measurable goals and how important it is to assess them and use them for demonstrated outcomes. He initiated a relationship with Wachovia Bank, now Wells Fargo, which began a discussion with CBC concerning home buying education. Rev. Elligan wrote a proposal which was later signed by Dr. Richard Cobble, the sixth president of CBC.

Rev. Richard Cobble served from 2010–2011, and he is pastor of Omega Holiness church. His major gift to CBC was his advanced empathy for the homeless veterans and for the substance abuse problems of the homeless. He emphasized Dr. King's concept of "The Beloved Community," and he was also mentored in the Ebenezer Baptist Church tradition.

Rev. Frank Brown was the seventh president of CBC. His term began in 2012, and he is the pastor of Mt. Olive Missionary Baptist Church. Like two other former presidents, he was mentored in the Ebenezer Baptist tradition. Less experienced than the others, he was nonetheless a gifted thinker, speaker, and preacher. His public leadership at the weekly forums was outstanding. His weekly updates of the public issues facing CBC were masterfully conceptualized and presented. He provided excellent leadership working with Wells Fargo Bank following up on the groundbreaking work initiated by Rev. Elligan and later signed by Dr. Cobble. Wells Fargo Bank provided a grant of $100,000 for holding educational seminars at local churches relating to housing foreclosures and affordable housing. Through their leadership, Rev. Brown and Wells Fargo have organized and carried out several successful housing education seminars for prospective home buyers and persons facing foreclosures. In addition, Brown worked with a committee of Mayor Kasim Reed on a novel approach to the homeless problem.

All these men brought pastoral imagination to the office of President of BC. Moreover, each person came to the presidency when there were critical problems facing the Atlanta community. For example, Bishop Henderson was the first president of CBC, and he was pastor at Ben Hill United Methodist Church when CBC was established, and the problem was what is now known as the "Murdered and Missing Children" case, which occupied the CBC in its founding days. Maynard Jackson was the first black mayor of Atlanta during this time.

The second president of CBC was Bishop McKinley Young, who was pastor of Big Bethel AME Church, and the major concern during this time was the building of the Georgia Dome. The concern during this time was the impact of the building of the Georgia Dome and the displacement of people and churches. Ambassador Andrew Young was mayor during this time, and CBC was a major player in helping the city to be more responsive to the needs of the community surrounding the Georgia Dome. James Allen Milner was very instrumental in helping CBC fulfill its mission to the homeless.

Other mayors of Atlanta included Bill Campbell, Shirley Franklin, and Kasim Reed. During the administration of these black mayors, CBC leadership addressed the concerns which had negative impacts on the poor and indigent communities.[14] The leadership of CBC achieved the following accomplishment through its pastoral imagination and public theological efforts: they helped to secure additional founding for indigent care at Grady Hospital from Dekalb and Fulton counties; initiated a 10,000 men and boys "March for Brotherhood" on May 18, 1991 to emphasize the need for black men to take more responsibility for the community; holds year-round voter registration and voter education efforts; addresses the concerns of juvenile justice, in particular "the disproportionate numbers" of African-Americans incarcerated; campaigns against the death penalty; addresses healthcare concerns such as the AIDS and HIV crisis, and partners with healthcare organizations to address a whole host of preventive medical concerns; worked against discrimination at Lockheed Martin, and against corporate injustice, and worked to assist people during the Camilla tornado, and the Marta Rapid Line Project; and received a grant of $100,000 to help Wells Fargo Bank conduct home foreclosure workshops and educational seminars on financing affordable housing.

In essence CBC leadership has been a proactive community organization working on behalf of the poor in Atlanta Community. Their efforts include advocacy, social responsibility, politics and justice, health and

[14] The Concerned Black Clergy of Metropolitan Atlanta, Inc., "History," accessed August 11, 2019, https://www.concernedblackclergy.com/cbc-history.

wellness, education, and workplace justice. CBC has a strong committee structure organized with Jay and clergy to address the following concerns: a Beltline Project Committee; an Economic Development Committee, an Education Committee, a Health Committee, a Juvenile Justice Committee, a Membership Committee, a Political Issues Committee, and a Public Policy/Safety Committee. Moreover, the heads of these committees make reports at every CBC Monday Morning Forum. Finally, CBC has a board of trustees, and holds monthly pastors' luncheons to provide education for clergy.

CBC has remained a viable organization because it is so responsive to the problems of the poor. Following the Civil Rights pastoral leadership model along with its organizational structure, CBC stands ready and able to respond to many of the important needs of the poor and underserved communities of Atlanta. Historically, CBC has provided a model of leaders who practiced advanced pastoral imagination drawing on the Civil Rights legacy of Dr. Martin Luther King.

Pastoral Leader and Public Theology

King brought his pastoral imagination to the public arena, and his everyday experience working with oppressed people informed everything he did in his public ministry. Pastoral imagination in King's mind involved reflecting on his own experience as a pastor working with his parishioners and people in the community, and he was able to visualize how the structures of oppression prevented them from being full participants in democracy. He brought to bear on his reflections about oppressed people his own understanding of Scripture, the Christian Gospel, the United States Constitution, non-violent resistance, and the Boston University philosophical tradition of Personalism.[15] From these sources of wisdom, he fashioned a public strategy for mobilizing the community to address the forces that prevented oppressed people from full participation in life. Informed by these various traditions along with the wisdom that came from his pastoral experience, he left a legacy which eventually was embraced by CBC. This practical and pastoral wisdom legacy enabled CBC to provide models of leadership, planning and evaluation for liberating people from oppression and enabling the poor, underserved, and downtrodden to do public theology by telling their own stories.

---

[15] Personalism is the philosophical and theological tradition characterized by understanding human beings and God as person (Persons) bringing a relational dimension to public discourse. See Carolyn A. Warren, "Dynamic Interpersonalism and Personhood," *Journal of the Interdenominational Theological Center* 25, no. 3 (1998): 8–32.

One of the important signature practices CBC developed from the King legacy is the public Monday morning Forum where the poor, oppressed, downtrodden, and those impacted by urban problems could come and tell their stories. Since its inception, this Forum has provided them an audience where they could be heard, taken seriously, and affirmed. This venue continues to enable the poor and downtrodden to speak for themselves, and their stories embolden CBC members to take action to speak for those who cannot speak for themselves—or are not heard or taken seriously—in the public arena.[16]

Interfaith and Interracial Relationships

From its inception, the CBC has been an interracial and interfaith effort. White Christians were involved and so were black Muslims. Many of the black pastors were members of the Christian Council of Atlanta, which had many white members, and the CBC and Black Muslims got together because of the Million Man March many years ago.

On May 18, 1991 10,000 men and boys joined the March for Brotherhood, which was organized to highlight the "commitment of men to take responsibility for our community."[17] This was a very successful march, and it laid the ground work for CBC and the Black Muslim community to form a committee to attend the Million Man March that was held in Washington, D.C. many years later.

Moving Forward

Similar to Dr. King, the black pastors who met periodically at Paschal's Restaurant also brought the wisdom of their own pastoral imaginations to the leadership of CBC. Both these pastors and the pastors who were presidents of CBC developed certain "signature responses" to the twentieth and twenty-first century cultural realities they encountered, responses once again infused with their particular pastoral imagination. This book both gives a historical account of the development and use of these "signature practices" and looks forward to how CBC will likely continue its legacy of public ministry utilizing these "signature practices."

---

[16] Helpful insight about the role of providing a public forum where those impacted by injustice and tell their stories comes from the publication of material related to the South African Truth and Reconciliation Commission headed up by Archbishop Desmond Tutu. See Dirk Smith, "Reform Faith, Justice and the Struggle Against Apartheid," in *Essays in Public Theology: Collected Essays 1* (Stellenbosch, South Africa: Sun Press, 2007), 27–49.

[17] "History," Concerned Black Clergy of Metropolitan Atlanta.

Conclusion

The sweep and power of Edward Wimberly's contributions to the field of pastoral theology and care shine through the chapters and articles included in this book. These writings communicate the convictions of a deeply faithful scholar, practitioner, and teacher who has helped shape the nature of the discipline. Edward Wimberly has never tired of striving to communicate the love of God for all people in the midst of the brokenness and strife that America's original sin—racism—has wrought. Wimberly has employed all the resources of pastoral care and its related disciplines in order to tell a different story: a story of resistance and hope, a story of a people's God-given value and worth.

For Wimberly, it is the love of God as revealed through Scripture and enacted in community that is the source of power to resist injustice in all its forms. He offers deeply effective ways to challenge the dehumanization and self-hatred that racism imposes. Going to the core of intra-personal as well as interpersonal and political struggles for wellbeing, Wimberly communicates a faith-inspired vision of a more holistic and life-giving social order, where communities of mutual concern support the flourishing of all people, including especially the least and the lost. By identifying the early pastoral care practices of the black church, Wimberly sketched the outlines of this alternative story, a story that includes both survival and liberation, infused by the recognition of God's enduring presence with and for African Americans.[1] At the same time, he challenged the dominance and power of white scholars in the field, even as he demonstrated the importance of understanding the deeply woven, contextual nature of care.

---

[1] See Carroll Watkins Ali, *Survival and Liberation: Pastoral Theology in African American Context* (St. Louis: Chalice, 1999).

Readers of this collection will see the evolution of Edward Wimberly's thought and care practices over time, as he gradually shifts his focus toward the prophetic dimensions of pastoral ministry, including public theology. Yet he never loses his convictions about *how* public theological discourse ought to be engaged, which is through networks of care such as in local congregations or in groups like the Concerned Black Clergy (described in chapter nine), where people come together to share their stories of struggle and to co-create solutions. By listening to the story of each member, the group can allow its theology and care practices—including political engagement—to be guided by a prophetic concern for "the welfare of the city" (Jer 29:7). Wimberly has held fast to his conviction that the wellbeing of each person is linked to the welfare of all.

Those who have read thus far will now have a sense of the substance and scope of Wimberly's corpus of work. The publication list included at the end of this volume represents the full record of his prolific scholarship. The impact of Wimberly's contributions is acknowledged in the literature of the field and beyond it: his books have garnered strong reviews in a diverse array of journals.[2] Wimberly's scholarship crosses over many dividing lines between people and institutions. His academic voice has reached the churches—numerous pastors and people in the pew have read and taught his books, gleaning wisdom for the everyday practice of ministry.[3]

Wimberly brought his focus on the black church to the previously almost all-white Society for Pastoral Theology (SPT), crossing over another line of division. He has stuck with the Society through times of turmoil and racial misunderstanding.[4] Along with other African American colleagues, he patiently explained the importance of racial contexts of care to those scholars who were or who still are, to varying degrees, oblivious. Also, as is evident in this collection, when feminist and womanist work was introduced to the Society, Wimberly began incorporating it into his thinking and writing.

Wimberly has been involved in wide-ranging conversations with biblical scholars, Wesleyan theologians, and theological educators from diverse fields. He has typically been quick to take in new ideas and awareness of various forms of injustice. He promptly discerned the resonance between

---

[2] Wimberly's work has been reviewed in diverse journals ranging from the *Journal of Pastoral Theology* and *Journal of the Interdenominational Theological Center* to *Review and Expositor* and the *Wesleyan Theological Journal*.

[3] Wimberly reports his total book sales at just over 89,000 copies, an unusually high number for academic books.

[4] For a brief description of this period in the history of SPT, see Loren Townsend, *Introduction to Pastoral Counseling* (Nashville: Abingdon, 2009).

his contextual approach to African American pastoral care and the wisdom of narrative therapy. He saw how narrative care could help underline the importance of sharing community stories, especially in poor and marginalized communities whose stories have been undervalued, and in situations of trauma.

Edward Wimberly, together with Anne Streaty Wimberly, has traversed international borders, not just visiting but teaching many times at Africa University in Zimbabwe. He has been both a teacher and a learner there, as evidenced in the way he absorbed the culture of the village in which they lived, and took in its significance for pastoral care. He came to use the concept of the village as a guiding metaphor for community relationships, and adapted the idea to inform pastoral care in the context of American individualism.

One of the signs of a scholar's influence on a field is the scholar's longevity. A scholar's ability to continuously plumb the depths and breadth of topics happens when the scholar is committed to critical inquiry. Not only has Wimberly's work spanned decades, his writings have been significant because he has continuously responded to the social issues of every era. From slavery to segregation through neo-Reconstruction, debates on family structure and family values, changing understandings of social interaction and counseling interventions, Wimberly has sought to attend to life's growing edges, especially the ways those growing edges have been experienced by African American people.

Wimberly has not only responded to the social conditions of those in crisis, giving particular attention to the traumas experienced by African Americans, he has also been attentive to the perspectives and reflections of his colleagues in the field. Each of his projects has taken seriously the theological positions of others, the socio-political environment, the usage of theory and the emergence of new theories, always part of his sustained commitment is to advocate pastoral intercession. He has kept the possibility of healing the social malaise as central to his work. Not only has he been informed by the works of others, he has, in his own compassionate way, challenged his colleagues to think through the implications of their reflections as they impact marginalized African American communities.

We, the editors, hope that Wimberly's reflections will inform the reader's scholarship and ministry. Whereas pastoral theology is a contextual and constructive theology, we hope that Wimberly's reflections on the African American context and his constructive presentations on African American pastoral care will inform the reader's theological methodology, approaches to context, and constructive reflections. We further hope that this *Reader* begins to fill out the historical record of the field of pastoral theology and care, which previously has offered very little to students and scholars wondering about the role of African Americans in the history of pastoral care. We invite others to continue the work of recognizing the historical contributions of African American scholarship to the field.

Credits

Chapter 1: Pastoral Care in the Black Church (1979)

"Pastoral Care in the Black Church" was previously published in Edward P. Wimberly, *Pastoral Care in the Black Church* (Nashville: Abingdon, 1979), 17–38 and associated notes. © 1979, Abingdon Press. Used by permission. All rights reserved.

Chapter 2: African American Men: Identity, Marriage, and Family (1997)

"Beyond African American Male Hierarchical Leadership" was previously published in Edward P. Wimberly, *Counseling African American Marriages and Families* (Louisville: Westminster John Knox, 1997), 1–10. Used by permission.

"Male and Female, God Created Them to Be Whole" was previously published in Edward P. Wimberly, *Counseling African American Marriages and Families* (Louisville: Westminster John Knox, 1997), 11–24. Used by permission.

"The Men's Movement and Pastoral Care of African American Men" was previously published in *The Care of Men*, edited by Christie Cozad Neuger and James Newton Poling (Nashville: Abingdon, 1997), 104–21 and associated notes. © 1997, Abingdon Press. Used by permission. All rights reserved.

Chapter 3: Narrative Care for Spiritual Renewal (1997)

"To Be Called Anew: Finding Spiritual Replenishment in Our Own Stories" was previously published in Edward P. Wimberly, *Recalling Our Own Stories: Spiritual Renewal for Religious Caregivers* (San Francisco: Jossey-Bass, 1997), 1–13. © 1997 by John Wiley & Sons, Inc. Reproduced with permission of John Wiley & Sons, Inc.

"Personal Myths: Stories That Empower Us or Leave Us Vulnerable" was previously published in Edward P. Wimberly, *Recalling Our Own Stories: Spiritual Renewal for Religious Caregivers* (San Francisco: Jossey-Bass, 1997), 14–33; and "The Possibility of Change: Reauthoring the Myths that Bind Us," in Edward P. Wimberly, *Recalling Our Own Stories: Spiritual Renewal for Religious Caregivers* (San Francisco: Jossey-Bass, 1997), 73–88. © 1997 by John Wiley & Sons, Inc. Reproduced with permission of John Wiley & Sons, Inc.

Chapter 4: Relational Refugees (2000)

"Adolescence and the Relational Refugee" was previously published Edward P. Wimberly, *Relational Refugees: Alienation and Reincorporation in African American Churches and Communities* (Nashville: Abingdon, 2000), 63–73 and associated notes. © 2000, Abingdon Press. Used by permission. All rights reserved.

"Poverty, Prosperity, and the Relational Refugee" was previously published in Edward P. Wimberly, *Relational Refugees: Alienation and Reincorporation in African American Churches and Communities* (Nashville: Abingdon, 2000), 75–84 and associated notes. © 2000, Abingdon Press. Used by permission. All rights reserved.

Chapter 5: Politics, Oppression, and Empowerment (2006)

"African American Pastoral Care and Counseling as Political Processes" was previously published in Edward P. Wimberly, *African American Pastoral Care and Counseling: The Politics of Oppression and Empowerment* (Cleveland: Pilgrim Press, 2006), 19–36. Used by permission.

"The Parish Context of African American Pastoral Counseling" was previously published in Edward P. Wimberly, *African American Pastoral Care and Counseling: The Politics of Oppression and Empowerment* (Cleveland: Pilgrim Press, 2006), 37–60. Used by permission.

Chapter 6: African American Narrative Pastoral Care (2008)

"A Narrative Approach to Pastoral Care" was previously published in Edward P. Wimberly, *African American Pastoral Care*, rev. ed. (Nashville: Abingdon, 2008), 1–15 and associated notes. © 2008. Abingdon Press. Used by permission. All rights reserved.

"Pastoral Care and Support Systems: Illness, Bereavement, and Catastrophic Loss" was previously published in Edward P. Wimberly, *African American Pastoral Care*, rev. ed. (Nashville: Abingdon, 2008), 31–45 and associated notes. © 2008. Abingdon Press. Used by permission. All rights reserved.

Chapter 7: Narrative Care in the Contexts of Trauma (2011)

"Story Telling and Managing Trauma: Health and Spirituality at Work" was previously published in *Journal of Health Care for the Poor and Underserved* 22, no. 3 (2011): 48–57. © 2011 Meharry Medical College. Reprinted with permission of Johns Hopkins University Press.

Chapter 8: Pastoral Theology in a Wesleyan Spirit (2011)

"Shame, Slavery, and Economics of Hope: Wesley's Public Theology" was previously published in Edward P. Wimberly, *No Shame in Wesley's Gospel: A Twenty-first Century Pastoral Theology* (Eugene, Ore.: Wipf & Stock, 2011), 78–93. ISBN 978-1-61097-193-5. www.wipfandstock.com. Used by permission.
"Practical Public Theology: Civil Rights and the Wesleyan Spirit" was previously published in Edward P. Wimberly, *No Shame in Wesley's Gospel: A Twenty-first Century Pastoral Theology* (Eugene, Ore.: Wipf & Stock, 2011), 94–109. ISBN 978-1-61097-193-5. www.wipfandstock.com. Used by permission.

Chapter 9: African American Pastoral Theology in Practice: The Gathering of the Village (2017)

"The Gift of Audience, Pastoral Imagination, and Public Theology" was previously published in Edward P. Wimberly, *The Gathering of the Village for Justice and Participatory Democracy: The Concerned Black Clergy of Atlanta* (Atlanta: ITC Press, 2017), 39–52. Used by permission.

The Works of Edward P. Wimberly

Books

Wimberly, Edward P. *Pastoral Care in the Black Church*. Nashville: Abingdon, 1979.

Wimberly, Edward P. *Pastoral Counseling and Spiritual Values: A Black Point of View*. Nashville: Abingdon, 1982.

Wimberly, Edward P., and Anne Streaty Wimberly. *Liberation and Human Wholeness: The Conversion Experiences of Black People in Slavery and Freedom*. Nashville: Abingdon, 1986.

Wimberly, Anne Streaty, and Edward Powell Wimberly. *One Household and One Hope: Building Ethnic Minority Clergy Family Support Networks*. Nashville: General Board of Higher Education and Ministry, United Methodist Church, 1988.

Wimberly, Edward P. *Prayer in Pastoral Counseling: Suffering, Healing, and Discernment*. Louisville: Westminster John Knox, 1990.

Wimberly, Edward P. *African American Pastoral Care*. Nashville: Abingdon, 1991.

Wimberly, Anne Streaty, and Edward Powell Wimberly. *The Language of Hospitality: Intercultural Relations in the Household of God*. Nashville: Cokesbury, 1991.

Wimberly, Edward P. *Using Scripture in Pastoral Counseling*. Nashville: Abingdon, 1994.

Wimberly, Edward P. *Counseling African American Marriages and Families*. Louisville: Westminster John Knox, 1997.

Wimberly, Edward P. *Recalling Our Own Stories: Spiritual Renewal for Religious Caregivers*. Religion-in-Practice. San Francisco: Jossey-Bass, 1997.

Wimberly, Edward P. *Moving from Shame to Self-Worth: Preaching and Pastoral Care*. Nashville: Abingdon, 1999.

Wimberly, Edward P. *Relational Refugees: Alienation and Reincorporation in African American Churches and Communities*. Nashville: Abingdon, 2000.

Wimberly, Edward P. *Claiming God, Reclaiming Dignity: African American Pastoral Care*. Nashville: Abingdon, 2003.

Wimberly, Edward P. *African American Pastoral Care and Counseling: The Politics of Oppression and Empowerment*. Cleveland: Pilgrim, 2006.

Wimberly, Anne E. Streaty, and Edward Powell Wimberly. *The Winds of Promise: Building and Maintaining Strong Clergy Families*. Nashville: Discipleship Resources, 2007.

Wimberly, Edward P. *African American History Month Daily Devotions 2009*. Nashville: Abingdon, 2008.

Wimberly, Edward P. *African American Pastoral Care: Revised Edition*. Nashville: Abingdon, 2008.

Wimberly, Edward P. *No Shame in Wesley's Gospel: A Twenty-First Century Pastoral Theology*. Eugene, Ore.: Wipf & Stock, 2011.

Wimberly, Edward P. *The Gathering of the Village for Justice and Participatory Democracy: The Concerned Black Clergy of Atlanta*. Atlanta: ITC Press, 2017.

Wimberly, Edward P. *Recalling Our Own Stories: Spiritual Renewal for Religious Caregivers*. With a new foreword by Tapiwa N. Mucherera. Fortress Press Edition. Minneapolis: Fortress, 2019.

Articles and Book Chapters

Wimberly, Edward P. "Pastoral Counseling and the Black Perspective." *Journal of the Interdenominational Theological Center* 3, no. 2 (1976): 28–35. doi:10.1177/002234097603000407.

Wimberly, Edward P. "Pastoral Counseling and the Black Perspective." *Journal of Pastoral Care* 30 (December 1976): 264–72. doi:10.1177/002234097603000407

Wimberly, Edward P. "Book Review: The Moral Context of Pastoral Care by Don S. Browning." *Journal of the Interdenominational Theological Center* 5, no. 1 (1977): 61–62.

Wimberly, Edward P. "Pastoral Care and Support Systems." *Journal of the Interdenominational Theological Center* 5, no. 1 (1977): 67–75.

Wimberly, Edward P. "The Suffering God." In *Preaching of Suffering and a God of Love*, edited by Henry J. Young, 56–62. Philadelphia: Fortress, 1978.

Wimberly, Edward P. "A Response to Morton T. Kelsey." *Journal of the Interdenominational Theological Center* 6, no. 2 (1979): 135–37.

Wimberly, Edward P. "The Pastor's Theological Identity Formation." *Journal of the Interdenominational Theological Center* 7, no. 2 (1980): 145–56.

Wimberly, Edward P. "Wholism in the Family: Implications for the Church from a Jungian Perspective." *Pastoral Psychology* 28, no. 3 (1980): 188–98.

Wimberly, Edward. "Using Our Wounds in the Service of Others." *Candler Ministry and Mission* 5, no. 4, Candler School of Theology (1980): 2, 7.

Wimberly, Edward P. "Contributions of Black Christians to the Discipline of Pastoral Care." *Reflections* 80, no. 2, a publication of Yale Divinity School (January 1983): 4–8.

Wimberly, Edward P. "The Healing Tradition of the Black Church and Modern Science: A Model of Traditioning." *Journal of the Interdenominational Theological Center* 11, no. 1 (1983): 19–30.

Wimberly, Edward P. "Minorities." In *Clinical Handbook of Pastoral Counseling*, edited by Robert J. Wicks, Richard D. Parsons, and Donald Capps, 300–317. Studies in Pastoral Psychology, Theology and Spirituality. Mahwah, N.J.: Paulist, 1985.

Wimberly, Edward P. "The Dynamics of Black Worship: A Psychosocial Exploration of the Impulses that Lie at the Roots of Black Worship." *Journal of the Interdenominational Theological Center* 14, nos. 1 and 2 (1986–1987): 195–207.

Wimberly, Edward P. "Response to the Paper Presented by Henry Young." In *Uncover the Myths: Proceedings of the Roundtable of Ethnic Theologians*, 91–93. Nashville: United Methodist Church and Division of Ordained Ministry, 1988.

Wimberly, Edward P. "The Black Christian Experience and the Holy Spirit." *Quarterly Review* 8, no. 2 (1988): 19–35.

Wimberly, Edward P. "Pastoral Counseling and the Black Perspective." In *African American Religious Studies*, edited by Gayraud Wilmore, 420–28. Durham, N.C.: Duke University Press, 1989.

Wimberly, Edward P. "Black American Pastoral Care." In *Dictionary of Pastoral Care and Counseling*, edited by Rodney J. Hunter, 92–94. Nashville: Abingdon, 1990.

Wimberly, Edward P. "Black Identity and Consciousness." In *Dictionary of Pastoral Care and Counseling*, edited by Rodney J. Hunter, 94–96. Nashville: Abingdon, 1990.

Wimberly, Edward P. "Black Issues in Psychology." In *Dictionary of Pastoral Care and Counseling*, edited by Rodney J. Hunter, 96–98. Nashville: Abingdon, 1990.

Wimberly, Edward P. "Black Populations." In *Clergy Assessment and Career Development*, edited by Richard A. Hunt, John E. Hinkle, and H. Newton Maloney, 149–53. Nashville: Abingdon, 1990.

Wimberly, Edward P. "Growth Counseling." In *Dictionary of Pastoral Care and Counseling*, edited by Rodney J. Hunter, 483–85. Nashville: Abingdon, 1990.

Wimberly, Edward P. "Men, Pastoral Care of." In *Dictionary of Pastoral Care and Counseling*, edited by Rodney J. Hunter, 704–6. Nashville: Abingdon, 1990.

Wimberly, Edward P. "Spiritual Formation in Theological Education." In *Clergy Assessment and Career Development*, edited by Richard A. Hunt, John E. Hinkle, and H. Newton Maloney, 27–31. Nashville: Abingdon, 1990.

Wimberly, Edward P., and Anne Wimberly. "Families, Society, Church and Sexuality: Issues and Solutions." In *Teaching Human Sexuality: A Collection of Resources for Teachers and Leaders*, edited by Cecile Beam. Nashville: General Board of Discipleship, 1990.

Wimberly, Edward P. "Indigenous Theological Reflection on Pastoral Supervision: An African American Perspective." *Journal of Supervision and Training in Ministry* 13 (1991): 180–89.

Wimberly, Edward P. "A Narrative Approach to Pastoral Care in an Intercultural Setting." In *Knowledge, Attitude and Experience: Ministry in the Cross-Cultural Context*, edited by Young-Il Kim, 84–103. Nashville: Abingdon, 1992.

Wimberly, Edward P. "Pastoral Counseling with African American Men." *Urban League Review* 16, no. 2 (1993): 77–84.

Wimberly, Edward P. "African American Spirituality and Sexuality: Perspectives on Identity, Intimacy and Power." *Journal of Pastoral Theology* 4 (Summer 1994): 19–31. doi:10.1080/10649867.1994.11745311.

Wimberly, Anne Streaty, and Edward P. Wimberly. "Pastoral Care of African Americans." In *Aging, Spirituality, and Religion: A Handbook*, edited by Melvin A. Kimble and Susan H. McFadden, 161–173. Minneapolis: Augsburg Fortress, 1995.

Wimberly, Edward P. "Reflections on African American Pastoral Care." *Journal of Pastoral Theology* 5, no. 1 (1995): 44–49. doi:10.1179/jpt.1995.5.1.006.

Wimberly, Edward P. "Oral-Narrative Culture and Pastoral Counseling with African American Males." In *Therapeutic Practice in a Cross-Cultural World: Theological, Psychological, and Ethical Issues*, edited by Carole R. Bohn, 59–75. Decatur, Ga.: Journal of Pastoral Care Publications, 1995.

Wimberly, Edward P. "Spirituality and Health: Caring in a Postmodern Age." *Caregiver Journal* 12, no. 4 (1996): 1–7.

Wimberly, Edward P. "Compulsory Masculinity and Violence." *Caregiver Journal* 13, no. 1 (1997): 18–19.

Thomas, Edith Dalton, Anne Streaty Wimberly, and Edward P. Wimberly. "Honoring and Sharing Our Elders' Wisdom." In *Honoring African American Elders: A Ministry in the Soul Community*, edited by Anne Streaty Wimberly, 171–85. San Francisco: Jossey-Bass, 1997.

Wimberly, Edward P. "The Men's Movement and Pastoral Care of African American Men." In *The Care of Men*, edited by Christie Cozad Neuger and James Newton Poling, 104–21. Nashville: Abingdon, 1997.

Wimberly, Edward P. "Methods of Cross-Cultural Pastoral Care: Hospitality and Incarnation." *Journal of the Interdenominational Theological Center* 25, no. 3 (1998): 188–202.

McCrary, Carolyn, and Edward P. Wimberly. "Introduction: Personhood in African-American Pastoral Care." *Journal of the Interdenominational Theological Center* 25, no. 3 (1998): 5–7.

Wimberly, Edward P. "The Cross-Culturally Sensitive Person." *Journal of The Interdenominational Theological Center* 25, no. 3 (1998): 170–87.

Wimberly, Edward P. "Liturgy and Narrative Psychology in the Formation of Self." In *Psychological Perspectives and the Religious Quest: Essays in Honor of Orlo Strunk, Jr.*, edited by Lallene J. Rector and Weaver Santaniello, 173–180. New York: University Press of America, 1999.

Wimberly, Edward P. "Reestablishing the Village: The Task of Pastoral Counseling." *Journeys* (Summer–Fall 1999).

Marshall, Joretta L., Bonnie J. Miller-McLemore, and Edward P. Wimberly. "Teaching Pastoral Theology: The Implications of Postmodernity for Graduate Programs." *Journal of Pastoral Theology* 10, no. 1 (2000): 47–63. doi:10.1179/jpt.2000.10.1.005.

Wimberly, Edward. "The Civil Rights Movement as a Potential Mentoring Model for Ending Domestic Abuse." *Journal of Religion and Abuse* 2, no. 1 (2000): 33–48.

Wimberly, Edward P. "Pastoral Care of Sexual Diversity in the Black Church." *American Journal of Pastoral Counseling* 3, no. 3–4 (2000): 45–58.

Wimberly, Edward P. "Homiletical Method: Pastoral Preaching." *African American Pulpit* 5, no. 3 (2002): 26–28.

Wimberly, Edward P. "The Formation of Wisdom and Human Sexuality." In *In Search of Wisdom: Faith Formation in the Black Church*, edited by Anne E. Streaty Wimberly and Evelyn L. Parker, 140–53. Nashville: Abingdon, 2002.

Wimberly, Edward P. "Wisdom Formation in Middle and Late Adulthood." In *In Search of Wisdom: Faith Formation in the Black Church*, edited by Anne E. Streaty Wimberly and Evelyn L. Parker, 125–39. Nashville: Abingdon, 2002.

Wimberly, Edward P. "Race and Sex in the Debate over Homosexuality in The United Methodist Church." In *Staying the Course: Supporting the Church's Position on Homosexuality*, edited by Maxie Dunnam and H. Newton Malony, 153–58. Nashville: Abingdon, 2003.

Wimberly, Edward P. "Minorities." In *Clinical Handbook of Pastoral Counseling*, vol. 3, edited by Robert J. Wicks, Richard D. Parsons, and Donald Capps, 60–76. Mahwah, N.J.: Paulist, 2003.

Wimberly, Edward P. "Pastoral Theological Method and Post-Nihilism." *Journal of Pastoral Theology* 13, no. 1 (2003). doi:10.1179/jpt.2003.13.1.004.

Wimberly, Edward P. "The Family Context of Development: African American Families." In *Human Development and Faith: Life-Cycle Stages of Body, Mind, and Soul*, edited by Felicity Kelcourse, 111–25. St. Louis: Chalice Press, 2004.

Wimberly, Edward P., Anne Streaty Wimberly, and Annie Grace Chingonzo. "Pastoral Counseling, Spirituality and the Recovery of the Village Functions: African and African-American Correlates in the Practice of Pastoral Care and Counseling." In *Spirituality and Culture in Pastoral Care and Counseling*, edited by John Fosket and Emmanuel Lartey. Cardiff Wales: Cardiff Academic Press, 2004.

Wimberly, Edward. "Black Pastoral Theology as Psychological Liberation." In *The Quest for Liberation and Reconciliation: Essays in Honor of J. Deotis Roberts*, edited by Michael Battle, 141–52. Louisville: Westminster John Knox, 2005.

Wimberly, Edward P. "Book Review: The Contemporary American Family: A Dialectical Perspective on Communication and Relationships by Teresa Chandler Sabourin." *Journal of Family Ministry* 19, no. 4 (2005): 62–63.

Wimberly, Edward P. "Book Review & Note: Our Home is Over Jordan: A Black Pastoral Theology." *Journal of Pastoral Care & Counseling* 59, no. 3 (2005): 303–4. doi:10.1177/154230500505900319.

Wimberly, Edward P. "The Bible as Pastor: An African American Perspective." In *Contact: Practical Theology and Pastoral Care: The Bible as Pastor*, 18–25. Cardiff, Wales: Cardiff University Press, 2006.

Wimberly, Edward P. "The Bible as Pastor: An African American Perspective." *Journal of Pastoral Theology* 16 (Spring 2006): 63–80.

Wimberly, Edward, Reuben Warren, and Anne Streaty Wimberly. "Exploring the Meaning and Possibilities of Black Fatherhood Today." In *Multidimensional Ministry for Today's Black Family*, edited by Johnny B. Hill, 41–56. Valley Forge, Pa.: Judson Press, 2007.

Wimberly, Edward P. "Beyond the Curse of Noah: African American Pastoral Theology as Political." In *African American Religious Life and the Story of Nimrod*, edited by Anthony B. Pinn and Allen Dwight Callahan, 179–89. New York: Palgrave Macmillan, 2008.

Wimberly, Edward P. "Book Review: Introduction to Pastoral Counseling by Loren Townsend." *Journal of Pastoral Theology* 19, no. 2 (2009): 138–41.

Wimberly, Edward P. "John Wesley and the Twenty-First Century: A Realistic Future." *Methodist Review: A Journal of Wesleyan and Methodist Studies* 1 (2009): 93–107. https://methodistreview.org/index.php/mr/article/view/27.

Adam, A. K. M., Richard S. Ascough, Sandra Gravett, Alice Wells Hunt, Dale B. Martin, Edward P. Wimberly, and Seung Ai Yang. "Should we be teaching the historical-critical method?" *Teaching Theology & Religion* 12, no. 2 (2009): 162–87.

Wimberly, Edward P. "Psychology of African Religious Behavior." In *African American Religious Cultures*, vol. 2, edited by Anthony B. Pinn, 593–605. Santa Barbara: ABC-CLIO, 2009.

Wimberly, Edward P. "It's A Girl: Challenges to African American Manhood and Birth of Daughters." In *Listen My Son: Wisdom to Help African American Fathers*, edited by Lee Butler, 73–82. Nashville: Abingdon, 2010.

Wimberly, Edward P. "No Shame in Wesley's Gospel." In *The Shame Factor: How Shame Shapes Society*, edited by Robert Jewett, 103–16. Eugene, Oreg.: Cascade Books, 2011.

Wimberly, Edward P. "Story Telling and Managing Trauma: Health and Spirituality at Work." *Journal of Health Care for the Poor and Underserved* 22 (2011): 48–57.

Wimberly, Edward P. "Unnoticed and Unloved: The Indigenous Storyteller and Public Theology in a Postcolonial Age." *Verbum Et Ecclesia* 32, no. 2 (2011). doi:10.4102/ve.v32i2.506.

Wimberly, Edward P. "Ethical Responsibility in Healing and Protecting the Families of the U.S. Public Health Service Syphilis Study in African American Men at

Tuskegee: An Intergenerational Storytelling Approach." *Ethics & Behavior* 22, no. 6 (2012): 475–81. doi:10.1080/10508422.2012.730007.

Wimberly, Edward P. "Forum-ing: Signature Practice for Public Theological Discourse." *HTS Teologiese Studies / Theological Studies* 70, no. 1 (2014). doi:10.4102/hts.v70i1.2079.

Wimberly, Edward P. "Prophetic-Pastoral Imagination in an Age of Sankofa and Post-racialism: The Concerned Black Clergy of Atlanta." *Journal of the Interdenominational Theological Center* 41 (Fall 2015): 55–69.

Wimberly, Edward P. "Mirrors of Hope: Eucharist and Pastoral Care as Hope for Life-long Ministry." *Journal of Pastoral Theology* 26, no. 2 (2016): 121–26. doi:10.1080/10649867.2016.1247619.

Bibliography

Akbar, Na'im. *Visions for Black Men*. Nashville: Winston-Derek, 1991.

Allen, Walter. "The Search for Applicable Theories of Black Family Life." *Journal of Marriage and the Family* 40, no. 1 (1978): 117–29.

Andrews, Dale P. *Practical Theology for Black Churches: Bridging Black Theology and African American Folk Religion*. Louisville: Westminster John Knox, 2002.

Ashby, Homer U., Jr. *Our Home Is over Jordan: A Black Pastoral Theology*. St. Louis: Chalice Press, 2003.

Axelson, Leland J. "The Working Wife: Differences in Perception Among Negro and White Males." *Journal of Marriage and the Family* 42, no. 2 (1980): 457–64.

Aymer, Margaret Patricia. "First Pure, Then Peaceable: Frederick Douglass Reads James." Ph.D. diss., Union Theological Seminary, New York, 2004.

Bagarozzi, Dennis, and Stephen A. Anderson. *Personal, Marital, and Family Myths: Theoretical Formulations and Clinical Strategies*. New York: Norton, 1989.

Becvar, Dorothy S. "The impact on the family therapist of a focus on death, dying, and bereavement." *Journal of Marital and Family Therapy* (2003): 469–77.

Berger, Peter, and Thomas Luckmann. *The Social Construction of Reality: A Treatise in the Sociology of Knowledge*. New York: Doubleday, 1966.

Berinyuu, Abraham Adu. *Pastoral Care to the Sick in Africa*. Frankfurt: Peter Lang, 1988.

———. *Towards Theory and Practice of Pastoral Counseling in Africa*. Frankfurt: Peter Lang, 1989.

Bidwell, Duane R. *Empowering Couples: A Narrative Approach to Spiritual Care*. Minneapolis: Fortress, 2013.

Billingsley, Andrew. *Climbing Jacob's Ladder: The Enduring Legacy of African-American Families*. New York: Simon & Schuster, 1992.

Bird, Phyllis. "Male and Female He Created Them." *Harvard Theological Review* 74 (April 1981): 129–59.

Browning, Don S. *A Fundamental Practical Theology: Descriptive and Strategic Proposals*. Minneapolis: Fortress, 1991.

Bowlby, John. "Pathological Mourning and Childhood Mourning." *Journal of the American Psychoanalytic Association* 11 (July 1963): 501.

Boyd-Franklin, Nancy. *Black Families in Therapy: A Multisystems Approach*. New York: Guilford Press, 1989.

Caldwell, Gilbert H. Foreword to *Relational Refugees: Alienation and Reincorporation in African American Churches and Communities* by Edward P. Wimberly, 11–14. Nashville: Abingdon, 2000.

Cameron, Norman. *Personality Development and Psychopathology: A Dynamic Approach*. Boston: Houghton Mifflin, 1963.

Cannon, Katie G. *Black Womanist Ethics*. Atlanta: Scholars Press, 1988.

Caplan, Gerald. *The Theory and Practice of Mental Health Consultation*. New York: Basic Books, 1970.

Capps, Donald. *Giving Counsel: A Minister's Guidebook*. St. Louis: Chalice, 2001.

Carey, Brycchan. "John Wesley's *Thoughts Upon Slavery* and the Language of the Heart." *Bulletin of the John Rylands University Library of Manchester* 85, nos. 2–3 (2003): 269–84.

Clandinin, D. Jean, and F. Michael Connelly. *Narrative Inquiry: Experience and Story in Qualitative Research*. San Francisco: Jossey-Bass, 2000.

Clebsch, William A., and Charles R. Jaekle. *Pastoral Care in Historical Perspective*. Englewood, N.J.: Prentice-Hall, 1964. Rev. ed., Northvale, N.J.: Jason Aronson, 1994.

Clinebell, Howard. *Basic Types of Pastoral Counseling*. Nashville: Abingdon, 1984.

Combs, Gene, and Jill Freedman. *Symbol, Story, and Ceremony: Using Metaphor in Individual and Family Therapy*. New York: W. W. Norton, 1990.

The Concerned Black Clergy of Metropolitan Atlanta, Inc. "History." Accessed August 11, 2019, https://www.concernedblackclergy.com/cbc-history.

Cone, Cecil Wayne. *Identity Crisis in Black Theology*. Rev. ed. Nashville: AMEC, 2003.

Cone, James H. *Black Theology and Black Power*. New York: Seabury Press, 1969.

———. *My Soul Looks Back*. Journeys in Faith. Nashville: Abingdon, 1982.

———. *My Soul Looks Back*. Maryknoll, N.Y.: Orbis Books, 1986.

———. *Risks of Faith: The Emergence of a Black Theology of Liberation, 1968–1998*. Boston: Beacon, 1999.

Crawford, A. Elaine. *Hope in the Holler: A Womanist Theology*. Louisville: Westminster John Knox, 2002.

Daniel, Vattell E. "Ritual and Stratification in Chicago Negro Churches." *American Sociological Review* (June 1942): 360–61.

Davis, Wayne R. "An Examination into the Process of Grief as Experienced by African American Males." Ph.D. diss., Southern Baptist Theological Seminary, 1994.

De La Cancela, Victor. "Coolin: The Psychosocial Communications of African and Latino Men." *Urban League Review* 16 (1993): 33–44.

Denborough, David. "A Storyline of Collective Narrative Practice: A History of Ideas, Social Projects and Partnerships." *International Journal of Narrative Therapy & Community Work* 1 (2012): 40–65

Doehring, Carrie. *The Practice of Pastoral Care: A Postmodern Approach.* Rev. ed. Louisville: Westminster John Knox, 2015.

————. *Taking Care: Monitoring Power Dynamics and Relational Boundaries in Pastoral Care and Counseling.* Nashville: Abingdon, 1995.

Earl, Riggins R., Jr. *Dark Symbols, Obscure Signs: God, Self and Community in the Slave Mind.* Maryknoll, N.Y.: Orbis Books, 1993.

Erickson, Beth M. *Helping Men Change: The Role of the Female Therapist.* Thousand Oaks, Calif.: Sage Publications, 1993.

Erikson, Erik. *Childhood and Society.* New York: W.W. Norton, 1963.

Fenn, Richard K. *The Dream of the Perfect Act: An Inquiry into the Gate of Religion in a Secular World.* New York: Tavistock, 1987.

Finch, Charles S., III. *Echoes of the Old Darkland: Themes from the African Eden.* Atlanta: Khenti, 1991.

Fluker, Walter Earl. "Recognition, Respectability, and Loyalty: Black Churches and the Quest for Civility." In *New Day Begun: African American Churches and Civic Culture in Post-Civil Rights America,* edited by R. Drew Smith, 113–41. Durham, N.C.: Duke University Press, 2003.

Foster, Charles R., Lisa E. Dahill, Lawrence A. Golemon, and Barbara Wang Tolentino. *Educating Clergy: Teaching Practices and Pastoral Imagination.* San Francisco: Jossey-Bass, 2006.

Foucault, Michel. *The Archaeology of Knowledge and the Discourse on Language.* New York: Pantheon Books, 1972.

————. *Birth of the Clinic: An Archaeology of Medical Perception.* New York: Vintage Books, 1973.

————. *The Care of the Self: The History of Sexuality.* New York: Vintage Books, 1988.

Franklin, Robert M. *Another Day's Journey: Black Churches Confronting the American Crisis.* Minneapolis: Fortress, 1997.

————. "Travelin Shoes: Resources for Our Journey." *Journal of the Interdenominational Theological Center* 25, no. 1 (1997): 3.

Frazier, E. Franklin. *The Negro Church in America.* New York: Schocken Books, 1964.

Freedman, Jill, and Gene Combs. *Narrative Therapy: The Social Construction of Preferred Realities.* New York: W. W. Norton, 1996.

Gabbard, Glen O. *Psychodynamic Psychiatry in Clinical Practice: The DSM-IV Edition.* Washington, D.C.: American Psychiatric Publishing, 1994.

Gilbert, Kenyatta R. *Exodus Preaching: Crafting Sermons about Justice and Hope.* Nashville: Abingdon, 2018.

Gill-Austern, Brita. "Love Understood as Self-Sacrifice and Self-Denial: What Does It Do to Women?" In *Through the Eyes of Women: Insights for Pastoral Care*, edited by Jeanne Stevenson-Moessner. Minneapolis: Fortress, 1996.

Glover-Wetherington, Miriam Anne. "Pastoral Care and Counseling with Women Entering Ministry." In *Through the Eyes of Women: Insights for Pastoral Care*, edited by Jeanne Stevenson-Moessner. Minneapolis: Fortress, 1996.

Goldberg, Michael. *Theology and Narrative: A Critical Introduction*. Nashville: Abingdon, 1981.

Gray-Little, Bernadette. "Marital Quality and Power Processes Among Black Couples." *Journal of Marriage and the Family* 44, no. 3 (1982): 633–46.

Guerin, Philip J., Jr., Leo F. Fay, Susan L. Burden, and Judith Gilbert Kautto. *The Evaluation and Treatment of Marital Conflict: A Four-Stage Approach*. New York: Basic Books, 1987.

Hale, Janice. *Black Children: Their Roots, Culture, and Learning Styles*. Provo, Utah: Brigham Young University Press, 1982.

Hamilton, Charles V. *The Black Preacher in America*. New York: Morrow, 1972.

Hansberry, Lorraine. *A Raisin in the Sun*. New York: Vintage Books, 1994.

Hare, Nathan, and Julia Hare. *Bringing the Black Boy to Manhood: The Passage*. San Francisco: Black Think Tank, 1985.

Harris, Frederick C. *Something Within: Religion in African-American Activism*. New York: Oxford University Press, 1999.

Harvey, Robin, Michael Smith, Nicholas Abraham, Sean Hood, and Dennis Tannenbaum. "The Hurricane Choir: Remote Mental Health Monitoring of Participants in a Community-based Intervention in the post-Katrina Period." *Journal of Health Care for the Poor and Underserved* 18, no. 2 (May 2007): 356–61.

Hauerwas, Stanley. *A Community of Character: Toward a Constructive Christian Social Ethic*. Notre Dame: University of Notre Dame Press, 1981.

Heitzenrater, Richard P. "The Poor and the People Called Methodists, 1729–1999." In *The Poor and the People Called Methodists*, edited by Richard P. Heitzenrater, 15–38. Nashville: Kingswood, 2002.

Herskovits, Melville J. *The New World Negro*. Bloomington: University of Indiana Press, 1966.

Hillman, James. *Healing Fiction*. Barrytown, N.Y.: Station Hill, 1983.

Hiltner, Seward. *Preface to Pastoral Theology*. Nashville: Abingdon, 1958.

Hobfall, Stevan E., Patricia Watson, Carl C. Bell, Richard A. Bryant, Melissa J. Brymer, Matthew J. Friedman, Merle Friedman, Berthold P. R. Gersons, Joop T. V. M. de Jong, Christopher M. Layne, Shira Maguen, Yuval Neria, Ann E. Norwood, Robert S. Pynoos, Dori Reissman, Joself I. Ruzek, Arieh Y. Shalev, Zahava Solomon, Alan M. Steinberg, and Robert J. Ursano. "Five Essential Elements of Immediate and Mid–Term Mass Trauma Intervention: Empirical Evidence." *Psychiatry* 70, no. 4 (2007): 283–315.

Hollies, Linda H., ed. *Womanist Care: How to Tend the Souls of Women*. Joliet, Ill.: Woman to Woman Ministries, 1991.

Holifield, E. Brooks. *A History of Pastoral Care in America: From Salvation to Self-Realization*. Nashville: Abingdon, 1983.

Hopewell, James. *Congregations, Stories, and Structures*. Philadelphia: Fortress, 1987.

Hughes, Langston. "I, Too." In *The Collected Poems of Langston Hughes*. New York: Knopf and Vintage Books, 1994.

Hulme, William. *Pastoral Care Come of Age*. Nashville: Abingdon, 1970.

Hunter, Rodney J., ed. *Dictionary of Pastoral Care and Counseling*. Nashville: Abingdon, 1990.

Jennings, Theodore W., Jr. *Good News to the Poor: John Wesley's Evangelical Economics*. Nashville: Abingdon, 1990.

Jewett, Robert. *Paul the Apostle to America: Cultural Trends and Pauline Scholarship*. Louisville: Westminster John Knox, 1994.

———. *Romans: A Commentary*. Minneapolis: Fortress, 2007.

———. *Saint Paul at the Movies: The Apostle's Dialogue with American Culture*. Louisville: Westminster John Knox, 1993.

———, ed. *The Shame Factor: How Shame Shapes Society*. Eugene, Ore.: Cascade Books, 2011.

———. "Tenement Churches and Pauline Love Feasts." *Quarterly Review: A Journal of Theological Resources for Ministry* 14, no. 1 (1994): 43–58.

Jewett, Robert, and John Shelton Lawrence. *The American Monomyth*. Lanham, Md.: University Press of America, 1988.

Johnson, Cedric. *Race, Religion, and Resilience in the Neoliberal Age*. New York: Palgrave Macmillan, 2016.

Johnson, James Weldon. "Lift Every Voice and Sing." Edward B. Marks Music Company, 1921.

Jones, Dionne J. "African American Males: A Critical Link in the African American Family." *Urban League Review* 16 (1993): 3–7.

Jung, C. G. *Modern Man in Search of a Soul*. Orlando: Harcourt Brace, 1933.

———. *Psychology and Education*. Bollinger Series. Princeton: Princeton University Press, 1954.

Karl, Jonathan, and Kevin Smith. "30 Years after Kerner Report, Some Say Racial Divide Wider." *CNN U.S. News*, March 1, 1998.

King, Martin Luther, Jr. *The Papers of Martin Luther King, Jr.: Advocate of the Social Gospel, September 1948–March 1963*. In vol. 6 of *Martin Luther King Papers*, edited by Clayborne Carson. Berkeley: University of California Press, 2007.

———. *Strength to Love*. New York: Harper & Row, 1963.

Kunjufu, Jawanza. *The Black Peer Group*. Chicago: African American Images, 1988.

———. *Countering the Conspiracy to Destroy Black Boys*. 3 vols. Chicago: African American Images, 1985.

————. *Hip-Hop Vs. MAAT: A Psycho-Social Analysis of Values*. Chicago: African American Images, 1993.

Lartey, Emmanuel Y. *In Living Colour: An Intercultural Approach to Pastoral Care and Counseling*. London: Cassell, 1997.

Lattimore, Vergel, III. "The Positive Contribution of Black Cultural Values to Pastoral Counseling." *Journal of Pastoral Care* 38, no. 2 (1982): 105–17.

Lawson, Erma J., and Cecelia Thomas. "Wading in the Waters: Spirituality and Older Black Katrina Survivors." *Journal of Health Care for the Poor and Underserved* 18, no. 2 (May 2007): 341–54.

Lawton, George. *John Wesley's English: A Study of His Literary Style*. London: Allen & Unwin, 1962.

Lewis, Diane. "The Black Family Socialization and Sex Roles." *Phylon* 36 (1975): 221–37.

Lindbeck, George A. *The Nature of Doctrine: Religion and Theology in a Postliberal Age*. Philadelphia: Westminster John Knox, 1984.

Lindemann, Erich. "Symptomatology and Management of Acute Grief." In *Crisis Intervention*, edited by Howard J. Parad, 7–21. New York: Family Service Association, 1976.

Lovin, Robin. "Human Rights, Vocation, and Human Dignity." In *Our Calling to Fulfill: Wesley's Views on the Church in Mission*, edited by M. Douglas Meeks, 109–23. Nashville: Kingwood, 2009.

Maddox, Randy L., and Jason E. Vickers, eds. *The Cambridge Companion to John Wesley*. New York: Cambridge University Press, 2010.

Majors, Richard, and Janet Mancini Billson. *Cool Pose: The Dilemmas of Black Manhood in America*. New York: Lexington Books, 1992.

Malony, H. Newton, and Richard A. Hunt. *The Psychology of Clergy*. Harrisburg, Pa.: Morehouse, 1991.

Marquardt, Manfred. *John Wesley's Social Ethics: Praxis and Principles*, translated by John E. Steely and W. Stephen Gunter. Nashville: Abingdon, 1992.

————. "Social Ethics in Methodist Tradition." In *T&T Clark Companion to Methodism*, edited by Charles Yrigoyen Jr., 292–308. New York: T&T Clark International, 2010.

Masamba ma Mpolo. "African Pastoral Care Movement." In *Dictionary of Pastoral Care and Counseling*, edited by Rodney J. Hunter, 11–12. Nashville: Abingdon: 1990.

————. "African Traditional Religion, Personal Care In." In *Dictionary of Pastoral Care and Counseling*, edited by Rodney J. Hunter, 12–13. Nashville: Abingdon: 1990.

Massey, Floyd, Jr., and Samuel B. McKinney. *Church Administration in the Black Perspective*. Valley Forge, Pa.: Judson Press, 1976.

May, Rollo. *Power and Innocence: A Search for the Sources of Violence*. New York: Norton, 1972.

Mays, Benjamin E., and Joseph W. Nicholson. *The Negro's Church*. New York: Institute of Social and Religious Research, 1933. Reprint, New York: Arno Press, 1969.

McCrary, Carolyn. Plenary presentation at the Society for Pastoral Theology Annual Meeting, Atlanta, Ga., June 2004.

McGoldrick, Monica. *You Can Go Home Again: Reconnecting with Your Family*. New York: Norton, 1994.

Meeks, M. Douglas. "A Home for the Homeless: Vocation, Mission, and Church in Wesleyan Perspective." In *Our Calling to Fulfill: Wesleyan Views of the Church in Mission*, edited by M. Douglas Meeks, 1–10. Nashville: Kingswood, 2009.

Melton, J. Gordon. *A Will to Choose: The Origins of African American Methodism*. New York: Rowman & Littlefield, 2007.

Messer, Donald E. *Contemporary Images of Christian Ministry*. Nashville: Abingdon, 1989.

Milner, J. Allen, *God's Special Provisions for the Poor*. Atlanta: Chapel of Christian Love Books, 2010.

Mitchell, Ella Pearson, ed. *Those Preachin' Women: Sermons by Black Women Preachers*. Vol. 1. Valley Forge, Pa.: Judson Press, 1985.

Mitchell, Henry, and Nicholas Lewter. *Soul Theology*. San Francisco: Harper & Row, 1986.

Morrison, Toni. *The Bluest Eye*. New York: Plume, 1994.

Moseley, Romney M. *Becoming a Self Before God*. Nashville: Abingdon, 1991.

Mucherera, Tapiwa N. *Glimmers of Hope: Toward the Healing of Painful Life Experiences through Narrative Counseling*. Eugene, Ore.: Wipf & Stock, 2013.

———. *Meet Me at the Palaver: Narrative Pastoral Counseling in Postcolonial Contexts*. Eugene, Ore.: Wipf & Stock, 2009.

Myers, William H. *God's Yes Was Louder than My No: Rethinking African American Call to Ministry*. Grand Rapids: Eerdmans, 1994.

National Committee of Negro Churchmen. "Black Power." *New York Times*, July 31, 1966.

Nelson, Marcia Z. *The Gospel According to Oprah*. Louisville: Westminster John Knox, 2005.

Neuger, Christie Cozad. *Counseling Women: A Narrative, Pastoral Approach*. Minneapolis: Fortress, 2001.

Nichols, William C., and Craig A. Everett. *Systemic Family Therapy: An Integrative Approach*. New York: Guilford, 1986.

Niebuhr, H. Richard. *The Meaning of Revelation*. New York: Macmillan Co., 1941.

Nouwen, Henri. *The Wounded Healer*. New York: Doubleday, 1972.

Oliver, William. *The Violent Social World of Black Men*. New York: Lexington Books, 1994.

Oglesby, William B. *Biblical Themes in Pastoral Care*. Nashville: Abingdon, 1980.

Parkes, C. M. "Disaster, public." In *Dictionary of Pastoral Care and Counseling*, edited by Rodney J. Hunter, 285–87. Nashville: Abingdon, 1990.

———. "Seeking and Finding a Lost Object: Evidence from Recent Studies of the Reaction to Bereavement." *Social Science and Medicine* 4 (1970): 187–201.

Passmore, John Arthur. *The Perfectibility of Man*. London: Gerald Duckworth, 1970.

Pasteur, Alfred B., and Ivory L. Toldson. *Roots of Soul: The Psychology of Black Expressiveness*. Garden City, N.Y.: Anchor Books, 1982.

Pattison, E. Mansell. *Pastor and Parish: A Systems Approach*. Philadelphia: Fortress, 1977.

Peare, Catherine Owens. *Mary McLeod Bethune*. New York: Vanguard Press, 1951.

Perryman, James. *Unfounded Loyalty: An In-Depth Look into the Love Affair between Blacks and Democrats*. Lanham, Md.: Pneuma Life Publishing, 2003.

Phelps, Jamie. "Black Spirituality." In *Spiritual Traditions for the Contemporary Church*, edited by Robin Maas and Gabriel O'Donnell, 332–51. Nashville: Abingdon, 1990.

Poling, James. *Deliver Us from Evil: Resisting Racial and Gender Oppression*. Minneapolis: Fortress, 1996.

Raboteau, Albert J. *Slave Religion: The "Invisible Institution" in the Antebellum South*. New York: Oxford University Press, 1978.

Ramsay, Nancy J., ed. *Pastoral Care and Counseling: Redefining the Paradigms*. Nashville: Abingdon, 2004.

———. "Resisting Asymmetries of Power: Intersectionality as a Resource for Practices of Care." *Journal of Pastoral Theology* 27, no. 2 (2017): 83–97.

Rediger, G. Lloyd. "A Primer on Pastoral Spirituality." *The Clergy Journal* (January 1996): 17–20.

Rizzuto, Ana-Maria. *The Birth of the Living God*. Chicago: University of Chicago Press, 1979.

Roberts, J. Deotis. *Liberation and Reconciliation: A Black Theology*. Philadelphia: Westminster John Knox, 1971.

Roberts, Stephen B., and Willard W. C. Ashley, Sr., eds. *Disaster Spiritual Care: Practical Clergy Responses to Community, Regional and National Tragedy*. Woodstock, Vt.: SkyLight Paths Publisher, 2008.

Rogers-Vaughn, Bruce. *Caring for Souls in a Neoliberal Age*. New York: Palgrave Macmillan, 2016.

Scheib, Karen D. *Pastoral Care: Telling the Stories of Our Lives*. Nashville: Abingdon, 2016.

Schüssler Fiorenza, Elisabeth. *In Memory of Her: A Feminist Theological Reconstruction of Christian Origins*. New York: Crossroad, 1992.

Sharpe, Joshua. "Continuing Coverage: Atlanta Child Murders." *Atlanta-Journal Constitution*. March 30, 2019. https://www.ajc.com/news/crime--law/says-escaped-the-atlanta-child-murders-suspect-now-talking/IHE056DNiE9FJZMgrFRpdM/.

Sipe, A. W. Richard. "Sexual Aspects of the Human Condition." In *Changing Views of the Human Condition*, edited by Paul W. Pruyser, 81–100. Macon, Ga.: Mercer University Press, 1987.

Smith, Archie, Jr. *Navigating the Deep River: Spirituality in African American Families*. Cleveland: United Church Press, 1997.

————. *The Relational Self: Ethics and Therapy from a Black Church Perspective*. Nashville: Abingdon, 1982.

Smith, Dirk. "Reform Faith, Justice and the Struggle Against Apartheid." In *Essays in Public Theology: Collected Essays 1*, 27–49. Stellenbosch, South Africa: Sun Press, 2007.

Smith, Warren Thomas. *John Wesley and Slavery*. Nashville: Abingdon, 1986.

Smith, Yolanda Y. "Anne Streaty Wimberly." Talbot School of Theology, *Christian Educators of the 20th Century*, Biola University. https://www.biola.edu/talbot/ce20/database/anne-streaty-wimberly.

Snorton, Theresa E. "The Legacy of the African-American Matriarch: New Perspectives for Pastoral Care." In *Through the Eyes of Women: Insights for Pastoral Care*, edited by Jeanne Stevenson-Moessner. Minneapolis: Fortress, 1996.

Staples, Robert. *Black Masculinity: The Black Man's Role in American Society*. San Francisco: The Black Scholar Press, 1982.

Swain, Storm. *Trauma and Transformation at Ground Zero: A Pastoral Theology*. Minneapolis: Fortress, 2011.

Taylor, Jill McLean, Carol Gilligan, and Amy M. Sullivan. *Between Voice and Silence: Women and Girls, Race, and Relationship*. Cambridge, Mass.: Harvard University Press, 1995.

Thornton, Edward E. *Professional Education for Ministry*. Nashville: Abingdon, 1970.

Toldson, Ivory A. "Massacres, Mental Health and Black Kids." *The Root*, December 27, 2012. https://www.theroot.com/massacres-mental-health-and-black-kids-1790894675.

Townes, Emilie. *A Troubling in My Soul: Womanist Perspectives on Evil and Suffering*. Maryknoll, N.Y.: Orbis Books, 1993.

Townsend, Loren. *Introduction to Pastoral Counseling*. Nashville: Abingdon, 2009.

Trible, Phyllis. *God and the Rhetoric of Sexuality*. Philadelphia: Fortress, 1978.

Van Kaam, Adrian. *Religion and Personality*. Garden City, N.Y.: Image Books, 1964.

Walker, Alice. *The Third Life of Grange Copeland*. New York: Pocket Books, 1988.

Walker, Clarence. *Biblical Counseling with African Americans*. Grand Rapids: Zondervan, 1992.

Walsh, Michelle. *Violent Trauma, Culture, and Power: An Interdisciplinary Exploration in Lived Religion*. New York: Palgrave Macmillan, 2017.

Warren, Carolyn A. "Dynamic Interpersonalism and Personhood." *Journal of the Interdenominational Theological Center* 25, no. 3 (1998): 8–32.

Washington, Joseph. *Black Sects and Cults*. Garden City, N.Y.: Doubleday, 1972.

Watkins Ali, Carroll A. *Survival and Liberation: Pastoral Theology in African American Context*. St. Louis: Chalice Press, 1999.

Wesley, John. "The Danger of Riches." In vol. 7 of *The Works of John Wesley*, edited by Thomas Jackson, 1–15. Grand Rapids: Baker, 1998.

———. *John Wesley's Sermons: An Anthology*, edited by Albert C. Outler and Richard P. Heitzenrater. Nashville: Abingdon, 1991.

———. *Journals and Diaries*. Vols. 18–24 of *The Works of John Wesley: The Bicentennial Edition*, edited by W. Reginald Ward and Richard P. Heitzenrater. Nashville: Abingdon, 1976.

———. "The More Excellent Way." In *Sermons I*, edited by Albert C. Outler. Vol. 1 of *The Works of John Wesley: The Bicentennial Edition*. 32 vols. Nashville: Abingdon, 1976.

———. *Thoughts Upon Slavery*. London: R. Hawes, 1774. http://gbgm-umc.org/umw/wesley/thoughtsuponslavery.stm, no longer available.

West, Cornel. *Prophetic Fragments*. Grand Rapids: Eerdmans, 1998.

———. *Race Matters*. New York: Vintage, 1993.

Whelchel, Henry L., Jr. "'My Chains Fell Off': Heart Religion in the African American Methodist Tradition." In *"Heart Religion" in the Methodist Tradition and Related Movements*, edited by Richard B. Steele, 97–125. Lanham, Md.: Scarecrow, 2001.

White, Michael. *Narratives of Therapists' Lives*. Adelaide, South Australia: Dulwich Centre Publications, 1997.

White, Michael, and David Epston. *Narrative Means to Therapeutic Ends*. New York: Norton, 1990.

Wiley, Christine Y. "The Impact of a Parish-Based Pastoral Counseling Center on Counselors and Congregation: A Womanist Perspective." DMin diss., Garrett-Evangelical Theological Seminary, Evanston, Ill., 1994.

Wimberly, Anne E. Streaty. *Honoring African American Elders: A Ministry in the Soul Community*. San Francisco: Jossey-Bass, 1997.

Wimberly, Anne E. Streaty, and Edward Powell Wimberly. *The Winds of Promise: Building and Maintaining Strong Clergy Families*. Nashville: Discipleship Resources, 2007.

Wimberly, Anne Streaty. "Overcoming Shame in Slave Songs and the Epistle to the Hebrews." In *The Shame Factor: How Shame Shapes Society*, edited by Robert Jewett, 60–85. Eugene, Ore.: Cascade, 2011.

———. *Soul Stories: African American Christian Education*. Nashville: Abingdon, 1995.

Wimberly, Anne Streaty, and Edward Powell Wimberly. *The Language of Hospitality: Intercultural Relations in the Household of God*. Nashville: Cokesbury, 1991.

———. *One Household and One Hope: Building Ethnic Minority Clergy Family Support Networks*. Nashville: General Board of Higher Education and Ministry, United Methodist Church, 1988.

Wimberly, Edward P. *African American History Month Daily Devotions 2009*. Nashville: Abingdon, 2008.

———. *African American Pastoral Care*. Nashville: Abingdon, 1991. Rev. ed., Nashville: Abingdon, 2008.

———. *African American Pastoral Care and Counseling: The Politics of Oppression and Empowerment*. Cleveland: Pilgrim, 2006.

————. "African American Spirituality and Sexuality: Perspectives on Identity, Intimacy and Power." *Journal of Pastoral Theology* 4 (Summer 1994): 19–31. doi:1 0.1080/10649867.1994.11745311.

————. "Beyond the Curse of Noah: African American Pastoral Theology as Political." In *African American Religious Life and the Story of Nimrod*, edited by Anthony B. Pinn and Allen Dwight Callahan, 179–89. New York: Palgrave Macmillan, 2008.

————. *Claiming God, Reclaiming Dignity: African American Pastoral Care.* Nashville: Abingdon, 2003.

————. "Compulsory Masculinity and Violence." *Caregiver Journal* 13, no. 1 (1997): 18–19.

————. *Counseling African American Marriages and Families.* Louisville: Westminster John Knox, 1997.

————. "The Family Context of Development: African American Families." In *Human Development and Faith: Life-Cycle Stages of Body, Mind, and Soul*, edited by Felicity Kelcourse, 111–125. St. Louis: Chalice Press, 2004.

————. "Forum-ing: Signature Practice for Public Theological Discourse." *HTS Teologiese Studies / Theological Studies* 70, no. 1 (2014). https://doi.org/10.4102/hts .v70i1.2079.

————. *The Gathering of the Village for Justice and Participatory Democracy: The Concerned Black Clergy of Atlanta.* Atlanta: ITC Press, 2017

————. "The Men's Movement and Pastoral Care of African American Men." In *The Care of Men*, edited by Christie Cozad Neuger and James Newton Poling, 104–21. Nashville: Abingdon, 1997.

————. "A Narrative Approach to Pastoral Care in an Intercultural Setting." In *Knowledge, Attitude and Experience: Ministry in the Cross-Cultural Context*, edited by Young-Il Kim, 84–103. Nashville: Abingdon, 1992.

————. *No Shame in Wesley's Gospel: A Twenty-first Century Pastoral Theology.* Eugene, Ore.: Wipf & Stock, 2011.

————. "Pastoral Care and Support Systems." *Journal of the Interdenominational Theological Center* 5, no. 1 (1977): 67–75.

————. *Pastoral Care in the Black Church.* Nashville: Abingdon, 1979.

————. *Pastoral Counseling and Spiritual Values: A Black Point of View.* Nashville: Abingdon, 1982.

————. "Pastoral Counseling and the Black Perspective." *Journal of Pastoral Care* 30 (December 1976): 264–72. doi:10.1177/002234097603000407.

————. "Pastoral Counseling with African American Men." *Urban League Review* 16, no. 2 (1993): 77–84.

————. *Recalling Our Own Stories: Spiritual Renewal for Religious Caregivers.* San Francisco: Jossey-Bass, 1997.

————. *Recalling Our Own Stories: Spiritual Renewal for Religious Caregivers.* With a new foreword by Tapiwa N. Mucherera. Fortress Edition. Minneapolis: Fortress, 2019.

————. "Reestablishing the Village: The Task of Pastoral Counseling." *Journeys* (Summer–Fall 1999): 5.

————. *Relational Refugees: Alienation and Reincorporation in African American Churches and Communities*. Nashville: Abingdon, 2000.

————. "The Significance of the Work of Cecil Wayne Cone." In *The Identity Crisis in Black Theology*, by Cecil Wayne Cone. Nashville: AMEC, 2003.

————. "Spiritual Formation in Theological Education." In *Clergy Assessment and Career Development*, edited by Richard A. Hunt, John E. Hinkle Jr., and H. Newton Malony, 27–31. Nashville: Abingdon, 1990.

————. "Story Telling and Managing Trauma: Health and Spirituality at Work." *Journal of Health Care for the Poor and Underserved* 22, no. 3 (2011): 48–57.

————. "Unnoticed and Unloved: The Indigenous Storyteller and Public Theology in a Postcolonial Age." *Verbum Et Ecclesia* 32, no. 2 (2011). doi:10.4102/ve.v32i2.506.

————. *Using Scripture in Pastoral Counseling*. Nashville: Abingdon, 1994.

Wimberly, Edward P., and Anne Streaty Wimberly. *Liberation and Human Wholeness: The Conversion Experiences of Black People in Slavery and Freedom*. Nashville: Abingdon, 1986.

Wimberly, Edward P., Anne Streaty Wimberly, and Annie Grace Chingonzo. "Pastoral Counseling, Spirituality and the Recovery of the Village Functions: African and African-American Correlates in the Practice of Pastoral Care and Counseling." In *Spirituality and Culture in Pastoral Care and Counseling: Voices from Different Contexts*, edited by John Foskett and Emmanuel Lartey, 15–30. Cardiff, Wales: Cardiff Academic Press, 2004.

Wimberly, Edward P., Reuben Warren, and Anne Streaty Wimberly. "Exploring the Meaning and Possibility of Black Fatherhood Today." In *Multidimensional Ministry for Today's Black Family*, edited by Johnny B. Hill, 41–56. Valley Forge, Pa.: Judson Press, 2007.

Wynn, Mychal. *Empowering African-American Males to Succeed*. South Pasadena, Calif.: Rising Sun Publications, 1992.

Yeo, Khiok-Khng. "Rhetorical Interaction 1 Corinthians 8 and 10: Potential Implications for a Chinese, Cross-Cultural Hermeneutic." Ph.D. diss., Northwestern University, 1993.

Index